THEORY AND INTERPRETATION OF NARRATIVE

James Phelan, Peter J. Rabinowitz, and Robyn Warhol, Series Editors

SOMEBODY TELLING SOMEBODY ELSE

A Rhetorical Poetics of Narrative

JAMES PHELAN

THE OHIO STATE UNIVERSITY PRESS

COLUMBUS

Library of Congress Cataloging-in-Publication Data
Names: Phelan, James, 1951– author.
Title: Somebody telling somebody else : a rhetorical poetics of narrative / James Phelan.
Other titles: Theory and interpretation of narrative series.
Description: Columbus : The Ohio State University Press, [2017] | Series: Theory and interpretation of narrative
Identifiers: LCCN 2017016909 | ISBN 9780814213452 (cloth ; alk. paper) | ISBN 0814213456 (cloth ; alk. paper)
Subjects: LCSH: Narration (Rhetoric) | American fiction—20th century—History and criticism—Theory, etc. | English fiction—History and criticism—Theory, etc.
Classification: LCC PS374.N285 P48 2017 | DDC 808/.036—dc23
LC record available at https://lccn.loc.gov/2017016909

Cover design by Lisa Force
Text design by Juliet Williams
Type set in Adobe Minion Pro

9 8 7 6 5 4 3 2 1

For the new generation, Abigail, Benjamin, Fox, and May

CONTENTS

PREFACE

I N 2000, fresh off his first victory in the Tour de France, Lance Armstrong wrote a book with Sally Jenkins called *It's Not about the Bike,* a title that led me to consider calling this book *It's Not about the Text.* (Of course, Armstrong's title now evokes the response, "We know—it's about the performance-enhancing drugs," but I ask you to leave that response in these parentheses.) Just as *It's Not about the Bike* signals that Armstrong's achievement was less about his equipment than about his agency, my title would signal that narrative is less about its materials (narrators, characters, events, techniques, and so on) than about how tellers use them to influence their audiences in particular ways. And just as the surprising negation in Armstrong and Jenkins's title implicitly acknowledges that the bike matters (notice that *It's Not Only about the Bike* would be a far less arresting title), so too would the hyperbolic negation in my title implicitly testify that I believe narrative texts remain important. In other words, it's *not entirely not about* the text. Finally, however, I decided my purposes would be better served by a positive expression of what I think narrative is about.

In previous work, I have proposed and explored a (default) rhetorical definition of narrative: somebody telling somebody else on some occasion and for some purposes that something happened. Using the opening of that definition as my title will, I hope, not just signal the continuity of this book with that work, but also call even more attention to the significance of tellers and audiences in narrative construction and communication. Thus, I want *Somebody Telling Somebody Else* to be shorthand for "somebody using the resources of narrative in order to accomplish certain purposes in relation to certain audiences."

Underlying this shorthand are the two key principles of rhetorical theory. The first I have already sketched: narrative is ultimately not a structure but an action, a teller using resources of narrative to achieve a purpose in relation to an audience. The second both complements and complicates the first: the presence and the activity of the somebody else in the narrative action is integral to its shape. In other words, the audience does not just react to the teller's communication; instead the audience and its unfolding responses significantly influence how the teller constructs the tale. The two principles also indicate why I label my project "rhetorical poetics." Like Aristotle and others committed to a poetics, I want to explain the *nature* of the elements of narrative—what I call resources. Again like Aristotle and others, I also want to explain the interrelations of these resources, and, more broadly, their functions. In order to do that, however, I have concluded that I need to nest my concern with poetics inside a rhetoric. In other words, I have become persuaded that the most compelling way to explain the nature, interrelations, and functions of narrative resources is by viewing them within the broader context of author-audience relationships. As I make the more detailed case for rhetorical poetics in this book, I hope to show that it offers (a) an understanding of narrative that provides distinctive and valuable insights into the mode and (b) sometimes greater explanatory power than other conceptions, especially those that are text-based and tied, implicitly or explicitly, to one degree or another, to structuralist narratology's view of narrative as a synthesis of story and discourse.

Just as I was tempted by a different title, I also contemplated a different subtitle: *Exercises in Rhetorical Reading* appealed to me not just as a description applicable to the individual chapters but also as a way of emphasizing my abiding interest in the acts of reading and of interpretation. To a large degree, the act of reading functions as both the ground and the test of rhetorical theory. In other words, it is (a) the basis for most of the paradigm's theoretical constructs (for example, the distinction between bonding and estranging unreliability, which I elaborate in chapter 5, seeks to capture differences in the readerly effects of the same technique) and (b) the standard against which the utility of such constructs can be measured (e.g., how well does the construct help capture one or more salient aspects of the reading experience?). In this way, the project of rhetorical poetics works inductively more than deductively by privileging narrative practice as the source of its theoretical constructs.

Furthermore, the project of rhetorical poetics views interpretation—and especially the understanding of author-audience relations in individual texts—as a fundamental raison d'etre. In that respect, the project stakes its claim to be worthwhile on its capacity to help users have richer encounters with narrative texts.

At the same time, however, my inquiries into individual narratives also aim for more general conclusions applicable to other narratives. Rhetorical reading informs rhetorical poetics and vice versa. In this way, rhetorical poetics wants its findings to be portable. To put this point another way, rhetorical poetics seeks to establish two-way traffic between practical inquiries into individual narratives and theoretical inquiries into (various dimensions of) author-audience relationships and/or the resources of narrative. The commitment to this methodology goes along with the principle that the project of rhetorical poetics is unlikely ever to be finished, since new theoretical conclusions typically generate new interpretive inquiries and these inquiries can lead to further extension or revision of the theory. Similarly, new narratives (or older narratives seen through new rhetorical lenses) can generate their own fresh lines of two-way traffic. For all these reasons, I regard *A Rhetorical Poetics of Narrative* as a perpetual work-in-progress.

Finally, both title and subtitle point toward the concerns of the individual chapters. I focus in them on (a) tellers: authors, narrators (especially character narrators), and characters in their dialogue with each other (a group who have been relatively neglected by narrative theory); (b) audiences: primarily authorial but in some chapters actual audiences as well; and (c) how the relations among tellers and audiences interact with other resources, including progressions, probability, ambiguity, and occasions, to create multiple effects that themselves ripple throughout a narrative.

In some of my previous work, I have not only staged extended engagements with other approaches but gave those engagements a prominent place in the development of my arguments. Indeed, in my first book, *Worlds from Words* (1981), I structured my whole inquiry into the role of language in fiction around my investigations into alternative theories about that role. In this book, I have subordinated engagements with others to the purpose of explaining the key principles and demonstrating the interpretive consequences of rhetorical poetics. Because I am a pluralist, I am not interested in arguing that rhetorical poetics is the most important or most powerful project in contemporary narrative theory. Indeed, if everyone became a rhetorical theorist, I would be unhappy because that would impoverish the field. In practical terms, my pluralism and my focus on rhetorical poetics mean that I take up the relation between my approach and others as that relation becomes especially relevant to clarifying my positions. Thus, for example, the argument in chapter 1 depends on a strong comparison and contrast between the narrative communication model in Seymour Chatman's structuralist narratology and the model I have developed, and in chapter 8, I demonstrate one way in which I think cognitive and rhetorical theory can work together. But in other chapters, my larger goal leads me to stay tightly focused on the two-way traffic between rhetorical theory and the interpretation of individual narratives.

Finally, a word on terminology: as I've noted elsewhere ("Voice"), I realize that many outsiders regard narrative theorists as what the late, largely unlamented Spiro Agnew might have called "nattering nabobs of needless neologisms." Although I do not share that view, I understand that sometimes the thick terministic screen of narrative theory impedes rather than facilitates the understanding of its concepts. To address that problem, I invite my readers to draw on two corollaries to Ockham's famous Razor, which states, "Do not multiply entities beyond necessity." Corollary 1 is what I call Phelan's Handle: concepts are more important than terms. Phelan's Handle means that the narrative theorist should be sure that terms are in the service of concepts, not vice versa. If a new term is proposed, it should not only be clearly tied to a concept, but it should also facilitate the understanding and the deployment of the concept. Corollary 2 is what I'll call Phelan's Shaver: some concepts are more central than others. Phelan's Shaver means that in any given study, readers should (a) distinguish between essential and ancillary concepts and (b) feel free to pay more attention to the central concepts than to the subordinate ones. Thus, for example, the distinction between unreliable and deficient narration (the first is intentional, the second is not) is a central concept, while the subtypes of deficient narration are ancillary. The purpose of elaborating the subtypes is to add both substance and nuance to the essential concept, and the elaboration allows for a deeper dive into the phenomenon. Phelan's Shaver means that I would not be disappointed to learn that readers of this book will not memorize the subtypes, but I would be disappointed to learn that they would not retain—because they would not find useful—the distinction between unreliable and deficient narration. Not surprisingly, I make only occasional references to Phelan's Shaver in the following chapters, but I invite my readers to wield it as they see fit.

THE VARIOUS PARTS of this book have been written over the last decade, and, in that time, I have accumulated intellectual and personal debts too deep and too numerous to settle in this preface. But I want at least to offer the academic's equivalent of the bankrupt's twenty cents on the dollar by expressing my affection and gratitude to the chief institutions and key people who have so frequently given me more credit than I deserve. The Department of English and the College of Arts and Sciences at Ohio State granted me a sabbatical in 2015–16 that enabled me to finish the book, and I am grateful to Debra Moddelmog and Peter Hahn, the department chair and divisional dean, for supporting my application. The International Society for the Study of Narrative has provided a vibrant intellectual community that has often offered what Porter Abbott, one of its active members, calls "friendly resistance"—and thus productive engagement—with many of the arguments I advance here. My colleagues in Project Narrative at Ohio State—Brian McHale, Robyn Warhol, Frederick Aldama, Jared Gardner, Sean O'Sullivan, Angus Fletcher, Amy Shuman, Julia Watson, and Katra Byram—extend not just "friendly affirmation" but also the commitment to a shared enterprise that creates a wonderful environment in which to work. Colleagues in the OSU Modernist Group organized by Steven Kern offer additional valuable contributions to that environment. I have benefited from exchanges with audiences at a range of conferences and universities, and I am especially grateful to the generous colleagues who have invited me to speak, especially Dan Shen, Jakob Lothe, Amy Elias, Arnaud Schmitt, Philip Goldstein, Henrik Skov Nielsen, Stefan Iversen, and John Simons. Genevieve Lively offered me a classicist's reassurance that what I have to say about Aristotle isn't totally bonkers. Lisa Zunshine encouraged me to think more about the relation between cognitive theory and rhetorical theory. Jim Battersby once again gave me the benefit of his sympathetic ear and his critical eye. Elizabeth Renker let me carry on about ideas in progress and responded with trenchant questions. Yonina Hoffman carefully copyedited the penultimate version of the whole manuscript and helped me both tighten the prose and avoid some gaffes. Nick Potkalitsky provided similar eagle-eyed work on the final manuscript and page proofs. Robyn Warhol, Peter Rabinowitz, and an anonymous reader for the press offered valuable advice that has improved the book. Peter's "close encounters" with numerous passages of my critical prose often led me to rethink both my ideas and my expression of them. In that way, his reading was, for me at least, a happy continuation of a conversation we've been having for over thirty years now. My greatest debt, the one I can never come close to repaying, is to Betty Menaghan, whose boundless love and support enriches every day of my life. Finally, I dedicate this book to my four grandchildren, Abigail, Benjamin, May, and Fox: may you all enjoy long and rich lives as storytellers and rhetorical readers.

ALTHOUGH NO CHAPTER in this book is a simple reprint of a previously published essay, most chapters do contain material that has appeared elsewhere. I am grateful for permission to reprint.

Chapter 1 contains material from "Rhetoric, Ethics, and Narrative Communication: Or, From Story and Discourse to Authors, Resources, and Audiences." *Soundings* 94.1–2 (2011): 55–75.

Chapter 2 from "Implausibilities, Crossovers, Impossibilities: A Rhetorical Approach to Breaks in the Mimetic Code of Narration." *A Poetics of Unnatural Narrative*. Ed. Jan Alber, Henrik Skov Nielsen, and Brian Richardson. Columbus: Ohio State University Press, 2013. 167–84.

Chapter 3 from "Rhetoric, Ethics, Aesthetics, and Probability in Fiction and Nonfiction: *Pride and Prejudice* and *The Year of Magical Thinking*." *Reception: Texts, Readers, Audiences, History* 2 (Summer 2010). <http://www.english.udel.edu/rsssite/toc2010.html>.

Chapter 4 from "Progression, Speed, and Judgment in Kafka's 'Das Urteil.'" *Franz Kafka: Narration, Rhetoric, and Reading*. Ed. Jakob Lothe, Beatrice Sandberg, and Ronald Speirs. Columbus: Ohio State University Press, 2011. 22–39.

Chapter 5 from "Estranging Unreliability, Bonding Unreliability, and the Ethics of *Lolita*." *Narrative* 15 (Spring 2007): 222–38.

Chapter 6 from "The Ethics and Aesthetics of Backward Narration in Martin Amis's *Time's Arrow*." *After Testimony: The Future of Holocaust Narratives*. Ed. Susan Suleiman, Jakob Lothe, and James Phelan. Columbus: Ohio State University Press, 2012. 120–41.

Chapter 7 from "'I affirm nothing': *Lord Jim* and the Uses of Textual Recalcitrance." *Joseph Conrad: Voice, Sequence, History, Genre*. Ed. Jakob Lothe, Jeremy Hawthorn, and James Phelan. Columbus: Ohio State University Press, 2008. 41–59.

Chapter 8 from "Rhetorical Theory, Cognitive Theory, and Morrison's 'Recitatif'": From Parallel Play to Productive Collaboration. *Oxford Handbook of Cognitive Literary Studies*. Ed. Lisa Zunshine. New York: Oxford University Press, 2015. 120–35.

Chapter 9 from "Conversational and Authorial Disclosure in the Dialogue Novel: The Case of *The Friends of Eddie Coyle*." *Narrative, Interrupted: The Plotless, the Disturbing, and the Trivial in Literature*. Ed. Markku Lehtimäki, Laura Karttunen, and Maria Makelä. Amsterdam: De Gruyter, 2012. 3–23. Also from "Privileged Authorial Disclosure about Events: Wolff's 'Bullet in the Brain' and O'Hara's 'Appearances.'" *Narrative Sequence in Contemporary Narratology*. Ed. Raphäel Baroni and Françoise Revaz. Columbus: Ohio State University Press, 2015. 51–70.

Chapter 10 from "The Implied Author, Deficient Narration, and Nonfiction Narrative: Or, What's Off-Kilter in *The Year of Magical Thinking* and *The Diving Bell and the Butterfly*?" *Style* 45.1 (2011): 127–45.

Chapter 13 from "Occasions of Narration in *Enduring Love:* Love, Logic, Madness, Contagion, and Narrative Communication." *Les Narrateurs Fous / Mad Narrators.* Ed. Nathalie Jaëck, Clara Mallier, Arnaud Schmitt, Romain Girard. Pesac: Maison Sciences de L'Homme de L'Aquitaine, 2014. 169–84. Also from "McEwan's *Enduring Love:* A Rhetorical Reader's Response to 'Appendix I' and 'Appendix II.'" *Anglistik* 24.2 (2013): 67–79.

PART 1

On the Explanatory Power of Rhetorical Poetics

Principles of Rhetorical Poetics

IN SEARCH OF A NEW PARADIGM

I N 1999 David Herman proposed the term *postclassical narratology* to describe the then-current state of narrative theory, a term designed to capture the field's many revisions of structuralist narratology. Since 1999, the postclassical movement has continued its robust activity, adding important developments in feminist, cognitive, and postcolonial narratology (to name a few) and developing new approaches, such as unnatural narratology and enactivist narratology. Nevertheless, the story/discourse distinction, arguably the foundational concept of structuralist narratology, remains an important staple for most narrative theorists. It is one of the first nutrients we take in, and it remains a source of nourishment that help shapes our maturation in the field. The distinction significantly influences our acquisition of narratological language, as we learn to say that story is the *what* of narrative and discourse the *how,* that story consists of events and existents, and that discourse consists of techniques for presenting those phenomena.

The distinction also shapes our narratological eyesight as we become disposed to identify other binary distinctions for analyzing narrative: mimesis and diegesis; kernel events and satellite events; filter and slant; order, duration, and frequency in the story versus order, duration, and frequency in the discourse; and so on. Consequently, even as current narrative theorists travel down their different postclassical paths, exploring the questions accompanying their particular approaches, their answers typically complement and complicate rather than replace the paradigmatic vision of narrative engendered by the story/discourse distinction: narrative is a structured sign system. In this respect, postclassical narratology has significantly revised but not fundamentally altered the paradigm of classical narratology.

With these observations in mind, I add two others: (1) The last fifty years of narrative theory, encompassing the classical and postclassical periods, have been enormously productive, generating major theoretical breakthroughs, several highly effective approaches, and countless insightful analyses of individual narratives. (2) Nevertheless, there are significant phenomena of narrative and its workings that the field has not yet adequately accounted for. I propose to make the case for the value of a rhetorical paradigm by demonstrating (a) that it can provide compelling accounts of those phenomena and (b) that the principles underlying those accounts have significant consequences for the way in which we think of other phenomena and narrative more generally.

In part 1, I begin to take up this challenge by zeroing in on two narrative phenomena that have so far been under-theorized. The first phenomenon, the focus of chapter 1, is a common feature of narrative texts that has been hiding in plain sight: character-character dialogue. The second phenomenon, the focus of chapter 2, is what Aristotle called probable impossibilities and what I will what I call *crossover phenomena in narrative progressions,* instances in which the logic of author-audience relationships trumps the logic of event sequence or of telling situations. In each chapter, I shall link the discussion of the phenomena to larger conclusions about the efficacy of the rhetorical paradigm.

In part 2, I shall thicken the description of this rhetorical paradigm and its consequences by means of multiple exercises in what Peter J. Rabinowitz and I have called theory-practice, that is, inquiries in which theory aids the work of interpretation even as that work allows for further developments in theory. These exercises address a range of issues, from probability to ambiguity, from unreliable and deficient narration to reliable narration, from character-character dialogue to occasions of narration. I discuss the logic underlying the arrangement of these exercises in the brief preface to part 2.

Before I launch into the exploration of character-character dialogue, I offer a sketch of ten key principles of the rhetorical paradigm that I and others working in the tradition have developed in previous work. I have expressed some of these points above, but I hope the advantages of putting them all in one place will outweigh the disadvantages of some redundant telling. This sketch seeks to be succinct in its explication, in part because the rest of the book will elaborate on the principles as it puts them to work and, in some cases, explicitly offers further commentary. I invite those readers who are familiar with the principles or are more interested in their application to jump to chapter 1 and return to this sketch as needed.[1]

(1) Rhetorical theory subsumes the traditional view of narrative as a structured sign system representing a linked sequence of events under the broader view that **narrative is itself an event—more specifically,** a multidimensional purposive communication from a teller to an audience. The concern with purpose informs the analysis of narrative phenomena, including the core elements: how has the teller tried to shape these materials in the service of her larger ends? The focus on narrative as *multileveled communication* follows from rhetorical theory's interest in accounting for the reading experience (and see principle number 5 for a gloss on "experience"). Consequently, rhetorical theory is at least as interested in a narrative's affective, ethical, and aesthetic effects—and in their interactions—as it is in that narrative's thematic meanings. Affective effects include the range of emotional responses (from empathy to antipathy) to characters, narrators, and even authors and to the narrative as a whole. Affective effects can follow from and/or influence ethical effects, and the quality of an audience's affective and ethical engagements with a narrative greatly influences its aesthetic effects.

(2) **The rhetorical definition of** *narrative,* **"somebody telling somebody else on some occasion and for some purpose(s) that something happened," describes a "default" situation rather than prescribes what all narratives should do.** The definition is designed to capture essential characteristics of most of those works that are widely considered to be narratives in our culture, even as I recognize that individual narratives may not conform exactly to every element of the definition. Thus, for example, I say "something happened," because the telling of events typically occurs after their occurrence. But I also recognize that the telling can sometimes be simultaneous with the events (as in J. M. Coetzee's *Waiting for the Barbarians*) or before the events (as in the ending of Dostoyevsky's *The Gambler*: "Tomorrow, tomorrow it will all be over!"). Characterizing the definition as "default" keeps one open to such deviations—and to the likelihood that they will be significant. See number 8 for a related principle.

(3) **Rhetorical interpretation and theory are based on an a posteriori rather than an a priori method.** This principle is closely connected to num-

---

1. This discussion of principles draws to some degree on the similar discussion Peter J. Rabinowitz and I offer in chapter 1 of *Narrative Theory: Core Concepts and Critical Debates.* But where that discussion identifies six principles, this one expands to ten. I am deeply grateful to Peter for his collaboration in that discussion and in so many others over the years.

ber 2. Rather than declaring what narratives invariably do or how they invariably do it, I seek to understand and assess the variety of things narratives have done and the variety of ways they have done it. In practical terms, this principle means that I try to reason back from the effects created by narratives to the causes of those effects in the authorial shaping of the narrative elements. I then try to draw appropriate generalizations about narrative as rhetoric. Since narrative communication is a complex, multilayered phenomenon, this reasoning process cannot be reduced to a formula, and its results yield hypotheses rather than dogmatic conclusions.

A related dimension of this principle is that rhetorical theory does not preselect for analysis certain matters of content, such as gender, race, class, age, sexual orientation, or (dis)ability, though it recognizes both that such methods have yielded valuable work on narrative and that some narratives do foreground such matters. More generally, rhetorical narrative theory maintains its interest in how authors seek to achieve their multidimensional purposes even as it strives to be sufficiently flexible to respond to the diversity of narrative acts. At the same time, of course, rhetorical theory is not a neutral, unmediated approach to narrative—as this present exposition of its principles amply demonstrates.

(4) **In interpreting a narrative, rhetorical narrative theory identifies a feedback loop among authorial agency, textual phenomena (including intertextual relations), and reader response.** In other words, the approach assumes that (a) texts are designed by authors to affect readers in particular ways; (b) those authorial designs are conveyed through the words, images, techniques, elements, structures, forms, and dialogic relations of texts as well as the genres and conventions readers use to understand them; and (c) those authorial designs are also deeply influenced by the nature of their audiences and their activity in responding to the unfolding communication. In a sense, my work in this book is a major elaboration of the consequences of this principle, one that starts from the idea that "there's a lot more here than initially appears." For now, I highlight a few of its practical consequences. The principle means that an interpretive inquiry can start with any point in the loop because questions about that point will inevitably lead to the consideration of other points. If, for example, I respond to a character's action with a negative ethical judgment, I will look for the textual sources of that judgment and the reasons why the author would have guided my judgment in that way, given her other purposes. In the course of asking and answering these questions, I may find that my negative judgment was too simplistic or otherwise inadequate, and I will therefore revise it.

Attending to all three points in the loop also sometimes makes rhetorical theory wary about thematic abstraction. For example, some critics have offered eloquent thematic defenses of Mark Twain's ending in *Huckleberry Finn*, but, while I admire the learning and reasoning in many of these arguments, I find them ultimately unpersuasive because they are insufficiently responsive to the readerly experience of that section. In focusing on thematic relevance, these analyses typically neglect the tedium most readers experience as they slog through Twain's account of Tom Sawyer's elaborate scheme for freeing Jim, and the disappointment they feel in Huck's ethical decline in his relationship with Jim. Because this response holds up after my examination of the textual phenomena of the Evasion section and my inferences about Twain's purposes, as revealed by the first two-thirds of the novel, I find it more convincing to view the ending as flawed.

(5) **The rhetorical approach theorizes "the somebody else" in narrative communication by identifying three audiences in nonfictional narrative and four audiences in fictional narrative.** The first audience is the actual audience, flesh-and-blood readers in all their differences and commonalities. The second audience is the authorial audience, the hypothetical group for whom the author writes—the group that shares the knowledge, values, prejudices, fears, and experiences that the author expected in his or her readers, and that ground his or her rhetorical choices. The authorial audience is neither wholly hypothetical nor wholly actual, but instead it is a hybrid of readers an author knows or knows about—or at least an interpretation of such readers—and an audience the author imagines. The third audience is the narratee, the audience addressed by the narrator, whether characterized or not. Typically, the more the narratee is characterized, the more important this audience is in the rhetorical exchange. Uncharacterized narratees in nonfiction are likely to be indistinguishable from the authorial audience. The fourth audience, exclusive to fiction, is the narrative audience, an observer position within the storyworld. As observers, the members of the narrative audience regard the characters and events as real rather than invented, and, indeed, they accept the whole storyworld as real regardless of whether it conforms to the actual world. Two of J. K. Rowling's inventions in her construction of Harry Potter's storyworld can be adapted to help explain the relation between the actual audience and the narrative audience. In entering the narrative audience, the actual audience puts on an Invisibility Cloak and apparates to the world of the fiction.

This point means that the degree of overlap between the beliefs of the authorial audience and those of the narrative audience can vary considerably. To stay with Rowling's construction by way of illustration, the narrative audience of the Harry Potter novels believes that the entire population of the world can be divided into two types: witches and wizards with magical powers, on the one hand, and humans without magical powers (muggles), on the other; the authorial audience, however, does not believe in witches and wizards. At the same time, the narrative audience does not necessarily accept the narrator's portrayal of everything as accurate, any more than the reader of a nonfictional text necessarily accepts everything represented as true. Finally, as an observer, a member of the narrative audience overhears the narrator's address to the narratee, even as the degree to which the observer can also feel addressed can vary from narrative to narrative. Typically, the variation will be tied to the narrative audience's similarity or difference from the narratee. Similarly, second-person narration in which the "you" is both protagonist and narratee can make all the audiences feel addressed. These points about the variability of the narrative audience–narratee relationship apply more broadly: the relationships among all audiences can vary from narrative to narrative, and some narratives make those relationships crucial to their effects while others do not.

Beyond distinguishing among audiences, rhetorical poetics makes several other assumptions about the "somebody else" of narrative communication: (1) Not all actual readers want to join the authorial audience. Those who do I call rhetorical readers, and those are the readers whose activity rhetorical poetics is most concerned with. Consequently, I will frequently use the phrase to refer to actual readers who have joined the authorial audience. To put this point another way, the authorial and, where relevant, narrative audience positions are roles that the rhetorical reader takes on, and examining those roles can provide insight into the experience of rhetorical readers. (2) In fiction, the authorial audience position includes the narrative audience position, since the authorial audience has the double-consciousness that allows it to experience the events as real and to retain the tacit knowledge that they are invented. (3) Rhetorical readers can and should evaluate the experiences they are invited to have in the authorial audience. Indeed, rhetorical readers do not complete their acts of reading until they take this second step. In the analyses in this book, this second step will often be implied in my endorsement of the author-audience relationships I perceive in the narratives, but at various points I will make that second step explicit, most notably in my discussion of "deficient narration" in chapter 9.

(6) In addressing narrative ethics, rhetorical theory distinguishes between the ethics of the telling and the ethics of the told. The ethics of the telling refer to the ethical dimensions of author-narrator-audience relationships as constructed through everything from plotting to direct addresses to the audience, while the ethics of the told refer to the ethical dimensions of characters and events, including character-character interactions and choices to act in one way rather than another by individual characters. In keeping with the a posteriori principle, I approach ethics from the inside out rather than the outside in. That is, rather than using a particular theory of ethics to interpret and evaluate the ethical dimension of narratives, I seek to identify the system (whether coherent, eclectic, or incoherent) an author has deployed (consciously or intuitively) in the narrative.

(7) **Rhetorical theory integrates history in multiple ways.** Because rhetorical theory emphasizes author-audience relations and because it views both as always already situated in historical and social contexts, rhetorical theory is not just compatible with but dependent on historical knowledge—and historical analysis—of all kinds: literary, cultural, social, political, and so on. The role of history in rhetorical analysis is itself governed by a principle of salience: what historical knowledge is especially significant for the construction of author-audience relations? To take just a few examples from the following chapters: In *The Friends of Eddie Coyle,* George V. Higgins relies on his audience to know something about both the Black Panthers and how they were perceived by white law enforcement. In *Pride and Prejudice,* Jane Austen relies on her audience to know about a wide range of social norms of England's Regency Period. In "Recitatif," Toni Morrison relies on her audience to know about the political controversies surrounding post-1960s school bussing programs in the United States. In "The Third and Final Continent," Jhumpa Lahiri relies on her audience to have some knowledge of the tradition of arranged marriages in India as well as of recent patterns of Indian immigration to England and the United States.

These examples also point to another common—but by no means universal—aspect of the relation between historical and rhetorical analysis. In each case, the historical knowledge is a necessary, not a sufficient, condition for understanding the author-audience relations. To get at sufficient conditions, the rhetorical analyst does a detailed, close analysis of the multiple factors that go into establishing that relationship—and, indeed, its trajectory over the course of a narrative. For the most part, my attention will be directed toward such analyses, but I remain aware that they are themselves dependent on a wide range of historical knowledge. One more example, about literary history, will help clarify this point. In approaching a novel such as *The Sound and the Fury,* a rhetorical reader benefits from knowing something about modernism and that Faulkner was a modernist. At the same time, such knowledge is only a starting point for the task of accounting for the detailed workings of the feedback loop among authorial agency, textual phenomena, and readerly response in Faulkner's novel.

(8) **The underlying rhetorical situation varies in different kinds of narrative, and it typically varies within individual narratives**. For instance, in fictional narratives such as Jhumpa Lahiri's "The Third and Final Continent" or Franz Kafka's "Das Urteil" (to take two narratives discussed in later chapters), the teller/audience situation is doubled: the narrators tell their stories to uncharacterized narratees for their own purposes, while the authors communicate both the events and the narrators' telling of them to their audiences for their own purposes. In such cases, the fictional narrative is a single text combining at least two tracks of rhetorical communication. I say "at least" because, as I shall argue in chapter 1, this commonsense description overlooks other tracks between author and audience commonly constructed via dialogue, juxtapositions of narrative segments, and other things. This description also overlooks the ways in which authors can construct synergistic relationships among these tracks that generate communications that are more than the sum of the transmissions along the individual tracks. In nonfictional narrative, the same tracks are available for the author's use, but sometimes the narrator-narratee track is indistinguishable from the author-audience track. In other words, sometimes authors of nonfiction speak directly in their own voices to their projected audiences, as, for example, Joan Didion does in *The Year of Magical Thinking*. But this common strategy in nonfiction is not a required one: authors of nonfiction can distance themselves from their narrators, as, for example, Frank McCourt does in *Angela's Ashes*.

(9) **The progression of a narrative—its synthesis of textual and readerly dynamics—is crucial to its effects and purposes.** Textual dynamics are the internal processes by which narratives move from beginning through middle to ending, and readerly dynamics are the corresponding cognitive, affective, ethical, and aesthetic responses of the audience to those textual dynamics. The bridge between textual dynamics and readerly dynamics consists of interpretive, ethical, and aesthetic judgments. These judgments constitute a bridge because they are encoded in the narrative yet made by rhetorical readers. Furthermore, by describing progression as a synthesis, I seek to capture the ways that textual dynamics and readerly dynamics influence each other. I will develop this point more fully in chapter 2.

Textual dynamics are themselves a synthesis of plot dynamics, governing the sequence of events, and narratorial dynamics, governing the relations among authors, tellers (whether narrators or characters), and audiences. Plot dynamics typically develop through patterns of instability-complication-resolution. That is, an author generates a plot through introducing one or more characters in unstable situations, he advances the plot by complicating those instabilities, and he ends the plot by resolving those instabilities to one degree or another—or thematizing the impossibility of resolution. Narratorial dynamics are diverse, but two broad patterns, which I will unpack more fully in part 2, are reliable and unreliable narration. Each pattern has consequences for how an author handles the plot dynamics and thus adds an important layer to the textual dynamics. Unreliable narration introduces tensions among authors, narrators, and audiences and the issue of whether these tensions will be resolved can become an important part of the textual dynamics. Readerly dynamics include both local and global interpretive, ethical, affective, and aesthetic responses to the unfolding textual dynamics. They also include such broader activities as configurations and reconfigurations of the various layers of the developing trajectory. Since analyzing the progression involves unpacking the underlying logic of the narrative—why it is the way it is and not some other way—it provides valuable insight into the narrative's purposes.

(10) **Rhetorical readers develop interests and responses of three broad kinds, each related to a particular component of the narrative: mimetic, thematic, and synthetic.** Responses to the mimetic component involve rhetorical readers' interest in the characters as possible people and in the narrative world as like our own, that is, hypothetically or conceptually possible; responses to the mimetic component include rhetorical readers' evolving judgments and emotions, their desires, hopes, expectations, satisfactions, and disappointments. Responses to the mimetic component of fiction are tied to rhetorical readers' participation in the narrative audience. Responses to the mimetic component of nonfiction are tied to rhetorical readers' sense of the fit between the actual world and its representation in the narrative. Responses to the thematic component involve rhetorical readers' interest in the ideational function of the characters and in the cultural, ideological, philosophical, or ethical issues being addressed by the narrative. Responses to the synthetic component involve rhetorical readers' interest in and attention to the characters and to the larger narrative as artificial constructs. The relationship among rhetorical readers' relative interests in these different components will vary from narrative to narrative depending on the nature of its genre and progression. Some narratives (including most so-called realistic fiction) are dominated by mimetic interests; some (including allegories and political polemics such as *Animal Farm*) stress the thematic; others (including the *nouveau roman* and postmodern metafiction) put priority on the synthetic. But the interests of many narratives are more evenly distributed among two or three of the components. Most narratives in the realistic tradition, for instance, promote both the mimetic and the thematic, and some narratives situate mimetic characters

in clearly anti-mimetic worlds. Furthermore, developments in the course of a narrative can generate new relations among those interests. Indeed, many narratives derive their special power from shifting rhetorical readers' attention from one kind of component to another: Nabokov's *Bend Sinister,* for instance, has the effect that it does in part because, in the closing pages, the mimetic is drowned out by the synthetic.

CHAPTER 1

Somebody Telling Somebody Else

AUTHORS, RESOURCES, AUDIENCES

WHY AREN'T CHARACTERS IN THE NARRATIVE COMMUNICATION MODEL?

ONE OF the most influential proposals of classical narratology is the narrative communication model proposed by Seymour Chatman in his aptly named *Story and Discourse* (1978) (entities within the brackets are located in the narrative text):

Since Chatman proposed this model in 1978, narrative theorists have suggested various revisions. Some theorists have proposed fewer agents—the implied author is the one most often given the axe—and some (e.g., moi in *Living to Tell about It*) have proposed moving the implied author outside the narrative text, but these proposals have only solidified the model's central place in narrative theory. To be sure, some theorists, including David Herman (2008), Richard Walsh, and Patrick Hogan have proposed alternative conceptions, but so far these alternatives have not displaced Chatman's model. In this way, the model is a good example of what Thomas Kuhn refers to as "normal science" in his work on *The Structure of Scientific Revolutions*; that is, it is an accepted way of doing work within an existing paradigm.

Looking at the model from a rhetorical perspective invites the questions: Where are characters? Why aren't they present? I seek to give some additional force to these questions by examining the fit between Chatman's model and a particular narrative. My choice is not a high-culture literary narrative (sorry, Jane Austen, Henry James, and Virginia Woolf, you have to sit this one out) but a crime novel set in the Boston underworld of the late 1960s by George V. Higgins, *The Friends of Eddie Coyle* (1970). To be sure, Higgins's novel has some significant admirers: Dennis Lehane, today's most accomplished Boston crime novelist, has recently called Higgins's book "the game-changing crime novel of the last fifty years" (vii), and Elmore Leonard claims he learned much of his craft from Higgins. Like David Simon's celebrated television series *The Wire*, *The Friends of Eddie Coyle* is a fascinating study of networks—both police networks and crime networks—and of the way information does and does not travel within and across those networks. The novel consists of thirty chapters, each of which is a scene of colorful dialogue. Collectively, these thirty scenes tell the story of how and why Eddie Coyle, a minor figure in the underworld, gets whacked by his so-called friends: the transmission of information in their network mistakenly leads these friends to conclude that he has ratted out some other so-called friends, with the result that one of the mob boss's favorite men gets killed in a shootout with the police. A subplot involves the fate of a gun dealer, Jackie Brown, someone whom Eddie has actually ratted out, in the vain hope that his informing the police will work in his favor at an upcoming sentencing hearing. The final chapter wraps up both the Jackie Brown subplot and the novel as a whole. I quote the first two paragraphs and then the closing dialogue between Jackie's defense lawyer, Foster Clark, and an unnamed prosecutor.

> Jackie Brown at twenty-seven sat with no expression on his face in the first row behind the bar of Courtroom Four of the United States District Court for the District of Massachusetts.
>
> The clerk called case number seventy-four-hundred-and-twenty-one-D, United States of America versus Jackie Brown. The bailiff motioned to Jackie Brown to rise. [. . .]
>
> "Good Christ," Clark said, "you guys want to put the world in jail. This is a young kid. He doesn't have a record. He didn't try to hurt anybody. He's never been in court before in his life. He doesn't even have a goddamned traffic ticket, for God's sake."

"I know that," the prosecutor said. "I also know he was driving a car that cost four grand and he's twenty-seven years old and we can't find a place he ever worked. He's a nice, clean-cut gun dealer, is what he is, and if he wanted to, he could probably make half the hoods and forty per cent of the bikies in this district. But he doesn't want to do that. Okay, he's a stand-up guy. Stand-up guys do time."

"So he's got to talk," Clark said.

"Nope," the prosecutor said, "he doesn't have to do a damned thing except decide which he wants to do more, talk, and make somebody important for us, or go down to Danbury there and get rehabilitated."

"That's a pretty tough choice to make," Clark said.

"He's a pretty tough kid," the prosecutor said. "Look, we don't need to stand here and play the waltz music. You know what you got: you got a mean kid. He's been lucky up to now: he's never been caught before. And you know what I got, too: I got him fat. You've talked to him. You saw him and you told him it was talk or take the fall, and he told you to go and fuck yourself, or something equally polite. So now you got to try the case, because he won't plead without a deal that puts him on the street and I don't make that kind of deal for machine gun salesmen that don't want to give me anything. So we try this one, and it'll take two days or so, and he'll get convicted. Then the boss'll tell me to say three, or maybe five, and the judge'll give him two, or maybe three, and you'll appeal, maybe, and some time around Washington's Birthday, he'll surrender to the marshals and go down to Danbury for a while. Hell, he'll be out in a year, year and a half. It isn't as though he was up against a twenty-year minimum mandatory."

"And in another year or so," Clark said, "he'll be in again, here or someplace else, and I'll be talking to some other bastard, or maybe even you again, and we'll try another one and he'll go away again. Is there any end to this shit? Does anything ever change in this racket?"

"Hey Foss," the prosecutor said, taking Clark by the arm, "of course it changes. Don't take it so hard. Some of us die, the rest of us get older, new guys come along, old guys disappear. It changes every day."

"It's hard to notice, though," Clark said.

"It is," the prosecutor said, "it certainly is." (179, 181–82)

This passage is very effective in its context, but I choose it in part because, if we look just at its textual features, it does not appear to be an especially innovative piece of storytelling. We've all read many other scenes of dialogue that work much like this one. Let's take a closer look at the passage and its fit—or lack thereof—with Chatman's model.

Three features of Higgins's communication stand out. First, Higgins relies heavily on the character-character dialogue to perform the standard functions of *narration, namely, reporting about characters and events, interpreting those reports, and evaluating them.* Higgins uses the prosecutor as his surrogate to convey not just to Clark but also to his audience how the legal system works. In that way, he initially uses Clark as a surrogate for his audience and then later as another surrogate for himself. Furthermore, as the prosecutor summarizes Jackie's behavior and predicts what will happen, he also interprets and evaluates these things for Clark's benefit. Higgins in turn uses the prosecutor's speech to inform his audience about how the legal system will respond to Jackie's behavior. Clark's response contributes his share of interpreting as he predicts the next chapter in the story of Jackie Brown versus the Legal System. In this way, Clark's response adds an important generalizing—and discouraging—evaluation about the events of that story. Higgins uses the prosecutor's final lines to offer both Clark and his own audience some comfort, however cold. And the ultimate agreement of the two men at the end of the passage endorses Higgins's communication to his audience about both the necessity and the limitations of the legal system.

As this analysis suggests, character-character dialogue, like character narration, simultaneously works along two communicative tracks. The first track is that between the characters and the second is that between the implied author and his or her audience. I shall call communication along the first track *conversational disclosure* and communication along the second track *authorial disclosure.* In part 2, chapter 10, I explore the complexities of the relationship between the two tracks more fully. Here I just note how seamlessly Higgins brings the two tracks together.

The second salient feature of the passage is that Higgins severely restricts the narrator's functions. Higgins not only gives the narrator very few lines but also limits his role almost entirely to that of a detached reporter who provides the necessary background for the dialogue (Jackie Brown sat; the clerk called; the bailiff motioned) and identifies its speakers (the prosecutor said; Clark said; and, in a very expansive mood, "the prosecutor said, taking Clark by the arm").

The third salient feature of the extract is the contrast between some aspects of the ethics of the told, which ultimately highlight ethical deficiencies in the legal system, and the ethics of the telling, which conveys a belief in rhetorical concord at the level of both character-character and author-audience interactions. The ethics of the told include both the ethical situations of the characters and the ethical values underlying the legal system described by Clark and the prosecutor. All three characters are responding to their situations in ways that Higgins implicitly endorses. Jackie faces the ethical choice of whether to help himself by informing on his associates or to do time by refusing to inform. His choice to do the time provides a stark contrast to Eddie Coyle's informing on Jackie for a possible but far from guaranteed reduction in his sentence. Not surprisingly, Jackie's choice earns the prosecutor's grudging respect ("He's a pretty tough kid"), and that respect in turn guides rhetorical readers' own ethical judgment of Jackie's choice. Clark and the prosecutor are both doing their jobs conscientiously, behavior that helps each earn the other's respect, and, indeed, helps form the basis for their eventual shared judgment of the legal system.

Higgins uses the dialogue to underline some significant tensions between the ethical dimensions of the legal system and a broader, more person-centered system of ethics. It is the legal system that presents Jackie with his ethical choice, and that presentation comes from an ethical hierarchy that puts convictions above friendship or loyalty or just about any other value. In addition, Higgins uses the dialogue to indicate that the legal system's efforts to find the appropriate balance among the various factors that go into punishment—age of the perpetrator, number of previous crimes, the right to a defense, the right to appeal, and so on—leads to a calculus that neither of our ethically sound characters finds particularly satisfactory. Rather than dispensing justice and moving perpetrators toward rehabilitation, they find themselves keeping a merry-go-round running.

The ethics of the telling involve Higgins's decisions to restrict his narrator to the minimal reporting function, to mediate his own views through the prosecutor and Clark, and to orchestrate the progression of their exchange in the way he does. Because Higgins positions the prosecutor as a surrogate for himself and initially positions Clark as a surrogate for his audience, their gradual movement from initial opposition to concord works in part as the vehicle for Higgins's effort to bring rhetorical readers into concord with himself. The mediation through the characters is crucial to the author-audience exchange here: Higgins gives rhetorical readers some subtle guidance but also invites them to complete the communication through their own judgments of Jackie, Clark, and the prosecutor, and of the legal system and its relation to the ethical tasks of dispensing justice. Thus, Higgins uses the surface tough-guy talk as a cover for his own telling that conveys both a spirit of cooperation and a respect for his audience's intelligence and discernment.

When I line up these three salient features of Higgins's communication— the telling functions of the dialogue, the restriction of the narrator, and the ethical dimension of the telling functions—against the standard model, I find myself asking the question that provides the title for this section with even more urgency: why aren't characters part of that model?

As I search for a plausible answer, I find myself in an on-the-one-hand/ on-the-other-hand dialogue of my own. On the one hand—let me call it the right—I can develop two defenses of the model: (1) *The Friends of Eddie Coyle*—and other dialogue narratives—only appear to pose a problem, because the model *implicitly* covers their ways of communicating: character-character dialogue is part of what the narrator reports to the narratee, and the speech tags are the formal signal of that reporting. The model leaves characters as implicit rather than explicit agents because, in the interests of efficiency and elegance, it names only the higher-level agents. (2) The passage I've examined, like countless other scenes of dialogue, displays a shift from the diegesis of narration to the mimesis of the character-character conversation. In that sense, the passage moves from the mediated transmission of narration to the unmediated transmission of scene. This defense is the one that I believe Chatman would offer, based on the evidence of his discussion of "nonnarrated stories," a category that for him includes narratives told in dialogue, and of his diagram at the end of *Story and Discourse,* designed to show the similarities and differences between mediated and unmediated narration:

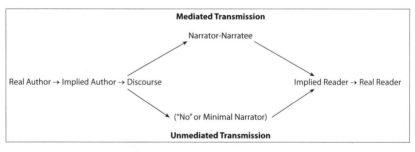

FIGURE 1.1. Mediated and Unmediated Transmission

On the other hand—the left—when I look back at the passage, I find both defenses of the standard model weak. The defense that the agency of the characters is subsumed under the agency of the narrator fails to account for the way Higgins's communication works. Because he restricts the narrator's role so severely, because he uses the characters to accomplish standard functions of narration, and because the ethics of the rhetorical exchange have so little to do with the narrator's functions and so much to do with those of the characters, any adequate model needs to identify the characters as distinct agents of narration. In other words, this defense preserves the model at the cost of its ability to adequately explain how communication in the passage works. Far better to say that characters are agents acting independently of the narrator.

The defense that the passage shifts from diegesis to mimesis fails because it packages that shift with the concept of unmediated transmission. While the scene of dialogue is itself an event in the storyworld, that dialogue is also doing a lot of mediated telling (as much as any passage of narration), and that mediated telling, as we have seen, is an integral part of the ethical dimension of the passage. It's hard not to conclude that the left hand wins the debate, well, hands down: the standard model, with its omission of characters, distorts our perception of the narrative communication here and in countless other scenes of dialogue. Consequently, the model needs—at a minimum—a substantial overhaul.

MULTIPLE CHANNELS OF COMMUNICATION AND SYNERGIES AMONG THEM

Before I sketch my version of this overhaul, I want to reflect on why it has taken so long for someone to argue that characters need to be part of the communication model. The reason, I believe, is the story/discourse distinction and its powerful effect on the perception of those who buy into it—which is to say the majority of narrative theorists. Because it has been bred in our bones, we have come to accept it as capturing something essential about the nature of narrative. Then, since characters fall on the story side of the binary distinction, and since the communication model is about discourse, we find it natural that characters are not part of it.

Once we recognize that their omission is a serious deficiency in the model, we have some good reasons to question the explanatory power of its enabling distinction. We need not renounce it, but we should replace the belief that it contains some immutable truth about narrative with an understanding that the distinction is a sometimes helpful—and sometimes not so helpful—heuristic. From this perspective, we can recognize that Chatman's model, though designed to explain narrative communication in general, actually describes a special case of it. More generally, reconfiguring the story/discourse distinction as a heuristic rather than a foundational truth liberates us to recognize that scenes of character-character dialogue often function simultaneously as events and as narration by other means, that is, as story and as discourse. Trying to decide which side of the binary such scenes fall on is like trying to decide whether Wittgenstein's famous figure (166) is either ultimately a representation of a duck (named Story) or of a rabbit (named Discourse).

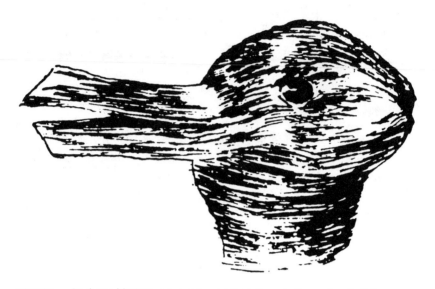

FIGURE 1.2. Duck or rabbit? Source: Jastrow, J. (1899). The mind's eye. *Popular Science Monthly,* 54, 299–312.

This recognition in turn allows us to recognize the continuity between two narrative techniques that the story/discourse distinction would put asunder: character narration and dialogue. Indeed, recognizing the continuity allows us to see scenes of dialogue as character narration on steroids. In each case, we have a single text with at least two tellers, at least two occasions, multiple audiences, and multiple purposes. Consequently, in both cases we are dealing with an art of indirection. With character narration, the implied author needs to motivate the telling according to the logic of the character narrator's occasion, audience, and purpose even as the implied author uses that motivated telling for his or her own different communications to the narrative, authorial, and actual audiences. With character-character dialogue, the implied author needs to motivate the conversational disclosures according to the logic of the occasion, the prior relationship between and among the characters, and the ongoing interpersonal dynamics of the conversation itself—even as the implied author uses the dialogue for his or her own different authorial disclosures to the other audiences.

These points lead to an even more significant conclusion: we can't revise Chatman's model simply by slotting characters into either or both of his diagrams. One or two diagrams won't be sufficient because adding characters to the model means that we now have at least *two mediated channels* (or tracks) of communication (author-narrator-audience and author-character-audience), that these channels will interact with each other, and that the second channel is also inseparable from story.

Furthermore, the interaction between the channels may be additive, as it is in the passage from *Eddie Coyle,* or it may be *synergistic.* Consider the initial communication in William Faulkner's *The Sound and the Fury.*

> Through the fence, between the curling flower spaces, I could see them hitting. They were coming toward where the flag was and I went along the fence. Luster was hunting in the grass by the flower tree. They took the flag out, and they were hitting. Then they put the flag back and they went to the table, and he hit and the other hit. Then they went on, and I went along the fence. Luster came away from the flower tree and we went along the fence and they stopped and we stopped and I looked through the fence while Luster was hunting in the grass.
>
> "Here, caddie." He hit. They went away across the pasture. I held to the fence and watched them going away.
>
> "Listen at you now." Luster said. "Aint you something, thirty three years old, going on that way. After I done went all the way to town to buy you that cake. Hush up that moaning." (3)

Among many other things, Faulkner communicates here that the trigger for Benjy's moaning is the word *caddie.* (I acknowledge the point that this communication is clearer on a second reading of the novel, but that point does not affect the comparison between Chatman's structuralist model and my rhetorical one.) The best Chatman's linear one-channel model can do with this communication that exceeds anything in the minds of characters or narrator would be something like this: the golfer's and Luster's lines of dialogue are embedded within Benjy's narration, and this embedding allows Benjy to unknowingly transmit the information about the cause of his moaning. Again, however, this account radically understates the role of the dialogue, and, even more significantly, it obscures our view of Faulkner's remarkable construction of interactive effects among Benjy's narration, the golfer's call, and Luster's dialogue.

Here's a better account: *Faulkner employs not one but three channels of communication, and he sets up a synergy among those channels to disclose the trigger for Benjy's moaning.* In addition to the *author-narrator-audience* channel identified by Chatman, Faulkner uses two *author-character-character-audience* channels that are functionally independent of that first channel and of each other, since Benjy does not alter or comment on the dialogue, and the golfer and Luster do not talk with each other. Faulkner deploys the author-golfer-caddie-audience channel to introduce the key word, and he deploys the author-Luster-Benjy-audience channel to tell us that Benjy moans. The synergy among these two communications and Benjy's naïve reporting prompts the audience's inference about the trigger. In this way, the communication arising from the interaction of the three channels is greater than the sum of the communication in each. In short, Faulkner's communication depends on characters, multiple channels, and synergy—all of which are absent from Chatman's model.

Again there is an ethical dimension to both the told and the telling. The ethics of the told involve the way Luster's treatment of Benjy is rooted in taken-for-granted assumptions about their relationship. Luster takes it for granted that he is Benjy's superior and that he has the right to object to Benjy's moaning and to tell him to hush. He also assumes that he is within his rights to call Benjy ungrateful—as if giving Benjy the cake obligated Benjy to behave in a certain way. At the same time, Luster is neither mean nor nasty. He just wants Benjy to be as little trouble as possible. The ethics of the telling arise from the contrasts between Benjy's narration and Faulkner's communication. Benjy is a naïve recorder/reporter, focused on the actions of others rather than himself, and unable to fully comprehend them, as his underinterpreting of the golf game and of Luster's searching in the grass indicate. His external focus has an appealing innocence that is set in relief by the sophisticated communication from Faulkner. Because Faulkner makes Benjy appealing even as he trusts his audience to make all those inferences, the ethics of his telling is itself appealing.

More generally, the passage is a striking example of what I venture to call the default ethics of the telling in literary narrative since modernism. This ethics is based on reciprocity and trust: the author and the audience assume that narrative communication is a shared enterprise, albeit one in which the author takes the lead. More specifically, the audience assumes that attending carefully to the author will result in a worthwhile reading experience. For his part, the author assumes that the audience can be trusted to recognize the synergies, fill in the gaps, and otherwise follow the art of mediated communication.

Lest we think that Faulkner is a high modernist outlier in his use of synergies, I turn to another, more recent example, a passage from Emma Donoghue's *Room* (2010). Donoghue's narrator is a five-year-old boy named Jack, whose mother has been kidnapped and locked for seven years in a one-room shed by a man whom Jack and his mother call Old Nick. Old Nick frequently shows up in the room and, in Jack's words, "creaks the bed" with Jack's mother. Jack's mother, whom he refers to only as Ma, has taught him that the whole world consists of their one room and Outer Space. The passage is part of Donoghue's communication about the night Old Nick visits after bringing Jack a remote-controlled Jeep as a belated birthday present. Jack, in a fit of Oedipal rage brought on by his sudden thought that Old Nick might be sucking at his mother's breast, uses the remote to send the Jeep off a shelf and down on top of Old Nick's head in the bed where he lays with Ma.

> SMASHSHSHSHSHSH.
>
> Old Nick roaring like I never heard him, something about Jesus but it wasn't Baby Jesus that did it, it was me. Lamp's on, light's banging in the slats at me, my eyes squeeze shut. I wriggle back and pull Blanket over my face.
>
> He's shouting, "What are you trying to pull?"
>
> Ma sounds all wobbly, she says, "What, what? Did you have a bad dream?"
>
> I'm biting Blanket, soft like gray bread in my mouth.
>
> "Did you try something? Did you?" His voice goes downer. "Because I told you before, it's on your head if—"
>
> "I was asleep." Ma's talking in a squashed tiny voice. "Please—look, look, it was the stupid jeep that rolled off the shelf."
>
> Jeep's not a stupid.
>
> "I'm sorry," Ma's saying, "I'm so sorry, I should have put it somewhere it wouldn't fall. I'm really really totally—"
>
> "OK."
>
> "Look, let's turn the light off—"
>
> "Nah," says Old Nick, "I'm done." (48)

Like Faulkner, Donoghue uses the synergy between the author-narrator-audience channel and the author-character-character-audience channel to communicate something that neither the narrator nor the characters report: Old Nick began to strangle Ma and then thought better of it. Jack can't report this event because it occurs while he has his eyes closed. Neither Old Nick nor Ma says anything directly about it because they don't have to: they've lived it and are focused on next steps. But by juxtaposing Jack's descriptions of Ma's voice with the dialogue between Ma and Old Nick, the implied Donoghue communicates the otherwise unreported event to her audience. Again, the synergy allows the author to communicate something greater than the sum of the information in each channel.

Furthermore, that synergy adds a rich layer to both the ethics of the told and the ethics of the telling. The dialogue itself captures the power dynamic between Old Nick and Ma and in so doing further underlines the violence that constitutes his instinctive reactions. Old Nick shouts at, accuses, and threatens Ma, while she first calmly tries to explain and then apologizes. She also seeks to get past the moment, but he simply dismisses her. Donoghue uses the juxtaposition of this power dynamic with Jack's innocent reporting to communicate vividly and efficiently the grim reality of Ma's life and, by extension, that of Jack's—and Ma's extraordinary but ultimately unsustainable effort to keep that reality from Jack.

The ethics of the telling here is another version of the default mode. Like Faulkner, Donoghue places considerable trust in her audience and asks that audience to reciprocate. Furthermore, there is a significant affective dimension to the ethics of the telling that goes along with the ethics of the told: the appeal of Jack's innocence is there in his voice just as the danger and desperation of Ma's situation is in hers. Together their voices create a remarkable combination of ethical appeal and ethical challenge that makes reading Donoghue's book such a powerful experience.

This attention to the author-character-character-audience channel and to its possible synergy with the author-narrator-audience channel invites us to look for other channels. *The Friends of Eddie Coyle,* with its thirty juxtaposed scenes of dialogue, calls attention to another one: author–structural arrangement–audience. In this third channel, the author skips over both the narrator and the characters in order to communicate to the audience through the arrangement of the narrative's disclosures of information, including through such devices as the ordering and juxtaposition of scenes and the placement of gaps in the temporal sequence. Again, since the author is not speaking directly, we ought to consider this channel as mediated communication.

In *Eddie Coyle's* penultimate chapter 29, Higgins uses the two mediated channels of communication to recount the events of the night Eddie gets whacked. Higgins again makes the dialogue the primary channel, and he again restricts the narrator to the reporting function. Eddie's so-called friend, Dillon, who has been hired by the mob bosses, carefully orchestrates the hit: he invites Eddie to attend a Bruins game with him and a younger man whom Dillon introduces as his wife's nephew but who is also getting paid by the mob bosses; Dillon gets Eddie drunk during the game so that he falls asleep in the stolen car that the kid drives; Dillon sits behind Eddie, and when they are safely out of the city, he leans forward with his revolver and plants nine rounds in Eddie's skull; finally, Dillon makes sure that Eddie's body won't be found for hours and that neither the gun he uses nor the car that takes them away from the scene can ever be traced to him.

Among the many things Higgins communicates by the juxtaposition of his final two chapters is something substantial about the ethics of the told. The juxtaposition develops a stark contrast between the smooth efficiency with which the underworld dispenses justice and the unsatisfactory inefficiency with which the legal system dispenses it. But the juxtaposition also emphasizes the catch: mob justice is much rougher, since Eddie is tried and wrongfully convicted by the rumor mill and then swiftly executed by Dillon. In this way, Higgins suggests that the legal system, despite its flaws and deficiencies that make good men question its efficacy, is far preferable. (I elaborate on this analysis in chapter 10.)

As for the ethics of the telling, Higgins gives his rhetorical readers even more room to complete the judgments about the ethics of the told than he does in the final chapter. There are no surrogates here: it's just his structuring and the audience's inferencing, his assumptions about his audience's capacities and the audience's trust that the juxtaposition is more purposeful than arbitrary. In both this juxtaposition and in the final chapter itself, Higgins provides another version of the default ethics of the telling since modernism.

AUTHORS, RESOURCES, AUDIENCES: A RHETORICAL VIEW OF NARRATIVE COMMUNICATION

One admirable feature of Chatman's diagram is its clarity. Can the rhetorical view generate something comparable? Given that the rhetorical model now identifies three mediated channels, each of which can interact with the other two, I cannot simply swap out Chatman's linear diagram for a new and improved one. Indeed, the rhetorical model cannot be diagrammed in the two dimensions available in the medium of the printed book. What I can do, however, is present a chart of possibilities. This chart identifies—and privileges—the two constants in the communication, the somebody who tells and the somebody who listens, even as it identifies the multiple resources the teller can deploy in order to connect with the audience. Here is that chart, the shorthand for which is ARA, for author, resources, and audience.

Let me highlight several salient features of this chart.

(1) As the Etc. at the end of the middle column suggests, the chart deliberately does not claim to cover all the possible resources authors can draw on. In part 2 for example, I will consider how authors can use ambiguity as a resource. In addition, different media have different resources.

(2) The chart deliberately does not specify the exact relationship among the constants and variables in any specific narrative communication. Those relationships can vary greatly from narrative to narrative and, indeed, even within the same narrative.

TABLE 1.1 CHART OF CONSTANTS AND VARIABLES IN NARRATIVE COMMUNICATION

AUTHOR	←----→	RESOURCES	←----→	AUDIENCE
ACTUAL/ IMPLIED				*AUTHORIAL AND ACTUAL (ESP. RHETORICAL)*
		Paratexts		
		Occasion		
		Narrator(s)/Narration		
		Characters/Dialogue		
		FID		
		Voice		
		Style		
		Space		
		Temporality		
		Arrangement/Gaps		
		Narratee/Narrative Audience		
		Genre/(Non)Fictionality		
		Intertextual References		
		Ambiguities		
		Etc.		

(3) With regard to the first column, I have included the slash between Actual Author and Implied Author for two reasons: (a) I find that the extended arguments about the efficacy of the concept of implied author have given the term so much baggage that it does not readily communicate what I would like it to, that is, the streamlined version of the actual author responsible for the construction of the narrative, including its ethical and thematic commitments. From the rhetorical perspective, designating an authorial agent is far more important than whether one calls that agent an author or implied author. To put this point another way, theorists who want to reject the implied author but retain the author as the constructor of the text have far more in common with me than those who want to reject the implied author because they believe meanings arise primarily out of text-audience interactions. That said, (b) I still find the concept of the implied author useful, and, in some cases, I find it all but indispensable. On its overall utility, see the discussion in chapter 9. On its indispensability, consider hoax memoirs and especially the negative responses the exposure of the hoax typically generates. In those cases, drawing on the difference between the actual author and implied author enables a clear and effective account of the teller-listener relationships. The actual author perpetrates the hoax by constructing a purported version of himself who tells

about the events as having actually occurred. In other words, the actual author constructs an implied author who unknowingly presents fabrications as facts, and the authorial audience takes them as such—and so too do those rhetorical readers who join the authorial audience. Once the hoax is exposed, rhetorical readers (and indeed, many other members of the actual audience) feel justifiably betrayed by the actual author's deceptions. Indeed, that negative ethical judgment is part of the rhetorical reader's step-two evaluation of the act of reading. But there is typically another group of readers who say that the deceptions don't matter much to them because they still value their reading experience. Such readers are typically responding to their relationship with the implied rather than the actual author.

(4) With audience, I break symmetry and don't include a slash between the authorial and actual readers for two reasons: (a) The difference is clear: while some theorists, such as David Herman (*Narrative Theory* 2012), find fault with the concept of an authorial audience, no one argues about its meaning; (b) The difference has a significant payoff in explaining how narrative communication works (or doesn't work) from a rhetorical perspective. The case of hoax memoirs is again a good example. But a more common situation also supports the point. As individual readers, we often find ourselves missing things in the authorial communication that we recognize (either while reading or in later conversation with other readers) that we are supposed to get. What we're experiencing on these occasions is the gap between the authorial and the actual audience—and we're also glimpsing the difficulty of being a successful rhetorical reader. See also number 6.

(5) I also locate the actual and authorial audiences together in the same column rather than putting the authorial audience in the resources column alongside the narratee and narrative audience for two reasons: (a) to emphasize the difference between text-specific devices employed by the author in the larger communication (narrative audience and narratee) and the authorial and actual audiences as the ultimate recipients of that larger communication and (b) to highlight the close relationship between the authorial and actual audiences in rhetorical reading—and thus, my use of the term *rhetorical readers* to identify those members of the actual audience focused on entering the authorial audience. As I noted in chapter 1, authorial audiences are typically a combination of an author's hypotheses about actual audiences and the author's decisions (conscious or intuitive) about the qualities she or he wants the audience to have. Actual rhetorical readers may have more or less difficulty in joining the authorial audience, but by definition, they want to.

(6) I also highlight the actual audience as a key constant in order to emphasize the point that the implied author's purpose in telling is to affect

real rather than hypothetical audiences. This conclusion, of course, is especially significant when we come to discuss the ethical consequences of reading. Furthermore, highlighting the actual audience prepares the way to the second step of rhetorical reading: moving outside of the authorial audience and evaluating the multilayered experiences offered by the narrative. I will discuss this point more fully when I take up the differences between unreliable and deficient narration in chapter 9.

(7) The second column, unlike Chatman's model, lists not just human agents but also other resources, such as occasion and arrangement, that authors deploy for significant communicative effects. I have already commented on how Higgins uses arrangement for his rhetorical and ethical purposes. As for occasion, think of how much Robert Browning in "My Last Duchess" communicates about the ethical character of the Duke of Ferrara with the artfully delayed disclosure that the Duke tells the story of his previous wife on the occasion of a visit from the representative of the father of his bride-to-be.

(8) I recognize that there is a considerable diversity among the resources—narrative audience and narratee are very different from paratexts, which in turn are different from voice and style. But placing them all in the same column highlights two points: they are all text-based, and in any given passage, some resources are likely to be more valuable than others (as further reflection on a category such as occasion suggests).

(9) Emphasizing the author/implied author as a constant and the narrator as a variable resource reorders their priority in narratological analysis. In Chatman's model, the implied author delegates just about everything to the narrator or to the nonnarrated mimesis. In my model, the implied author typically does not tell directly, but he or she does more than hand over the telling to the narrator, as my focus on the channel of narrative arrangement suggests.

Here is another example from *Eddie Coyle*: The first sentence of the novel is "Jackie Brown at twenty-six, with no expression on his face, said that he could get some guns" (3). The first sentence of chapter 19 is "With no expression on his face, Jackie Brown sat in the outer office, his cuffed hands in his lap" (114). And as quoted above, the first clause of the last chapter is "Jackie Brown at twenty-seven sat with no expression on his face" (179). The echo contributes substantially to the communication of the ethics of the told: in all three moments, despite the changes in experience and especially the changes in his understanding of Eddie Coyle, Jackie Brown is essentially the same tough guy—though in the second two situations he sits in silence rather than making deals.

Who is the agent constructing these echoes? Given that Higgins makes minimal use of the narrator, typically restricting his function either to identifying speakers or to straightforward reporting of events, I find it implausible to attribute that construction to the narrator: such an attribution would give him a strange and inconsistent self-consciousness. I therefore understand the echo as constructed only by the implied Higgins. Just as Browning, not the Duke of Ferrara, is the agent responsible for the iambic pentameter couplets in "My Last Duchess," so too the implied Higgins, not the restricted narrator, is responsible for these echoes in *Eddie Coyle*. In this way, the implied Higgins is using the resource of his reliable but highly restricted narrator to communicate to his audience over the head or behind the back of that narrator. Notice that these metaphors are the ones theorists of unreliable narration use to talk about that technique. In this way, the new model, with its emphasis on the implied author as the ultimate somebody who tells, allows us to recognize that even the valuable distinction between reliable and unreliable narration is less important than the overarching issue of how the implied author uses the various resources of narrative communication at his disposal. I will return to this point in my discussion of reliable narration in chapter 11. Notice, too, how this recognition heightens the collusion between implied author and rhetorical readers—how, in other words, it is another variation on the default ethics of the telling.

(10) While Chatman's model conceives of narrative communication as unidirectional, highlighting the audience as a constant helps us recognize that audiences exert their influence on the author's deployment of resources. If Donoghue were to write *Room* for children, she would write it very differently. If Higgins were to write *Eddie Coyle* for children, he would have to make even more radical revisions. So far, so obvious. But when we add the temporal dimension to the rhetorical exchange—that is, the way that the communication unfolds over time—then the audience's role in that communication can become even more significant. I seek to demonstrate this point in the next chapter.

CHAPTER 2

Somebody Telling *Somebody Else*

AUDIENCES AND PROBABLE IMPOSSIBILITIES

"I broke my hip!" Mrs. Croft announced, as if no time had passed.

"Oh dear, madame."

"I fell off the bench!"

"I am so sorry, madame."

"It was the middle of the night! Do you know what I did, boy?"

I shook my head.

"I called the police!"

She stared up at the ceiling and grinned sedately, exposing a crowded row of long gray teeth. Not one was missing. "What do you say to that, boy?"

As stunned as I was, I knew what I had to say. With no hesitation at all, I cried out, "Splendid!"

Mala laughed then. Her voice was full of kindness, her eyes bright with amusement. I had never heard her laugh before . . .

—JHUMPA LAHIRI, "THE THIRD AND FINAL CONTINENT" (194–95;
    MY EMPHASIS)

FIGURE 2.1. A turning point in *Stitches,* part I. David
Small, *Stitches* (253).

FIGURE 2.2. A turning point in *Stitches,* part II. David Small, *Stitches* (255).

> The poet should prefer probable impossibilities to improbable possibilities.
>
> —ARISTOTLE, *POETICS*, CHAPTER 24

DESPITE THEIR obvious differences—in content, technique, and media—these extracts from *Stitches* and "The Third and Final Continent," when viewed through ARA's lens and its focus on reading experiences, have three salient commonalities: (1) In each, as I will explain shortly, the implied author violates the dominant logic governing the probability of cause-effect relationships in the narrative. (2) In each, both the actual and authorial audiences are not likely to notice the violation or to be bothered by it, if they do. (This claim indicates that I do not regard the violation in *Stitches* to be Small's depiction of his psychiatrist, Dr. Harold Davidson, as the White Rabbit from *Alice in Wonderland*, a point that I'll return to in the next paragraph.) (3) In each, the author's violation increases the experiential effectiveness of the narrative.

In the case of "The Third and Final Continent," the dominant cause-effect logic is that of fictional mimesis: Lahiri constructs characters who could plausibly exist and events that could plausibly occur in the extratextual world. Lahiri violates that mimetic logic by having her character, Mala, perform a specific action (laughing) at this specific moment, because that action deviates from the chain of cause and effect set up in the storyworld. In the case of *Stitches*, the logic is that of memoir, a logic that allows for the expression of subjective truths within a representation ultimately bound by reference to actual people and events. The violation does not involve Small's drawing of the psychiatrist as the White Rabbit from *Alice in Wonderland*, since that is a clearly marked excursion into fictionality designed to capture the subjective truth of their relationship. The violation instead involves the probability of the psychiatrist making these pronouncements to David on the occasion of his first visit.

Violations such as these are as old as narrative itself, but I believe that rhetorical theory has something new to say about them, especially about what they reveal about the importance of audiences for the very construction of narrative. Aristotle called out such violations in the *Poetics* with the famous dictum that I have used as my third epigraph: "The poet should prefer *probable impossibilities* to improbable possibilities" (24.10; my emphasis), and he offers an example from the work commonly regarded as the first narrative in the Western literary tradition: Achilles' solo pursuit of Hector in book 22 of the *Iliad* (the incident is "impossible" because Achilles' fellow soldiers would not have let him go it alone). Aristotle goes so far as to pronounce Achilles' pursuit as "justified," but, unfortunately, he doesn't offer much explanation of that assessment beyond the general point that it renders the epic "more striking" (25.5). Commentators on Aristotle such as Andrew Ford (more on Ford below) regard his dictum as consistent with his emphasizing that poets should shape their plots for maximum effect on their audiences. If the violation of probability productively adds to the effect, it can be justified. I agree with that reading of Aristotle, but I find that there's a lot more to unpack in the phenomena of probable impossibilities and other implausibilities (and for my purposes, I consider probable impossibilities and implausibilities as two subtypes of the larger phenomenon of justified deviations from the dominant system of probability in a narrative). I also acknowledge at the outset that some narratives contain unjustified deviations—unconvincing improbabilities and impossibilities such as the phenomena covered by the term *deus ex machina*.[1] These improbabilities and impossibilities are unconvincing because they arise out of an authorial need to have something happen rather than out of the logic of the progression. For my purposes, these unjustified deviations are worth noting, because they, like Dorothea Brooke's poor dress, set in relief the beauty of something else.

In order to begin my unpacking of probable impossibilities and related phenomena, I will look closely at the case of *Stitches*—and some other cases of implausibility that help with that unpacking. I will return to Lahiri in chapter 11 because I want to show how she integrates her handling of (im)probability with her handling of other resources—character-character dialogue, reliable narration, and the synergies between them—that I will discuss in more detail between now and then. But my major claim about the phenomena associated with improbabilities applies to both cases. In them, *the implied author relies (consciously or intuitively) on the authorial audience's unfolding responses to the narrative progression as he or she constructs new parts of the text. In other words, these unfolding responses in the trajectory of readerly dynamics not only have a discernible effect on the textual dynamics but they also justify the deviations from probability.* To put this point another way, readers regard the impossibilities or implausibilities as probable because of a "crossover effect" between readerly and textual dynamics. Moreover, *these probable deviations are not one-off or anomalous phenomena but instructive examples that indicate how tellers frequently rely on the unfolding of readerly dynamics in their construction of textual dynamics.* In other words, authors often construct narrative progressions that so deeply intertwine textual and readerly dynamics

---

1. For an illuminating discussion of such cases, see Ryan, "Cheap Plot Tricks."

that readerly dynamics become not just a consequence of textual dynamics but also a force that shapes them. Furthermore, *this crossover effect is itself an especially strong manifestation of a phenomenon more central to the construction and reception of narrative than has previously been recognized: the mutual influence of authorial and readerly agency on the shape of narrative texts.*

To develop these points, I will start with Aristotle and then turn to the neo-Aristotelian Sheldon Sacks, who worked in his own instructive way on the interconnection between textual and readerly dynamics.[2] I will then look at some other cases that further prepare the way for the analysis of *Stitches.*

ARISTOTLE ON PROBABILITY

In chapter 9 of the *Poetics,* Aristotle declares that "it is not the function of the poet to relate what has happened, but what may happen—what is possible according to the law of probability or necessity" (9.1). This declaration not only fits well with Aristotle's claims that tragedy is an imitation of an action and that there is pleasure in imitation, but it also provides the basis for his claim that poetry is more philosophical than history. By following the law of probability and necessity, poetry, unlike history, can go beyond what has happened to what may happen and thus go beyond the particular to the universal. With this cluster of claims and conclusions, then, Aristotle identifies necessary conditions for an effective poetic construction. By the same reasoning, a poet who violates the law of probability and necessity would be introducing error into the imitation, as Aristotle himself says early on in chapter 25. Strikingly, however, Aristotle, for all his systematic rigor, doesn't stop there, but goes on to his famous dictum that the poet should prefer probable impossibilities to improbable possibilities, citing the pursuit of Hector as a "justified error."

In "Literary Criticism and the Poet's Autonomy," Andrew Ford offers what I believe is a standard explanation of Aristotle's thinking. Aristotle, he explains, views literary works as following "rules inherent in the form," and he therefore believes a work may contain "distortions of reality or even untruths" if such materials contribute to the poem's overall effect more powerfully than strict adherence to reality or truth would allow it to do (149). With regard

2. I approach Aristotle in the same spirit that the first-generation Chicago School theorists did. R. S. Crane nicely captured this spirit in his introduction to *Critics and Criticism,* when he noted that he and his fellow contributors have reconstructed an Aristotle "that is not [identical to] the Aristotle of [his scholarly] commentators. It may not, indeed, except in a general way, be Aristotle at all!" (17). In other words, I want to make a plausible reconstruction of Aristotle's thought, but I am less concerned about having that reconstruction pass muster with classicists than I am with using it as a launching point for productive explorations into the logic of literature that was never dreamed of in Aristotle's philosophy.

to the example of Hector, Ford brings in Aristotle's longer discussion of it in chapter 24, where Aristotle (a) commends the incident for adding to the marvelous effects of the *Iliad* and (b) notes that the impossibility of the scene, which would be "ludicrous" on the stage, is less conspicuous in epic narration (24.8). On the stage, the audience would see Achilles waving the Greek soldiers away, an impossible scenario given the norms of military combat (the scenario would be akin to an American football player on defense waving away his teammates so that he would be the only one who could tackle the ball carrier).

I find that this commentary is good as far as it goes but that it underestimates the consequences of Aristotle's discussion in chapter 25.[3] First, it's worth pausing over the terms *probable impossibilities* and *improbable possibilities*: they make sense only if there are two systems of probability at work: (a) the law of probability and necessity referred to in chapter 9, which exists external to the work, and (b) the system of probability internal to the work, a system that arises from the poet's selection and arrangement of events and their leading to certain expectations in the audience. In the term *probable impossibilities,* the adjective refers to the text-internal system and the noun to the text-external system. And so too with the term *improbable possibilities.* Second, when Aristotle stipulates that the poet should follow the law of probability and necessity, he indicates that the two systems are interrelated but that the external should govern the internal.

Third—and here's where things get fascinating—by expressing his preference for probable impossibilities and by claiming that they can be justified, Aristotle indicates that sometimes the text-internal system can override the text-external system. At that point, he has introduced a loophole in his chapter 9 dictum large enough for the Greek army to march through. Fourth, Aristotle's choosing the pursuit of Hector as his case in point takes Aristotle to the brink of reversing the hierarchy of the two systems. To put this point another way, the choice of example takes Aristotle to the brink of subordinating poetics, with its focus on textual structures, to rhetoric, with its focus on authors and audiences. My reading of the *Poetics* takes him over that brink.

If Aristotle wanted just to qualify what he says about probability and necessity in chapter 9, he could have cited an example of a justifiable probable impossibility by referring to an event that plays a minor but necessary

---

3. Classicists believe that *Poetics* 25 is a digest of Aristotle's lost book on Homeric Problems, and that in discussing the pursuit of Hector he is addressing a problem identified by some commentator who regards Achilles' keeping his fellow Greeks at bay with a nod of his head or a wave of his hand as a violation of probability. My main interest is in how Aristotle's handling of this problem complicates the overall view of probability in the *Poetics.* I am indebted to Genevieve Lively for sharing her expertise about Aristotle with me.

role in its larger work or to an event whose impossibility would not be readily apparent. But the pursuit of Hector is a far more radical choice for several reasons. It is, as Aristotle has just noted in chapter 24, an event that in itself is ludicrous, and, thus, easily recognizable as impossible by Homer's audience. Yet it is not just a major part of book 22 but also a major part of the climax of the whole epic. Furthermore, Homer highlights its importance by elaborating on the role of the gods in the chase, by giving each character major speeches, and by showing the effects of Achilles' killing of Hector on Priam, Hecuba, and Achilles' fellow Greeks. In other words, Aristotle's example is impossible, major, and not at all concerned about its audience being able to detect the impossibility.

This discussion leads me to two other conclusions: (1) Aristotle provides a model of the a posteriori method underlying rhetorical poetics, as he reasons back from effects to their causes in the construction of the work. If Aristotle were using an a priori method, he would apply the dictum that the poet must follow the law of probability and necessity and conclude that Homer's "error" could not be justified. However, because book 22 of the *Iliad* is so affectively powerful and because its power is so appropriate to the story of the wrath of Achilles, Aristotle decides that the "error" is justified. (2) For Aristotle, the text-internal system of probability itself has two dimensions: a logic of the unfolding action and a logic of the audience's unfolding affective responses to that action. "The error may be justified," he writes, "if the end of the art be thereby attained . . . if, that is, the effect of this or any other part of the poem is thus rendered more striking" (25.5). For Aristotle, effects are primarily affective ones, as his focus on pity, fear, and catharsis and his discussion of the desirable effects of the marvelous in chapter 24 all indicate.

The pursuit of Hector, then, is justified because by book 22 author and audience both need the one-on-one confrontation between the two principal figures on each side of the Trojan War. Homer needs it as a climax in his shaping of the story of Achilles' wrath, and the audience needs it as a climax in the overall trajectory of emotional responses generated by Homer's shaping of Achilles' story. Indeed, by this logic, the pursuit of Hector is not an "error" at all but a brilliant contribution to both parts of the text-internal system of probability. This logic, as I trust is now evident, is that of rhetorical poetics.

SHELDON SACKS ON READERLY INFERENCES ABOUT GENRE

Although Sheldon Sacks is primarily known today as the founding editor of *Critical Inquiry,* he wrote both *Fiction and the Shape of Belief* (1964), an important book about how choices of genre strongly influence the ways in which authors of fiction embed their ethical beliefs in their narratives, and some remarkable essays about the power of genre.[4] In his 1968 essay "The Psychological Implications of Generic Distinctions," Sacks proposed two intriguing hypotheses about genre: "traditional generic distinctions . . . are forms of intuitive knowledge actually used by readers to comprehend and writers to create literary works" (106), and "there is at least a strong probability that more abstract knowledge underlying [generic] distinctions are . . . innate dispositions of the human psyche" (111). While I join most of Sacks's readers in finding the second hypothesis fascinating but untenable, I find the first hypothesis fascinating, sound, and, when appropriately modified, extremely valuable for rhetorical poetics. Let me explain by telling a story about Sacks's teaching of a text whose narrative turns on a probable impossibility, and then returning to his essay on generic distinctions.

In the spring of 1973, at the end of my very difficult MA year, I took Sacks's course in the eighteenth-century British novel. That course turned out to be the transformative event in my academic career because it gave me a nascent understanding of how what readers did as they followed novels from page to page could serve as the basis for formal academic interpretation and theory. One way Sacks taught the thirty or so of us in that course was by emphasizing the power of textual patterns on our readerly intuitions about genre. He illustrated the point throughout the course in our discussions of all the novels we read. I can't say I still have the syllabus because Sacks never gave us one, but memory tells me they were *Pride and Prejudice, Pamela, Tom Jones, Rasselas, Gulliver's Travels, Humphry Clinker,* and *Tristram Shandy.* One day, however, Sacks decided to step back from the intricacies of these works and use a much simpler text to illustrate his larger points. In fact, he started by giving us only part of the text, whose author he identified as that prodigious and diverse figure "Anonymous."

Expenses for the Month

Oct. 1	Ad for female stenographer	1.00
Oct. 4	Violets for new stenographer	1.50
Oct. 6	Week's salary for new stenographer	45.00
Oct. 9	Roses for stenographer	5.00
Oct. 10	Candy for wife	.90
Oct. 13	Lunch for stenographer	7.00
Oct. 15	Week's salary for stenographer	60.00

4. For some thoughtful engagements with Sacks's work, see Springer, Lipking, Kincaid, and Rader, "Literary."

Oct. 16 Movie tickets for wife and self	1.20
Oct. 18 Theatre tickets for steno and self	16.00
Oct. 19 Ice cream sundae for wife	.30
Oct. 22 Mary's salary	75.00
Oct. 23 Champagne & dinner for Mary & self	32.00[5]

In 2017 what stands out in this text, besides the amazingly low prices and salaries, is its deep reliance on gender stereotypes and heteronormative assumptions. Sacks noted the stereotypes but didn't dwell on them. I find them more troubling, but I am also optimistic that my readers don't share them. In any case, Sacks asked us to write the ending. I'll pause here and invite you to do the same.

WHAT DID YOU come up with?

Our suggestions in 1973 were about various ways to resolve what we regarded as the unstable triangle involving the record keeper, his wife, and the stenographer. The most common proposal was for an entry such as "October 30 Retainer for divorce lawyer 100," although some of my classmates proposed entries that gave more agency to the record keeper's wife. None of us, however, anticipated the final entries Sacks wrote on the board:

Oct. 25 Doctor for stupid stenographer	375.00
Oct. 26 Mink stole for wife	1,700.00
Oct. 28 Ad for male stenographer	1.50
Total expenses for month	$2,321.90

Sacks then engaged us in a discussion about the inferences we drew from these entries, a discussion that led to a consensus that the record keeper paid for an abortion, that he bought the mink out of guilt, and that he advertised for a male stenographer so as not to succumb to temptation again. (Today we'd probably have added "or so as to make sure that the next stenographer

---

5. I'm using the version of the story used by Ralph Rader in his 1974 *Critical Inquiry* essay, "Fact, Theory, and Literary Explanation," and reprinted in *Fact, Fiction, and Form* (though I have added the title, which I believe Sacks also used). I know that Rader and Sacks had discussed the story and no doubt influenced each other's takes on it. Sacks's treatment of it in class was in line with Rader's discussion of it in his essay, so what I say here applies to Rader's commentary as well. But since Rader didn't agree with Sacks about the psychological implications of generic distinctions, and I want to get at something that I see as crucial to Sacks's argument for those implications, I've chosen to keep my focus on Sacks's teaching of the story.

could not become pregnant." More seriously, today we'd also have discussed the misogynistic assumptions upon which the whole story is built.) Sacks also drew our attention to how these inferences both fit with and reconfigured the patterns of the first twelve entries, resulting in a conclusion that this ending was better than anything we had come up with because of its deft management of an appropriate surprise. Most importantly, we could recognize this ending as better because we had intuitively grasped the genre of the story: it's a joke that takes the form of a punitive comedy designed to provoke laughter; its structural logic is one in which the protagonist is given a temporary license to advance his interests by transgressing the ethical norms of his world, only to have the license taken away and to end up appropriately and comically punished for his transgressions.

Sacks had all of us nodding, but he wasn't finished. He called our attention to the glitch in the story, its probable impossibility (though I don't recall that he used the term). In 1973, let alone the unknown year further in the past in which the story is set, it would not be possible within the time frame of the story for the stenographer to be pregnant by the record keeper and know it. What to do? Sacks identified two main options with an additional choice accompanying the first one: (1) Change or reinterpret the story so that its events remain within the realm of the possible. The change would involve having the same events play out over a time span long enough for the stenographer to know that her employer was the father of her unborn child. The reinterpretation would involve inferring that the stenographer got involved with the record keeper in order to entrap him into paying for her abortion. (2) Accept the impossibility as a "justified error," or in Sacks's terms, a minor flaw necessary for the story to deliver the effect appropriate to its genre of punitive comedy.[6]

Sacks preferred the second option for several reasons: (1) The affective punch of this punitive comedy depends on its brevity and pace; changing the story so that it extends over a longer period of time would weaken its appeal. (2) Reinterpreting the story would entail flipping the relationship between victim and victimizer, and that flip goes against the grain of our intuitive apprehension of the punitive comedy underlying the joke. (3) The story is not otherwise greatly concerned with extratextual probability, as a little reflection on the mix of personal and business expenses and the restriction of what's included in the ledger indicate (no phone bill or other nonrelationship matters).

---

6. Rader opts for a version of this second option, calling the glitch "an unintended and unavoidable negative consequence" of the execution of a "positive constructive intention" ("Fact, Theory" 38).

In 1973 I was fully persuaded by Sacks's reasoning. Now I'm still persuaded by his conclusion but want to revise his reasoning to some degree. While I agree with reasons 1 and 3, I worry that Sacks's assigning the story to a particular genre involves some a priori thinking on his part: the inference about genre seems to control Sacks's consideration of the alternative. More than that, I think that Sacks's reliance on the significance of genre obscures something more fundamental to the feedback loop among authorial agency, textual phenomena, and readerly response in the story: the role of the audience's unfolding responses to the progression on the very construction of that progression. Let's look more closely at the hypothesis that the textual signals of the story should lead us to reinterpret it.

We might justify the reinterpretation (that the stenographer was already pregnant) by arguing that it is well-grounded in Anonymous's use of temporality as a communicative resource. In this account, Anonymous follows external probability and uses the temporality as a signal to prompt our reconfiguration of character and events and our understanding of the story's genre. Rather than being a joke built on the genre of punitive comedy, the story would become a more serio-comic tale in which Anonymous, while appropriately punishing the record keeper, also gives significant covert agency to the stenographer and puts some affective and ethical weight on her experiences. Note that reasons 1 and 3 for preferring the "probable impossibility" reading don't work against this hypothesis, and thus, at this point, appealing to genre isn't sufficient for adjudicating between the hypotheses.

What does work against the reinterpretation, however, is something prior to the inference about genre, the more detailed and textured unfolding of readerly experience, which, I suggest, follows what I shall call the Rule of Dominant Focus: once an author shapes the textual dynamics to establish a dominant focus for the audience, the author relies on that focus in the construction of new elements of the progression—even if those new elements lead the audience to reinterpret the dominant focus. (I will return to this rule later in the chapter.) Let me explain by briefly shifting away from the story's ending to the entry for Oct. 22: "Mary's salary 75.00." In the course of our discussion, Sacks asked, "Who is Mary?" and we confidently and promptly answered, "The stenographer." But when Sacks then asked, "How do you know that Mary is not some other employee?," we realized that we could not cite any definitive textual evidence. Instead, as Sacks pointed out, both the answer and the conviction with which we gave it arise from the interplay between the textual patterning, our inferencing about it, and the effects that follow from that inferencing. More generally, inferring that Mary is the stenographer involves privileging the text-internal system of probability (which "of course" indicates that Mary has to be the stenographer) over the text-external system (which gives rise to the question of whether Mary is another employee).

I want to extend Sacks's point to what I now see as a more radical one: Anonymous relies on his audience's unfolding responses as he writes this minimalist entry. In other words, Anonymous knows that the audience will infer that Mary is the stenographer rather than some other employee because he infers that the audience will have intuited the pattern of growing intimacy between employer and employee and will therefore infer that his switching from referring to her by her job title to referring to her by her name perfectly fits that pattern. Furthermore, Anonymous relies on these inferences to heighten the audience's negative ethical judgments of the record keeper's character, which are in turn crucial to the audience's laughter at and satisfaction in the reversal of fortune that occurs at the end of the month. Note that all of these responses to the entry are distinct from any definitive conclusion about the story's genre.

Furthermore, this inferencing is all about the playing out of the stereotypical triangle of the record keeper, his female employee, and his unnamed wife—indeed, an additional inference is about the significance of the record keeper naming the employee but not his wife. In other words, the Dominant Focus of the story is on (a) the ethical character of the record keeper and (b) the rapid playing out—and the twist—of the stereotypical narrative. For better and worse, the focus of the story is not on the ethical character of either the wife or the stenographer. Reinterpreting the story entails piling up inferences about the ethical character of the stenographer rooted not in the Dominant Focus but only in the need to keep the story within the bounds of the possible: she astutely assesses her boss's ethical character and his relationship with his wife in order to manipulate him into paying for her abortion, and so on. In this respect, the reinterpretation, while still, of course, possible, looks more and more like an overreading of the recalcitrant detail. To put this point another way, paying attention to the Dominant Focus of the textual and readerly dynamics means that the "probable impossibility" reading of the story is more probable (!) than the reinterpretation.[7]

Extrapolating from this discussion of "Expenses for the Month," I find additional confirmation for the conclusion that the text-internal system is a synthesis of two progressions, that of the representation of the events and that of the audience's responses to that representation. Furthermore, the synthesis makes the system recursive: the audience's responses to early parts of the text

---

7. For a related argument about probability, albeit one grounded in a historicist analysis of the mode of sentimentality, see Chandler.

influence the construction of later parts, which in turn influence the audience's responses to those parts, and so on and so on.

These conclusions influence my reading of "The Psychological Implications of Generic Distinctions." In that essay, Sacks poses the problem of how to explain an audience's confident interpretations of potentially ambiguous events as unambiguous parts of unfolding genres. He notes, for example, that at the beginning of chapter 2 of *Pride and Prejudice,* the narrator reports that "Mr. Bennet was among the earliest of those who waited on Mr. Bingley. He had always intended to visit him, though to the last assuring his wife that he should not go; and till the evening after the visit was paid, she had no knowledge of it." Sacks argues that

> in theory it would be possible to interpret the information conveyed to us in the stylistically neutral sentences as evidence that we are to regard Mr. Bennet with horror since, in one sense, the information is final proof that the first chapter had revealed an intelligent and ironic man pointlessly tormenting his ignorant and vulgar wife. (107)

Sacks contends that this theoretical possibility is so rarely actualized by readers because, by the end of chapter 1, they have intuited that the novel is a comedy and that intuition governs their reading of those stylistically neutral sentences.

But why should readers coming to the novel for the first time intuit a comic genre, since there is no one-to-one correspondence between any set of textual signals and the inference of comedy? Sacks's answer consists of two main moves: (1) He posits the assumption that "a finite—perhaps even a very limited—number of formal aesthetic ends are known in advance by any reader capable of reading a comedy as a comedy, or, indeed, by any writer capable of writing one" (110). With a limited number of options, the reader can more easily make correct choices with exposure to just a few signals of the generic pattern. (2) Sacks deduces an account of how readers and writers acquire their knowledge of this finite number of artistic ends by developing an analogy with language acquisition, especially as understood through Noam Chomsky's work on generative grammar. Chomsky's work indicates that linguists cannot explain the human ability to construct and understand new sentences unless they conceive of the mind as having some innate disposition to learn the grammar of a language. The actual acquisition of the grammar, of course, depends on some combination of "innate ideas and external experience" (111). So, too, says Sacks, does the acquisition of generic distinctions. We are not born with generic patterns imprinted on our minds, but we are born with a mental disposition to intuit such patterns after exposure to specific instances of them. When we encounter a new work, our knowledge of the limited number of patterns allows us to place it in the appropriate genre—sometimes as early as the second chapter.

Sacks admits that his argument for the second hypothesis is speculative, and, as I noted above, I find the speculations more fascinating than persuasive. Sacks does not provide sufficient warrant for the assumption about the limited number of genres, and the argument by analogy is vulnerable from multiple directions, including that it overlooks the differences between learning a first-order sign system (language) and a second-order sign system (generic distinctions). Attending to the differences would seriously complicate the argument because it would mean giving a much larger role to culture's influence on the second-order sign system. Furthermore, applying a posteriori reasoning leads me to be skeptical of the hypothesis: the vast corpus of narratives in the world does not seem to be reducible to only a few genres.

On the other hand, Sacks's point about how readers typically respond to the beginning of chapter 2 of *Pride and Prejudice* does invite further thought about intuitive knowledge in our reading. Rather than locating that intuitive knowledge in the apprehension of a genre, I propose a more flexible conclusion: the unfolding responses of the audience function as tentative, open-ended frames within which they comprehend new parts of literary works. These unfolding responses can include but would not be restricted to the apprehension of a work's genre. In the case of the first few sentences of chapter 2 of Austen's novel, such an inference about genre is not necessary. Instead, because Austen in chapter 1 so closely aligns the voice and values of Mr. Bennet with the voice and values of her narrator, it is going to take something more egregious than his actually doing what his wife wants him to do and not telling her until after the fact to alter our ethical judgments of him.

BEYOND ARISTOTLE AND SACKS: IMPLAUSIBILITIES AND READERLY DYNAMICS

I turn now to elaborate on my claim in the introduction to this chapter that *probable deviations are not one-off or anomalous phenomena but rather instructive examples that indicate how tellers frequently rely on the unfolding of readerly dynamics in their construction of textual dynamics* by looking at two cases of implausible narration, one in *Adventures of Huckleberry Finn* and the other in *The Great Gatsby*. These analyses will then prepare the way for my discussion of the panels from *Stitches* that serve as my first epigraph.

Before turning to Twain's novel, I want to note differences and similarities between probability as it applies to events and probability as it applies to narration. Probability as it applies to events is primarily about an unfolding sequence of causality: how probable is the initiating event (in light of what we know about character and storyworld), and how probably does cause X within the constraints of this storyworld lead to event Y? Probability as it applies to narration is primarily a question of epistemology: How can such and such a narrator in such and such a situation know what he or she knows? Alternatively, how can a naïve, unself-conscious narrator withhold important information until its revelation has maximum effect? (Gérard Genette has labeled situations in which narrators tell more than they seemingly should be able to know paralepsis, and situations in which narrators tell less than they know paralipsis [*Narrative Discourse* 195].) But underneath this epistemological question is a concern with causality: how this effect (this narrator's knowing or withholding this information) can be reconciled with what appear to be insufficient causes to produce it (the limitations of what such and such a narrator in such and such a situation can be presumed to know, or the limitations that unself-conscious naïveté put on a narrator's command of the telling).

There is an additional important consideration about probability as it applies to narration: the role of conventions. For example, there is a convention in fictional narrative that authorizes omniscient narration, and there is a convention in nonfictional narrative that authorizes memoirists to quote long-past conversations verbatim. The existence of such conventions is instructive for two reasons: (1) It indicates that authors and audiences have found it worthwhile to suspend the laws of extratextual probability in exchange for the positive effects on the overall feedback loop that the conventions make possible. (2) Once established, a convention can function as part of the dominant probability scheme of a narrative. In practical terms, then, an omniscient narrator in a nineteenth-century novel is neither an impossibility nor an improbability, and a memoirist quoting long-ago conversations is not a liar. This point about conventions also entails a point about history: since conventions change over time, what counts as a violation at one period may become conventional at another.

Although the *Adventures of Huckleberry Finn* includes some outlandish episodes, Mark Twain, in the first two-thirds of the novel, primarily operates with the probability system of fictional mimesis: Huck is designed to be a plausible adolescent and his adventures are designed to follow extratextual patterns of cause and effect. In the beginning of chapter 2, Huck reports two events that occur on a nighttime excursion he has with Tom Sawyer, events that are consistent with this system of probability. Tom helps himself to some candles from the Widow Douglas's kitchen, leaving a five-cent piece for them on the kitchen table, and then plays a practical joke on Jim, who has fallen asleep in the yard. Tom slips Jim's hat off and hangs it on a nearby tree. Before continuing with Huck's account of the night's adventures, however, Twain has Huck flash forward to recount Jim's response to these events:

> Afterwards Jim said the witches bewitched him and put him in a trance, and rode him all over the State, and then set him under the trees again, and hung his hat on a limb to show who done it. And next time Jim told it he said they rode him down to New Orleans: and, after that, every time he told it he spread it more and more, till by and by he said they rode him all over the world, and tired him most to death, and his back was all over saddle-boils. . . . Niggers is always talking about witches in the dark by the kitchen fire; but whenever one was talking and letting on to know all about such things, Jim would happen in and say, "Hm! What you know 'bout witches?" and that nigger was corked up and had to take a back seat. Jim always kept that five-center piece round his neck with a string, and said it was a charm the devil give to him with his own hands, and told him he could cure anybody with it and fetch witches whenever he wanted to just by saying something to it; but he never told what it was he said to it. Niggers would come from all around there and give Jim anything they had, just for a sight of that five-center piece; but they wouldn't touch it, because the devil had had his hands on it. Jim was most ruined for a servant, because he got stuck up on account of having seen the devil and been rode by witches.[8] (36)

Twain designs Huck's digressive prolepsis to be amusing, though rhetorical readers will notice that it trades in racist stereotypes about the gullibility and superstitions of African Americans. But for my purposes, the most salient aspects of the passage are that (a) it is highly implausible (though not outright impossible) for Huck to know all that he reports here and (b) even dedicated rhetorical readers are likely to miss that implausibility. Furthermore, overlooking the implausibility is not a consequence of previous readerly responses to Jim or to Huck as character or narrator, since Twain uses this scene to introduce Jim, since Huck has no role in the proleptic action, and since Huck's narration has not established a pattern of deviating from his epistemological limitations.[9] Why, then, is it so easy for readers not to register the implausi-

---

8. I am grateful to Henrik Skov Nielsen for directing my attention to this passage.

9. One could argue that by beginning with metalepsis in the very first paragraph—Twain has Huck break the ontological boundary between his world and the extratextual world by having Huck comment on Twain's veracity in the *Adventures of Tom Sawyer*—Twain does prepare

bility? Let me first clarify its nature, which is rooted in issues of access and temporality.

If, as Huck's narration implies, he heard directly or heard from a third party about Jim's successive embellishments of the story, then his life at the Widow's has a significant dimension that does not otherwise appear in his narrative. Either he hangs out with the slaves even when they gather to tell stories in their own space ("in the dark by the kitchen fire"), or he has a friend among the slaves who reports all this information to him. But each of these hypotheses preserves the mimetic probability of Huck's knowing in one way only to disrupt it in another. Each generates a different kind of implausibility, a withholding of information from the narratee—about how Huck spends his days or about his friend among the slaves—that does not fit with Huck's generally naïve openness.

As for temporality, the issue involves the relation of the time span of Jim's exploits as storyteller to the time span of Huck's stay at the Widow Douglas's. We soon learn that Huck is on the scene only another five or six months: Tom's band of robbers is active for "about a month" (41); it's another "three or four months" (43) that takes them through winter; then Pap turns up, and it's another six weeks or so until Pap takes Huck away from the Widow "one day in the spring" (49). Could Jim have perfected his stories and become a regional legend in such a short time? Or is Huck reporting a sequence of events that could not have occurred within the time frame of the dominant action? The vagueness of the reach of the flash forward makes it impossible to answer for certain, but that very vagueness in combination with Huck's unlikely knowledge indicates that in this passage Twain has departed from the basic law of probability he has been observing, which is that the events in the fictional world operate under the same constraints as events in the actual world. Furthermore, Twain's vagueness about the time span of Jim's exploits suggests both that he does not want to call attention to this departure and that he is more concerned with disclosing certain information to his audience and creating certain effects than with conforming to the constraints of mimetic probability.

As noted above, Twain wants, first, to entertain his audience, and he effectively draws on the combination of Jim's flight of fancy, the credulity of the other slaves, and Huck's own naïveté (notice that Huck never questions Jim's silence about the devil's magic words) to accomplish that goal. In part, then,

---

his audience for other deviations from strict probability. But given that Huck's narration does not deviate between that opening and this passage, that metalepsis does not provide the same kind of unfolding reader response that influences the construction of the narrative in the way that unfolding responses to the entries in "Expenses for the Month" influence the construction of "Oct. 22 Mary's salary 75.00."

audiences are willing to overlook the implausibility because doing so enables that entertainment. But Twain also uses the passage for his initial characterization of Jim, and, indeed, that goal guides the rest of his choices in the narration. This prolepsis is the first time in the novel that Huck is not himself an actor in the events, and Twain designs Huck's narration so that Jim is front and center. Furthermore, the passage goes a long way toward characterizing him: he has an active imagination, he stands out among the other slaves, and he is an extremely proud man. In addition, Jim is remarkably and intuitively resourceful: he takes the events of falling asleep and waking up to find his hat hung on a tree limb and a five-cent piece on the kitchen table and parlays them into the means to elevate his status among his fellow slaves. Finally, Twain shows that Jim believes in a supernatural realm that is different from, although somewhat related to, the supernatural realm of the Christianity that the Widow Douglas and Miss Watson have been trying to teach Huck. By allowing himself these implausibilities, Twain establishes Jim as a remarkable and arresting man, one whom Huck is then very fortunate to meet up with on Jackson's Island. The audience's understanding of Jim's character in turn informs their judgments about Huck's responses to Jim throughout their relationship, especially when Huck treats him as an object of fun and when Huck makes his decision to go to hell rather than send Jim back to slavery.

This analysis provides a good backdrop for my next step of proposing seven reasons why readers are not likely to notice Twain's departure into implausible narration until some close-reading, probability-obsessed narrative theorist points it out. Each reason is tied to the experience of reading, which is to say that each has some roots in the actual and authorial audience's unfolding responses to the progression—though as I noted above, these responses do not themselves shape the construction of the passage. I shall dub the seven reasons the five Rules and two Meta-Rules of Thumb (that is, tendencies or even conventions but not laws) about Readerly Engagement with Breaks from the Dominant System of Probability. The two Meta-Rules underlie the five Rules and, applying Phelan's Shaver (see the preface), they are the most important ones to remember. But the five Rules offer a deeper dive into the particular ways authors use resources to guide audiences' responses to deviations from strict probability.

(1) The passage is relatively brief, and thus suggests the **Rule of Duration**: the briefer the break, the less likely audiences will notice it; the more extended the break, the more likely audiences will notice it.[10]

---

10. One important qualification here: sometimes a break can extend for such a long duration and be so compelling that readers (a) accept it as the new normal and (b) focus their attention on what is being disclosed rather than on the break that makes the disclosure possible.

(2) The voice in the passage remains recognizably Huck's and thus creates continuity with the dominant code. Here we have the **Rule of Partial Continuity**: when the break is restricted to one aspect of the narration, audiences are less likely to notice it. This Rule is closely tied to the Rule of Dominant Focus, which, as I suggest below, deserves to be called a Meta-Rule.

(3) The transitions into and out of the break are smooth and matter-of-fact: it begins in mid-paragraph with the adverb "Afterwards" and ends where the quotation above ends. The next paragraph accomplishes the transition back to the present time of the action with a simple "Well," followed by "when Tom and me got to the edge of the hill-top" (36). Similarly, the passage does not call attention to the signs of its break in perceptual field (or vision). Huck's knowledge of what Jim said to the other slaves is simply presumed by his act of narration—nothing is done to explain or justify it. In these ways, Twain follows the **Rule of Self-Assurance**: if the narration or other textual elements do not call attention to the break, audiences are less likely to notice it. To put this point from the perspective of authors: when you break from the dominant system, it is better to ask for forgiveness than permission—and, if your break is relatively unobtrusive, chances are you won't need to ask for forgiveness.

(4) When we first come upon this passage, the issue of temporality is not a concern because we do not know the length of the temporal interval between this night and Pap's taking Huck from the Widow's. Even in retrospect, the vagueness of the temporality will hide the implausibility from most readers. Here we have the **Rule of Temporal Decoding**: if the break in the code is detectable right away, audiences are more likely to notice it than if it is not detectable until later in the narrative progression.

(5) As I noted above, Twain designs the passage to be amusing because it communicates the outlandish outcomes of Jim's imagination working on the relatively mundane events Huck has just narrated. This aspect of the passage and its effects points to the **Rule of Extraordinary Revelation**. If breaking the code introduces remarkable, marvelous, or otherwise extraordinary material, audiences are more likely to focus on those revelations than they are on the deviations from the dominant code. In other words, what is being revealed is likely to distract attention from how it is being revealed. Even if the extraordinary nature of the disclosures leads rhetorical readers to question its probability or plausibility, such questioning remains focused on the what rather than the how of the narration.

(6) **The Meta-Rule of Dominant Focus**: I previously defined this one as follows: once an author shapes the textual dynamics to establish a dominant focus for the audience, the author relies on that focus in the construction of new elements of the progression. Here I describe it from the perspective of

audiences. Once audiences infer that narratives are committed to a certain set of interests—characters in action in a world like our own (the general realm of the mimetic); a self-reflexive look at their own responses to narrative resources (the general realm of the synthetic, as in metafiction); a narrative's particular philosophical or ideological agenda (the general realm of the thematic); and so on—they will continue to interpret new information in light of that dominant focus until the textual phenomena provide sufficient recalcitrance to frustrate those efforts. The question of how much recalcitrance is sufficient is best answered on a case-by-case basis because the application of this Meta-Rule will depend in part on how relevant the other five Rules are to each case. For example, this Meta-Rule combines with the Rule of Partial Continuity to explain why breaks in the perceptual field (or vision) of the narration are less likely to be noticed when they are not accompanied by a shift in voice.

(7) **The Meta-Rule of Value Added**: Readers overlook or do not take issue with breaks in the probability code when those breaks enhance the reading experience. This Meta-Rule applies to probable impossibilities such as Achilles' pursuit of Hector or the stenographer's pregnancy by the account–book keeper in "Expenses for the Month" (in Sacks's reading). It also applies to situations in which the break in the probability code allows audiences access to material—relevant information, events, characterizations—that would not be available without those breaks but that also enhance the audience's unfolding experiences.

LET'S NOW CONSIDER a more egregious example of implausibly knowledgeable narration (one which is a clear-cut example of what Genette would call paralepsis) in which most readers either don't notice or don't mind the break in the probability code. In chapter 8 of *The Great Gatsby*, F. Scott Fitzgerald has Nick Carraway report in considerable detail how George Wilson spent the night after his wife Myrtle's death.[11] The Rules of Duration and Temporal Decoding guide the judgment of this break as more egregious than the one in

---

11. I discuss this same stretch of narration in *Narrative as Rhetoric*, but I return to it not just to comment on some different passages but also because I believe the Rules and especially the Meta-Rules shed further light on how author-reader relations affect audiences' responses to the break in the probability code. In *Narrative as Rhetoric*, I emphasized that readerly judgments of mimetic probability depend in part on conventions and that "those conventions are somewhat elastic and the criterion 'what is probable or possible in life' can sometimes give way . . . to the criterion 'what is needed by the narrative at this point'" (110). My discussion in this chapter seeks to provide a richer, more nuanced account of how and why the conventions of mimetic probability can be elastic.

Huck Finn: Nick's report goes for more than four pages and every aspect of the break is immediately apparent—if one is looking for such a break. Furthermore, Fitzgerald's break is more radical than Twain's because Fitzgerald gives Nick the privilege not only of reporting events he did not witness but also of focalizing the scene through other characters—primarily Michaelis, Wilson's neighbor who kept an eye on him that night, and, secondarily, Wilson himself. Consider, for example, this excerpt, which begins with Michaelis asking Wilson a question, continues with Michaelis's vision, and then shifts to Wilson's.

> "Maybe you got some friend that I could telephone for, George?"
>
> This was a forlorn hope—he was almost sure that Wilson had no friend: there was not enough of him for his wife. He was glad a little later when he noticed a change in the room, a blue quickening by the window, and realized that dawn wasn't far off. About five o'clock it was blue enough outside to snap off the light.
>
> Wilson's glazed eyes turned out to the ashheaps, where small gray clouds took on fantastic shapes and scurried here and there in the faint dawn wind. (167)

Given that the implausible knowing in Nick's narration is so much more pronounced than it is in Huck's, why do most readers either not notice the break or not find it troubling if they do? The Rules of Partial Continuity and Self-Assurance begin to provide an answer: Although we have a shift in perceptual field, we still have Nick's voice. And, although Nick does explicitly call attention to a shift in his narration, he focuses on a shift in temporality rather than perception: "Now I want to go back a little and tell what happened at the garage after we left there the night before" (163–64). In line with the Rule of Self-Assurance, Nick just plunges right into his reporting.[12]

But with two rules pointing toward notice of the break and two pointing against such notice, the more compelling explanation can be found in the Meta-Rules of Added Value and Dominant Focus. Nick's implausibly knowledgeable narration adds considerable value to the narrative. It fulfills a significant gap in the audience's knowledge of events, even as it heightens our mimetic engagement with Wilson. The focalization through Michaelis means that Fitzgerald's audience still sees Wilson from the outside, while the dialogue and the occasional focalization through Wilson give that audience some

---

12. In chapter 7, Nick notes that Michaelis was the principal witness at the inquest, and the narration that immediately follows is clearly built on Michaelis's testimony. But it is implausible to conclude that Michaelis's testimony would be as detailed and as focused on the blow-by-blow of cognition as the account Nick gives in chapter 8.

sharper sense of his psychological state (notice that he sees the clouds as having "fantastic" shapes), even as it stops short of revealing all that he is thinking. This mimetic engagement becomes all the more important as chapter 8 continues to its climactic revelation of Gatsby glimpsing an "ashen, fantastic figure gliding toward him" (169)—Wilson. Nick's implausibly knowledgeable narration not only allows Fitzgerald's audience to connect the dots between Myrtle's death and Gatsby's but it also foregrounds issues of character and motive as they apply to Wilson. This foregrounding in turn reinforces prominent issues in the novel: Who is Gatsby, and why does he throw his parties? Who is Daisy, and why does she stay married to Tom? And so on. Given the audience's focus on these issues, this reinforcement of its interests either occludes or renders insignificant its perception of the implausibility.

RHETORICAL THEORY AND UNNATURAL NARRATOLOGY

Before I turn to the crossover phenomenon in *Stitches*, I want to address the relation between my rhetorical approach to these deviations from probability and the approach of unnatural narratologists such as Jan Alber, Stefan Iversen, Henrik Skov Nielsen, and Brian Richardson.[13] I admire the work of the unnatural narratologists and its salutary effect on the field. This work has called attention to the various ways in which narrators, characters, plots, space, and time—all the components of narrative—can be anti-mimetic or unnatural. Storytellers in the long tradition of unnatural narrative deliberately opt out of following the law of probability and necessity and other strictures that tie narrative representation to extratextual reality. Instead, these storytellers give free rein to the pleasures of the imagination, and they affirm the value of exploring what is not possible in extratextual reality as an alternative way of offering insight into that reality. The unnatural narratologists quite rightly contend that in order to account for the anti-mimetic tradition, narrative theory requires expansion and revision of much of its received wisdom, and they have taken important steps in that project.

With regard to the phenomena I discuss in this chapter, however, I believe that unnatural narratology and rhetorical theory have some significant differences, arising from their different investments in the "somebody else" of narrative communication. I find it telling that Brian Richardson in *Narrative Theory: Core Concepts and Critical Debates* cites with approval work in rhe-

---

13. See their cowritten essay ("Unnatural Narratives") as well as the coedited volume by Alber, Nielsen, and Richardson (*A Poetics*), and the individual works by Alber, Nielsen, and Richardson in the Works Cited.

torical theory on "textual dynamics" but is silent about its work on "readerly dynamics" ("Time, Plot, Progression" 78). For the unnatural narratologists, textual phenomena are more significant than audiences, whereas for rhetorical theorists, that hierarchy is reversed. Consequently, where I emphasize the "probable" side of a "probable impossibility," the unnatural narratologists would emphasize the "impossibility." Thus, when presented with the cases I have looked at so far, I believe that an unnatural narratologist would highlight the impossibilities or implausibilities and then thematize them. That is the procedure Richardson uses, for example, in his analysis of the "impossible" temporality in Shakespeare's *Macbeth*. While this approach has its virtues— it explains the link between techniques and their signification in a way that narratological interpretation has long valued—the approach does not address rhetorical theory's concern with how the interaction between readerly and textual dynamics illuminates the experience of reading. Furthermore, this difference means that rhetorical theory's concerns cut across the mimetic/anti-mimetic divide. Nick's narration remains within the realm of the mimetic—as do the passages from *Stitches* and "The Third and Final Continent"—even as all these cases break with the probability codes set up by the textual dynamics. To put this point another way, rhetorical poetics cuts across unnatural narratology because it roots its judgments of unnaturalness not just in anti-mimetic textual phenomena but also in the ways that the trajectory of readerly dynamics establishes its own set of expectations and even requirements about the boundaries of the mimetic in a given narrative.

CROSSOVER PHENOMENA: DAVID SMALL'S *STITCHES*

With *Stitches*, I turn to probability in nonfiction memoir and I move from the affordances of wholly verbal print to those of the graphic medium, even as I return to an instance of a probable impossibility. As I noted earlier, the dominant cause-and-effect logic of memoir allows for the expression of subjective truths within a representation ultimately bound by reference to actual people and events. Thus, Small's depiction of Dr. Davidson as the White Rabbit is not an impossibility because it is not a break in the dominant logic. Instead it is a clearly signaled move to local fictionality (Small knows that his audience knows that the psychiatrist is not the White Rabbit), and it is designed to capture the experiencing-David's sense of having escaped from the grim reality of everyday life in his dysfunctional family into the alternate reality constituted by the Wonderland of Dr. Davidson's office. The probable impossibility resides in Dr. Davidson's telling David that his mother doesn't love him just a few minutes into their first appointment. Indeed, by the usual rules of probability, such a pronouncement would mark Dr. Davidson as an incompetent psychiatrist, and, thus, would signal that the appointment itself, which has been arranged by David's mother, is another sign of her deficient parenting. To put this point another way, it is impossible for Dr. Davidson to have acted this way during this first appointment with David *and* to be the excellent therapist that Small represents him to be.

I have taught *Stitches* multiple times, including to a group of two dozen medical students, and only a few readers have wondered about Dr. Davidson's competence in making his pronouncement so soon after meeting David. Furthermore, no one has commented on the scene as either an impossibility or an implausibility until I raised the issue. I do not think that my students are inattentive readers. Instead, I submit that they are properly registering the scene as plausible, and that this plausibility arises from a crossover effect in the narrative progression: *readerly dynamics—rhetorical readers' unfolding responses to the progression—cross over into textual dynamics and lend a logic to the events that is more powerful than the logic of external probability.* Because Dr. Davidson's pronouncement is not impossible in the way that Achilles' pursuit of Hector or the stenographer's becoming pregnant by her employer is, I do not want to call the scene a probable impossibility. Instead it is a probable implausibility, that is, an unlikely event according to the logic of character and action that becomes all but inevitable in the unfolding progression. Small's reliance on the crossover is all the more remarkable because the scene is also the turning point in his memoir. Let us look more closely.

The textual dynamics of Small's memoir immediately establish the global instability as his difficult relationship to his parents, especially his mother. He titles the first chapter "I Was Six," and he skillfully uses his black-and-white drawings to depict his isolation in his unhappy family. His first self-representation depicts his six-year-old self alone with his drawing materials, working (in a bit of foreshadowing) on a picture of a rabbit. The retrospective verbal narration begins to identify some of the specific unhappiness of this unhappy family. "Mama had her little cough" (15) are the first words of the narration, and Small continues by reporting the other wordless communications in his family: his mother's slamming of cupboards, his father's hitting a punching bag, his brother's banging on his drums, and his own frequent illnesses. The global instability gets complicated with just about every panel, and Small depicts his mother as especially cold and angry. As if that's not bad enough, young David's interest in *Alice in Wonderland,* which he exhibits by putting on an Alice-like head scarf, makes him an object of ridicule for other kids in the neighborhood. David's response is to imagine his own escape into an underground Wonderland.

These textual dynamics evoke considerable sympathy for David's painful situation and clear ethical judgments about the deficiencies of his parents and his peer group. But Small's skill with his black-and-white drawings, his diverse panels and page layouts, and his overall mastery of the graphic medium provide an aesthetic dimension to the readerly dynamics that partially offsets the dismal affective dimension of those dynamics. In addition, this aesthetic dimension also serves as a tacit signal that, although we are focused on the Portrait of the Young Artist in a Dysfunctional Family, that young artist becomes the remarkable implied author whose rich communications we are engaging with on every page.

The most egregious complications of the global instability involve the responses of David's parents to a growth on David's neck when he is eleven. It is diagnosed as a sebaceous cyst, but his parents do not have it taken care of until three and a half years later. Their ethical deficiency becomes all the more outrageous—and the corresponding affective responses to them and to David all the more contrasting—because shortly after the initial diagnosis, his parents go on a spending spree, purchasing a new car, furniture, and many appliances. Conspicuous by their absence are any purchases for David.

Small's account of the surgery and its aftermath highlights the emotional and ethical deficiencies of his parents and maximizes the audience's sympathy for him. The cyst has morphed into cancer, which requires two operations. David loses his thyroid gland and one of his vocal cords and gains the stitches that give the memoir its title. Furthermore, in perhaps the most telling evidence of their inability to empathize with David, to see the world from his perspective, his parents decide not to tell him about the cancer. Even after David later confronts them for not telling him, his father angrily replies, "You didn't need to know anything then . . . and you don't need to know about it now. That's *final!*" (238).

Small uses multiple techniques to highlight the experiencing-David's feelings of being lost and abandoned and to deepen the audience's sympathy for him. Especially notable is a remarkable sequence of images that Small places shortly after the ordeal of the operation. He depicts David's dream of a bat caught in the rain coming upon an umbrella whom it calls "Mama!" But rather than sheltering the bat, the umbrella gets totally shredded by the rain, leaving the bat at the mercy of the elements. Yet Small never has David explicitly articulate that he is an unloved child. For example, when David awakens, he only mutters to himself, "Crazy goddamn dream" (201).

As Small begins the scene of David's meeting with Dr. Davidson/the White Rabbit, he follows the real-world script for a patient's first meeting with a therapist. That script says that patient and therapist will focus on getting to know each other and establishing a working relationship built on mutual trust. In addition, the therapist will focus on learning about the patient by asking such questions as why the patient has sought therapy, what current symptoms she or he may be especially concerned about, and what, if any, is the relevant medical history. The script allows for the therapist to make an initial diagnosis, but the overriding maxim is that the therapist ought not rush to judgment. Small focalizes the scene through David as he and Dr. Davidson begin the process of getting to know each other. A voice calls David into the office and invites him to have a seat. David looks at the furniture, asks questions, and ventures opinions about how things work: "Do I have to lie on the couch?" (249); "I suppose you'll be giving me drugs or hypnotizing me, or something like that"; and the voice replies, "No, David. No drugs. No hypnosis. In here, we talk, that's it" (250). Then Small departs from the script and lets the crossover from the unfolding readerly dynamics be his guide to the construction of the textual dynamics. For now I will set aside the issue of the accuracy/distortion in Small's depiction of the scene, but I will return to it later.

The first departure from the standard script comes when Small connects the psychiatrist's voice to a body—the body of the White Rabbit, dressed very much as John Tenniel dresses him in Carroll's *Alice*. Taking advantage of the resources of the graphic medium in this way, Small simultaneously deploys the Rules of Extraordinary Revelation and of Self-Assurance not only to depict David's subjective truth but also to signal to the audience that the usual script will not entirely fit. As the scene proceeds, Small departs further and further from the script, as Davidson/the White Rabbit barely listens to David and instead both reconstructs and authoritatively interprets David's story for him.

The Rabbit begins with an invitation, "Now tell me, what's on your mind?" and David, in the time-honored fashion of adolescent boys in the West, says, "Nothing." True to character, the Rabbit responds, "Nothing? That's curious" (251), and then reports that David's mother had said he's been "acting crazy, doing crazy things." When David replies, "I guess so," the White Rabbit turns the conversation, giving his own description of David that implicitly challenges his mother's characterization of him: "A boy who has had cancer . . . A boy whose parents and doctors did not tell him he had cancer . . . A boy who had to find out the truth on his own . . . Is this crazy?" (252).

Small works the crossover by pushing the Meta-Rule of Dominant Focus to its logical endpoint. In giving his litany, the Rabbit has just summarized the key events that Small's audience has experienced and responded to. In hav-

FIGURE 2.3. A turning point in *Stitches,* part II. David Small, *Stitches* (255).

ing the Rabbit ask his question to David, Small is simultaneously asking it to his audience, who of course are primed to answer "no." Small completes the crossover in two more steps: the White Rabbit asserts that "you have been living in a world full of nonsense" (253), and then delivers the most crucial truth his audience already knows (see figure 2.3).

This revelation is all the more powerful because it comes from the figure of authority (and note here that Small uses the close-up to give a kind of double exposure to the figure: he is simultaneously White Rabbit and human psychiatrist). Furthermore, the revelation is far more powerful than it would have been had Small followed the standard script, since doing so would have involved his going over so much ground that the audience already knows well, and that redundancy would have greatly attenuated the Rabbit's articulation of the truth. The sudden, authoritative revelation is far more effective. In this way, the crossover has considerable Added Value.

The effects of the Rabbit's truth-telling are immediate. Because David had not allowed himself to think that his mother didn't love him, he is initially shocked by Davidson's pronouncement. But within that shock, David also recognizes the truth of his experience. Small expresses David's coming to terms with that truth through another remarkable set of graphic depictions: David cries, he holds on to Dr. Davidson's leg, his tears turn to rain and the rain falls all over his small world until it finally becomes cleansing and peaceful. In this way, the scene functions as the turning point in the whole progression. Once David accepts its truth and has Dr. Davidson to help him deal with its consequences, he starts down the path that leads him to become the accomplished artist who creates this powerful memoir.

Within the internal logic of the progression, then, the probable implausibility is amply justified. But this analysis raises questions about nonfiction's responsibility to extratextual referentiality. Does such an implausibility represent an abdication of that responsibility, an abandonment of the implicit promise to tell the truth? Does the analysis expose a huge problem in the ethics of Small's telling? Have I used rhetorical theory to do for *Stitches* what TheSmokingGun.com did for James Frey's *A Million Little Pieces*—that is, reveal its deviation from the truth in a way that undercuts the audience's trust in the author to tell it like it was?

No, no, and no. The difference between Small and Frey is that Small's representation of what happened between him and Dr. Davidson refers to actual events that occurred in their sessions, while Frey invented events that never happened. If there were no Dr. Davidson, or if he did not warrant Small's gratitude in the acknowledgments ("my special thanks to Dr. Harold Davidson for pulling me to my feet and placing me on the road to the examined life" [331]), then Small would be guilty of the ethical breaches Frey has admitted to. What matters for Small's story is not the strict referential accuracy of what he and Dr. Davidson said to each other during their first session but that David's therapy generated the insights that helped him change the direction of his life. The departure from the standard script and the deployment of the probable implausibility via the crossover allows Small to communicate in an especially effective manner just how powerfully transformative his experience with Dr. Davidson was. It's hard to imagine any reader who would prefer a representation of their first meeting that eschewed the probable implausibility for the predictable probability of script following. I shall return to the ethical issues related to probability in the next chapter.

A SPECTRUM OF (IM)PROBABILITY

The work of this chapter, along with some previous work on breaks in the probability code in character narration in *Narrative as Rhetoric* and *Living to Tell about It,* leads me to propose a spectrum of (im)probability, as seen through the lens of rhetorical theory. At one end is the default case in which the implied author constructs the textual dynamics so that they consistently follow the narrative's dominant system of probability (whether it is mimetic or anti-mimetic) and the audience responds accordingly. At the other end is the case of a strong crossover from readerly dynamics to textual dynamics, such as we see in *Stitches*. In the middle of the spectrum are such phenomena as redundant telling, paradoxical paralipsis, and plausible paralepsis. In redundant telling, an implied author will have a character narrator improbably tell a narratee something that the narratee already knows in order to communicate it to the authorial audience. The Meta-Rules of Dominant Focus and Value Added can explain why some redundant narration is effective. When Robert Browning in line 49 of "My Last Duchess" has the Duke of Ferrara say to the envoy from the father of his next duchess that "the Count *your master's* known munificence" (emphasis mine) allows the Duke to be confident about settling her dowry, the possessive phrase is redundant telling: the envoy knows very well that the Count is his master, and the Duke's story about what he did to his last duchess is ample warrant that no inference about the envoy's heightened awareness of his own subordinate position should be disallowed. But the unobtrusive reference does not disturb the dominant focus on Browning's revelation of the Duke's character, even as it adds enormous value to that revelation: it reveals to Browning's audience the identity of the Duke's narratee, a revelation that enables rhetorical readers to more fully grasp the outrageousness of the Duke's act of telling to this person on this occasion.[14]

In one common version of paradoxical paralipsis, an author will have a naïve character narrator retrospectively tell a story about the loss of her naïveté without the new knowledge informing the narration. This improbable withholding is typically not noticed—or if noticed, not deemed objectionable—by the audience because it becomes apparent only after the audience has experienced the naïve telling about the events that led to the loss of naïveté.[15]

Plausible paralepses are instances of implausibly knowledgeable narration that audiences welcome, such as we have examined in chapter 8 of *The Great Gatsby*. And the previous section of this chapter seeks to explain the logic of crossover phenomena. Figure 2.4 is a sketch of the spectrum, with the arrow pointing in the direction of increasing power of the readerly dynamics to shape the construction of the textual dynamics.

---

14. Sarah Copland has also pointed out to me that the second half of the first line of Browning's poem, "That's my last duchess painted on the wall" is an instance of redundant telling, since the envoy knows he is looking at paint on a wall, but Browning needs to impart that information to his audience. In this case, the redundancy is necessary for establishing the dominant focus on the Duke and his storytelling about his last duchess. Like other techniques, redundant telling can have a range of effects, depending on how it is deployed and how it interacts with other aspects of a narrative. Browning does his best to keep the redundancy hidden; other authors will call attention to it for different effects. In *Living to Tell about It*, I compare and contrast Browning's practice with that of Sandra Cisneros in "Barbie-Q." Cisneros, I contend, flaunts her redundant telling (1–30).

15. See my discussion of Hemingway's use of this technique in "My Old Man" in chapter 4 of *Narrative as Rhetoric*.

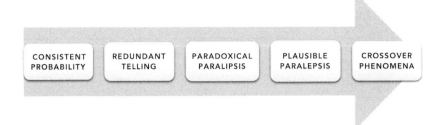

FIGURE 2.4. From probability to plausible violations of probability to probable implausibilities and impossibilities.

Having given this overview of the explanatory power of rhetorical poetics, including its capacity to account for the important role of author-audience relations in the deployment of narrative elements, I turn in part 2 to more in-depth looks at a range of resources of narrative, including character narration, character-character dialogue, and occasions of narration. But even as I bring these resources to the front and center of the discussion, I shall remain ultimately concerned with how authors use them to achieve certain effects on audiences, how the details of those uses are in turn influenced by the knowledge and responses of audiences, and how the effects of those author-audience interactions relate to the authors' overall purposes.

PART 2

Resources

GENERIC FRAMES, TECHNIQUES, OCCASIONS— AND SYNERGIES

Constructing a Rhetorical Poetics

N KEEPING with this book's focus on "somebody telling somebody else," I choose in the following chapters to examine resources of narrative that help unpack the multifarious relationships among those three terms. Just as chapter 1 gave primary attention to the *somebody* and chapter 2 to the *somebody else,* these chapters give primary attention to resources—and how they're deployed by particular tellers in relation to particular audiences. Here I offer just a brief sketch of the logic governing the sequence of my theory construction. It is, to a large degree, a chain-link logic: theoretical issues in one chapter get looped into issues in the next, even as all those issues are explored in relation to particular narratives. Partially because of this interest in rhetorical reading, I do not construct all the links as symmetrical, and, indeed, some are both larger and thicker than others. My ultimate goal is to construct a comprehensive rhetorical poetics, but since that goal is not attainable in a single book, my secondary goal is to indicate what such a poetics would look like through detailed development of some parts of it and illustrative sketches of others.

More specifically, I begin the chain-link process of theory construction in chapter 3 by extending the discussion of probability in chapter 2, but I also shift the focus to how authors' and audiences' shared assumptions about fiction and nonfiction influence authors' handlings of and audiences' responses to plotting and probability. My test cases are Jane Austen's *Pride and Prejudice* and Joan Didion's *The Year of Magical Thinking*. In chapter 4, I continue the probability chain, even as I bring in a resource I call stubbornness—a textual phenomenon that won't yield to interpretive mastery but nevertheless contributes to the effectiveness of a narrative. To come to terms with Franz Kafka's use of stubbornness in his remarkable short story, "Das Urteil," I also examine his use of other resources, especially narrative speed and progression toward a surprise ending.

Chapters 5–13 depart from the probability link and fashion links focused on authors telling audiences by means of (a) character narrators telling narratees and (b) characters telling/talking to each other. This section of the book draws on and deepens the work I began in *Living to Tell about It: A Rhetoric and Ethics of Character Narration*. But this section also widens the scope of rhetorical poetics, and I discuss other issues, including ambiguity and occasion, as I take up some connections between the project of rhetorical poetics and those of other approaches.

Chapter 5 itself focuses on how an author can use the same resource in the service of radically different ends as it posits a spectrum of unreliability that runs from estranging to bonding effects between narrators and audiences. It then deploys the spectrum in an examination of the ethics of the telling in Vladimir Nabokov's *Lolita*. In chapter 6, I continue forging character narration links, as I examine Martin Amis's handling of "backwards narration" (telling that proceeds in reverse temporal order) in *Time's Arrow* and its consequences for the ethics and aesthetics of Amis's rhetorical communication. In chapter 7, I form the next link in the character narrator chain by analyzing Joseph Conrad's handling of his participant-observer narrator Marlow in *Lord Jim* and how Conrad uses Marlow's telling as part of the construction of a different kind of stubbornness than I examined in "Das Urteil," this one focused on the protagonist himself. In chapter 8, the ambiguity/stubbornness chain gets further developed along with the character narrator chain, as I examine the interaction between the two resources in Toni Morrison's "Recitatif." In this chapter, I also situate rhetorical poetics in relation to cognitive narratology, since Morrison's story lends itself to illumination by both approaches.

In chapter 9, the character narration link moves back to the front and center of my theory construction, as I develop an account of what I call deficient narration (telling that leads the actual audience to resist entering the authorial audience) through a return to Didion's *Year of Magical Thinking* and a look at Jean-Dominique Bauby's *The Diving Bell and the Butterfly*. In chapter 10, I switch the focus to character-character dialogue and pick up the discussion of the technique from chapter 1, as I again pair a return—this time to

George V. Higgins's *The Friends of Eddie Coyle*—with the fresh examination of another narrative, John O'Hara's "Appearances." In chapter 11, I then loop this link into those on character narration, as I theorize reliable narration and consider the synergies between narration and dialogue in Jhumpa Lahiri's "The Third and Final Continent." That discussion also completes the discussion of probable improbabilities in chapter 2. In chapter 12, I pull together the various links in my discussion of character narration, as I offer an overview of reliable, unreliable, and deficient narration. Finally, in chapter 13, I finish this book's chain-link construction of rhetorical poetics by examining the interactions between character narration, occasions of telling, and the arrangement of narrative segments in Ian McEwan's *Enduring Love*.

Even as I engage in this chain-link examination of resources, my rhetorical poetics remains grounded in the principles I articulate in the introduction. The clearest evidence of that grounding is my recurring attention to narrative progression and to the affective, ethical, and aesthetic effects of author-audience interactions.

CHAPTER 3

Probability in Fiction and Nonfiction

PRIDE AND PREJUDICE AND
THE YEAR OF MAGICAL THINKING

I N THIS CHAPTER, I extend the discussion of probability from chapter 2, even as I shift the purpose of that discussion. Having established that authors often construct their narratives in light of their sense of their audience's unfolding responses, I now take up the issue of how rhetorical theory's privileging of authors and audiences over textual phenomena provides the basis for an intervention in the debate about the distinction between fiction and nonfiction. More specifically, I focus on how authors and audiences approach issues of probability in one way in fiction and in a distinctively different way in nonfiction. These differences depend on both a shared understanding of the purposes and appropriate means of fiction and nonfiction and on how particular authors deploy that understanding in relation to particular projects. I come at these issues through some observations about the phenomenon of fraudulent memoirs.

In the world of creative nonfiction, the first two decades of the twenty-first century will likely be known as the Age of the Fraudulent Memoir. With James Frey's *A Million Little Pieces,* Matt McCarthy's *Odd Man Out,* Margaret B. Jones's *Love and Consequences,* and several other books, we have witnessed an all-too-familiar narrative of reception. Chapter 1: Initial reviewers and readers enthusiastically praise the memoir as an affectively powerful and ethically rewarding performance; they use adjectives such as *intense, lacerating, eye-opening, humane,* and *deeply affecting.* Chapter 2: Skeptics and fact-checkers produce convincing evidence that the events could not have happened the way the memoirist represents them. Chapter 3 has two main variants, each of which also has a significant ethical dimension. In the first, the memoirist plays defense, either by denying that the difference between the actual experiences and the representation of them is a matter of any consequence or by playing the subjective truth card. That is, the memoirist argues that the narrative is not seeking historical truth but rather recounting the experiences as he or she remembers them. In the second variant, the memoirist admits to the distortions or fabrications but offers an ends-justifies-the-means defense. In all the celebrated cases, the memoirist's rationalization ultimately fails. Chapter 4: The audience splits into three main groups in their final assessment: many find the author guilty of lying to them, others say that they'll just read the memoir as fiction, and still others contend that the distinction between fiction and nonfiction is not important because "a good story is a good story" regardless of its generic status.

This narrative of reception raises—or revives—some larger questions about the connections among narrative, ethics, rhetorical reading, and the fiction-nonfiction distinction: Can we identify any bottom-line distinction between fiction and nonfiction, and if so, how? If we can, what does it suggest about the efforts at genre-switching that the second group of readers opt for? If we can't, should we then side with the third group and just focus on the quality of the narrative independent of its status as fiction or nonfiction? In this chapter, I will make a case for the viability—and power—of the distinction by arguing that the differences in our tacit readerly assumptions about fiction and nonfiction have significant consequences for judgments about the probability, plotting, ethics, and aesthetics of a narrative. Furthermore, although narratives often do not contain explicit markers of their fictionality or nonfictionality, comparing hypotheses about whether the textual details are parts of a fictional or a nonfictional narrative often leads to a clear outcome. As a result, we can conclude that the same textual phenomena can have very different effects depending upon the larger generic frame in which authors construct and audiences respond to them. This conclusion in turn means that placing a narrative in one generic frame or another matters a great deal for both its construction and its consumption. I will carry out these arguments by focusing on two representative examples, Jane Austen's *Pride and Prejudice* and Joan Didion's *The Year of Magical Thinking*.

I am, of course, only the latest in a long line of narrative theorists who have addressed the fiction-nonfiction distinction, though my predecessors reach a variety of conclusions. Hayden White, for example, has emphasized the similarities of selection and plotting in both fiction and history, and his work has often been cited by those who want to blur the boundaries between the two genres. Dorrit Cohn, on the other hand, has identified what she regards as distinctive textual features, or "signposts," that differentiate fiction from nonfiction. Marie-Laure Ryan uses classical narratology and possible-worlds theory to argue for the viability of the distinction. And recent work on fictionality by Richard Walsh, Henrik Skov Nielsen, Simona Zetterberg Gjerlevsen, and others relies on the distinction even as it looks to separate fictionality (defined as a nondeceptive departure from the actual) from generic fictions such as the novel, short story, and fiction film. I have contributed to that work on the pervasiveness of fictionality, but my focus here is on how readerly assumptions about the fiction-nonfiction distinction interact with both textual and readerly dynamics in generic fictions and generic nonfictions.

RHETORICAL THEORY'S ASSUMPTIONS ABOUT FICTION AND NONFICTION

The most significant tacit assumption underlying the writing and reading of generic fiction is that its audience maintains a double perspective on the characters and the action. (For the purposes of this chapter, I will bracket metafiction, which sometimes plays with this tacit assumption—except to say that such play highlights its importance.) Readers of fiction simultaneously participate in the illusion that the characters are independent agents pursuing their own ends and remain aware that the characters and their trajectories toward their fates are part of an authorial design and purpose. Ralph Rader's definition of the novel (as it emerged in the work of Samuel Richardson and Henry Fielding) captures this tacit assumption very well: the novel, says Rader, is "a work which offers the reader a focal illusion of characters acting autonomously as if in the world of real experience within a subsidiary awareness of an underlying constructive authorial purpose which gives their story an implicit significance and affective force which real world experience does not have" ("Emergence of the Novel" 206). I would slightly revise the end of Rader's definition to read "an underlying constructive authorial purpose which gives the story *a thematic, ethical, and* affective significance and force which real world experience does not have."

As noted in the introduction to this book, rhetorical theory connects its understanding of the readerly experience of fiction to this double consciousness: the narrative audience responds to characters as if they were acting autonomously, while the authorial audience remains tacitly aware of the fiction's construction and thus interested in its "underlying . . . authorial purpose." Both audiences are roles that rhetorical readers take on. Furthermore, rhetorical theory regards reading as a two-step process: first, reading within the authorial and narrative audiences, and then, second, assessing that reading experience in relation to one's own beliefs and values.

From the perspective of the author, this tacit assumption about the double consciousness of readers helps reveal one of the fundamental challenges of writing successful realist fiction: to preserve the illusion that the characters are acting autonomously while also designing their actions and the consequences of those actions so that the audience recognizes their thematic, ethical, and affective significance and force. In this way, we can describe the author's task as one that involves a particular combination of freedom and constraint. The author of realist fiction is free to invent characters and events, but the successful author accepts the constraint that she cannot sacrifice the illusion of autonomy on the altar of underlying authorial purpose. Similarly, the author is free to invent characters and events, but the successful author accepts the constraint that their invention must somehow contribute to the larger significance of the fiction. Our experience as readers teaches us that the most successful fiction writers are the ones most adept at negotiating this relationship between freedom and constraint.

Jane Austen's revision to the ending of *Persuasion* provides an excellent illustration of this last point. *Persuasion* is different from Austen's other novels because it is a tale not of the discovery of love but rather a tale of its rediscovery. Eight years before the main action of the novel takes place, Anne Elliot had been persuaded by Lady Russell and her own conscience that she should reject Frederick Wentworth's marriage proposal. For Wentworth, Anne's rejection signals the end of their relationship and, he thinks, the end of his love for Anne. Although Anne never stops loving Frederick, she does stop believing that there is any chance he will forgive her and return to her. In the main action of the novel, events conspire to bring them back within each other's social orbit, and Wentworth gradually comes to rediscover his love for Anne—though he thinks that his awakening has come too late since it appears that she is on the verge of becoming engaged to William Elliot. At this point, Austen needs to find a way to overcome this final obstacle and reunite Anne and Frederick. In Austen's first effort, she transforms an awkward meeting into the moment of happiness. Wentworth's brother-in-law, Admiral Croft, who is renting the Elliot family home, commissions Wentworth to tell Anne that he will give up the lease once she is married to William. When Anne assures Wentworth that there will be no such marriage, the two exchange a very meaningful look and voila!—"all Suspense and Indecision were over. They were re-united. They were restored to all that had been lost" (263).

This ending is relatively effective, and it respects the major parameters of freedom and constraint governing the novel. The characters appear to be acting autonomously even as the ending includes two ethically satisfying elements: (a) William's self-interested pursuit of Anne helps to bring about her engagement to Wentworth, and (b) Wentworth's misdirected anger at Anne eventually leads to the early part of this scene in which he experiences a mild comic punishment before his ultimate happiness. But Austen wasn't satisfied with this ending and replaced it with one in which Anne has a much more active role. She delivers a deeply felt speech to Captain Harville about the greater constancy of women, a speech that Wentworth overhears and that gives him the hope and the courage to renew his proposal.

The revision is a significant improvement because it better completes the unfolding pattern of action with its corresponding thematic, ethical, and affective force that Austen had been constructing prior to this point. Although Wentworth is the character who needs to change, and although Anne faces the strong restrictions on a woman's behavior imposed by her society, Austen has been constructing a pattern in which Anne functions as the main agent in bringing about Wentworth's change of understanding and feeling—and ultimately her own happiness. The original ending, despite its virtues, fails to follow through on this pattern, as it once again reduces Anne's agency. The revision, however, brilliantly completes the pattern, and in so doing, dramatically enhances the thematic, ethical, and affective force of Austen's novel.[1]

The case of *Persuasion* also helps us identify a key tacit assumption of authors and audiences of nonfiction, because it reminds us that we can applaud Austen's revision without having to worry about fact-checking it. Jane-ites need not live in fear that one day TheSmokingGun.com will prove that the first ending is actually the one supported by the historical evidence or, indeed, that both of Austen's endings are bogus, because their reporters have found evidence that a desperate Anne, on the first night of the trip to Lyme Regis, snuck into Wentworth's room and then ran off with him the next morning to Gretna Green. Jane-ites need not worry because these scenarios are based on a category mistake that entails treating fiction as if it were nonfiction. That mistake in turn reveals the main tacit assumption about nonfiction: it claims to represent people and events external to the textual world—and therefore can be contested by other representations of them. By contrast, when one fiction contests another, as, for example, when Jean Rhys's *Wide Sargasso Sea* contests Charlotte Brontë's *Jane Eyre,* the second work may lead us to revise our interpretations and evaluations of the first, but its contestation

---

1. This discussion draws on my previous analysis of Austen's revision in *Experiencing Fiction.* See also Robyn Warhol's fine analysis in *Narrative Theory.*

does not lead any readers to feel betrayed by Brontë in the way that so many felt betrayed by James Frey.

These considerations lead to a definition of literary nonfiction narrative parallel to Rader's definition of the novel: a work that offers the reader a representation of actual people and events that is simultaneously responsible to their existence outside the textual world *and* shaped in the service of some underlying authorial purpose designed to give the people and events a thematic, affective, and ethical significance and force that would not be apparent without such shaping. This conception means that literary nonfiction operates with a different relationship between freedom and constraint than the novel does. The author of literary nonfiction is free to shape the characters and events into his or her vision of their thematic, affective, and ethical significance within the limits imposed by the necessary responsibility to the extratextual existence of those characters and events. This conception of nonfiction also means that we do not read it with the double consciousness operating in our reading of fiction, and, thus, we do not need to invoke a narrative audience distinct from the authorial audience. Furthermore, because we do not read with such a double-consciousness, the default assumption—one that operates until the implied author signals that it does not apply—is that the "narrating-I" is a reliable representative of the implied author.

As we have seen in chapter 2's discussion of the crossover between textual and readerly dynamics in *Stitches,* this relationship between freedom and constraint in nonfiction does not necessarily entail a strict one-to-one correspondence between extratextual realities and narrative representations of them. Instead, it involves a constant negotiation between the twin demands of referentiality and the communication of thematic, affective, and ethical significance. This point in turn sheds light on the problem with fraudulent memoirs. In most of these cases, the authors become so enamored of their visions of the larger thematic, affective, and ethical purpose of the narrative that they no longer observe the constraint of being responsible to the extratextual existence of the characters and events. They buy into the temptation of inventing events because "they make for a better story"—where "better" means "more vivid, more deeply affecting, more thematically powerful." By sacrificing responsibility to the extratextual dimensions of their narratives on the altar of heightened effects, authors of fraudulent memoirs construct narratives that are deficient in their ethics of the telling. In these cases, the authors are not constructing "probable impossibilities or plausibilities" but inventing events that have no basis in the extratextual raw materials of their narratives.

This rhetorical conception of the fiction-nonfiction distinction underlies my strong claim that our tacit readerly assumptions often lead us to respond very differently to the same kinds of textual phenomena in the two genres—and that authors' knowledge of this readerly response influences their construction of their narratives. But I also want to temper—or at least clarify—this claim in two ways. First, I want to underline that I say "often" rather than "always." I recognize the wide diversity of fictional and nonfictional narratives as well as the class of narratives that seek to trouble the fiction/nonfiction distinction, and I believe that such diversity should make theorists suspicious of claims that apply to all cases. Second, reading a narrative with the assumptions that apply to nonfiction is not necessarily sufficient for us to be able to recognize whether a given memoir is fraudulent: the internal structures of some fraudulent memoirs do not allow their audiences to detect their inventions. Sometimes we need TheSmokingGun.com.

PLOTTING AND PROBABILITY IN *PRIDE AND PREJUDICE*

In *Pride and Prejudice,* Austen famously tells a story about the transformation of negative "first impressions" (the phrase was her initial title for the book) into well-grounded feelings of passionate love. The easy part of her task is the representation of those negative first impressions. Austen manages that task with characteristic economy by bringing Elizabeth and Darcy together at the first ball and by having Elizabeth overhear Darcy's cold response to Bingley's offer to introduce him to her: "She is tolerable; but not handsome enough to tempt *me*; and I am in no humour at present to give consequence to young ladies who are slighted by other men" (12). With that stroke, Austen clearly establishes Darcy's unfavorable first impression of Elizabeth and motivates hers of him. But this beginning also creates a certain problem for Austen's efforts to give her characters autonomy while also achieving her underlying purpose.

Since the two characters won't voluntarily seek each other's company, how can Austen both preserve the illusion of their autonomy and still bring about their eventual union? Austen goes with the most logical solution of having "circumstances" bring them into the same circles,[2] but her different attention to the workings of circumstance early and late in the narrative reveals something significant about the relationship between the illusion of characters'

---

2. Austen also establishes some givens for the narrative that make possible some of the workings of circumstance. The most significant given is that Lady Catherine de Bourgh is both Mr. Collins's employer and Darcy's aunt, which of course makes it easy for Austen to have Darcy visit Lady Catherine at the same time that Elizabeth visits her good friend Charlotte Lucas Collins.

autonomy and authorial purpose, both in *Pride and Prejudice* and the realist novel more generally. Early on, Austen goes to considerable lengths to have the apparently autonomous actions of different characters be the means for bringing Darcy and Elizabeth together, but later on, she is content to rely heavily on the good offices of the novelist's dangerous friend, Chance—and, just as important, most readers, rhetorical and otherwise, are content with her contentment. Readers' contentment with Austen's reliance on Chance is another example of the Meta-Rule of Dominant Focus and of how readerly dynamics influence the construction of textual dynamics.

The first extended interaction between Elizabeth and Darcy after the ball occurs at Netherfield during the period when Elizabeth provides company and assistance to her ill sister Jane. In order to bring about this situation, Austen draws on the apparently autonomous actions of numerous characters. By my count, Austen takes six main steps in her plotting, each of which is carefully grounded in probabilities of character and circumstance. First, Caroline Bingley invites Jane to dine at Netherfield on a day when her brother and Darcy are out dining with officers. Both the absence of the gentlemen and the invitation fit with the social norms of the time and the characters of those involved. Second, although Jane asks to borrow the family carriage, Mrs. Bennet proposes that she go on horseback because "it seems likely to rain and then you'll have to stay all night"—and thus, spend at least some time in Mr. Bingley's company. Mrs. Bennet's proposal is wholly in keeping with her character ("the business of her life was to get her daughters married" [5]), but the more sensible Mr. Bennet—and Jane—are forced to accept that proposal because the horses that would drive the carriage are needed in the Bennet farm. Third, it rains hard as Jane rides to Netherfield. Of course it is Austen who assigns the horses to the Bennet farm and who controls the weather in the storyworld, but there is no strong intrusion of authorial purpose into the characters' autonomy here because it is perfectly natural for horses to work on a farm and for heavy rain to fall in Hertfordshire in the autumn.

Fourth, the hard rain brings on Jane's illness, and Mr. Bingley and his sister, as gracious hosts, insist on her staying at Netherfield until she gets well. Fifth, Elizabeth insists on going to visit Jane for a day, even if it means walking across the muddy fields—which it does. Sixth, when Elizabeth prepares to leave at the end of the first day's visit, Jane is so concerned that Miss Bingley insists that Elizabeth stay. Again, with these last three steps, everything is fully in keeping with nature (or beliefs about the connection between getting wet and becoming ill), with the social norms of the time, and with the characters of those involved. After these elaborate arrangements, Austen then devotes the next five chapters to Elizabeth's time at Netherfield in the company of

Darcy, a time during which Darcy begins to feel the danger of his attraction to Elizabeth.

By contrast, Austen's arrangements for Elizabeth and Darcy's meeting at Pemberley are far less elaborate and far more dependent on Chance. First, it just so happens that the Gardiners are required to change their planned trip with Elizabeth so that they go to Derbyshire, the location of Pemberley, rather than the Lake Country. Second, once in Derbyshire, the Gardiners naturally want to see Pemberley. Elizabeth is reluctant to go, given that she has by this time rejected Darcy's marriage proposal and done so in a manner that she now deeply regrets. But after receiving assurances from the chambermaid at their hotel that Darcy is away for the summer, Elizabeth consents. Third, Darcy then turns up "unexpectedly." We might conclude that his arrival is a contrivance, an event motivated by authorial purpose that works against the illusion of the characters' autonomy. But most readers don't regard the meeting as something that violates the mimetic illusion, and I believe our tacit assumptions about fiction—and the overall readerly dynamics of the novel's progression—help explain why.

These assumptions help us recognize that Darcy's arrival at Pemberley is unexpected by the narrative audience, that is, the audience engaged with the characters as autonomous actors, but wholly expected by the authorial audience, that is, the audience that knows the autonomy is an illusion. Here Sheldon Sacks's arguments about the power of genre that I discussed in chapter 2 (and in this context, *genre* means not simply "fiction" but "fictional comedy of fulfillment") do apply. If the first chapter supplies insufficient evidence for a solid inference about this genre, the progression in the rest of the beginning and the middle supplies ample evidence. The most significant evidence is Austen's handling of Mr. Collins's proposal to Elizabeth. Austen's representation of Collins's many defects, from unwarranted pride to an overall lack of good sense, combined with Mrs. Bennet's desire to have Elizabeth accept the proposal, means that Elizabeth faces a genuine threat to her happiness, present and future. Austen resolves the instability by means of Mr. Bennet's wittily expressing the choice Elizabeth faces: "From this day you must be a stranger to one of your parents.—Your mother will never see you again if you do *not* marry Mr. Collins, and I will never see you again if you *do*." Austen uses both this resolution and its manner as strong signals to her audience that in this narrative, the various threats to Elizabeth's happiness will never be wholly realized. Furthermore, the interactions between Darcy and Elizabeth at Netherfield and at Lady Catherine's before Darcy's first proposal reinforce her audience's expectation that Darcy and Elizabeth will eventually marry. Consequently, the authorial audience's response to the disastrous first proposal scene includes the inference that it represents a temporary, albeit serious, obstacle to their union. This inference is reinforced by both Darcy's letter to Elizabeth, explaining the behavior that her imperfect knowledge and prejudices had led her to regard as ethically reprehensible, and Elizabeth's self-criticism after reading the letter. In addition, the readerly dynamics of the progression include the authorial audience's desire for the union.

Thus, as soon as the Gardiners and Elizabeth get near Pemberley, the authorial audience both expects and desires that Elizabeth will cross paths with Darcy. Consequently, Austen can rely on the Meta-Rule of Dominant Focus to license her skipping the kind of preparation in the textual dynamics for Darcy's arrival at Pemberley that she goes through for Elizabeth's stay at Netherfield. Austen simply has the housekeeper at Pemberley update the chambermaid's information with the report that Darcy is expected the next day with a large party and then, after Darcy shows up, has him explain that "business with his steward" (256) made him arrive a few hours ahead of the others. In other words, Austen's reliance on Chance here is not a problem because (a) she has scrupulously avoided Chance in establishing the initial pattern of the progression in the textual dynamics and (b) those dynamics establish readerly inferences about the genre of fictional comedy of fulfillment, and those inferences in turn lead the audience to expect the meeting. To put the point another way, the interaction of the textual and readerly dynamics in the progression across the beginning and the middle of the novel converts what looks like Austen's reliance on Chance into a reliance on probability. From this perspective, it would be far more improbable for Darcy and Elizabeth to miss each other during Elizabeth's visit to Pemberley.

Now, if this narrative were nonfictional, would Austen's handling of the meeting at Pemberley need to be different? Yes, but not because it relies on the workings of Chance, since Chance often does work in the extratextual world. Since the default of nonfiction is that the author has freedom to shape the narrative structure within the constraints of being responsible to the extratextual world, the meeting at Pemberley would not be understood as part of the author's invention of events. Thus, its justification cannot simply be that the meeting fits the pattern that the author has been arranging. Instead, it must both fit that pattern and observe the constraints of being responsible to the extratextual existence of characters and events. Consequently, if *Pride and Prejudice* were nonfiction, the author would need to address the apparent workings of Chance more fully than Austen does in the novel. The author could choose among various strategies, including calling explicit attention to the workings of Chance (the functioning of Chance would add to the tellability of the narrative) and showing that what has the surface appearance of

Chance is actually the convergence of Elizabeth's and Darcy's different purposes. The larger point of this analysis, then, is that the tacit assumptions underlying authors' and readers' engagements with fiction and with nonfiction significantly influence both the construction and reception of narrative events. Readers' different assumptions about fiction and nonfiction mean that the same event (a chance meeting) requires different authorial treatment in nonfiction than it does in fiction.

FREEDOM AND CONSTRAINT IN *THE YEAR OF MAGICAL THINKING*

As I turn to *The Year of Magical Thinking,* I ask you to try the thought experiment of coming to it without knowing whether it is fiction or nonfiction. Here's a passage from very early in the narrative:

> In outline.
>
> It is now, as I begin to write this, the afternoon of October 4, 2004.
>
> Nine months and five days ago, at approximately nine o'clock on the evening of December 30, 2003, my husband, John Gregory Dunne, appeared to (or did) experience, at the table where he and I had just sat down to dinner in the living room of our apartment in New York, a sudden massive coronary event that caused his death. Our only child, Quintana, had been for the previous five nights unconscious in an intensive care unit at Beth Israel Medical Center's Singer Division, at that time a hospital on East End Avenue (it closed in August 2004) more commonly known as "Beth Israel North" or "the old Doctors' Hospital," where what had seemed a case of December flu sufficiently severe to take her to an emergency room on Christmas morning had exploded into pneumonia and septic shock. This is my attempt to make sense of the period that followed, weeks and then months that cut loose any fixed idea I had ever had about death, about illness, about probability and luck, about good fortune and bad, about marriage and children and memory, about grief, about the ways that people do and do not deal with the fact that life ends, about the shallowness of sanity, about life itself. (6–7)

If we assume that this passage is fiction, then our dual perspective means that we also assume that the "I" who narrates this passage is a character distinct from Didion the implied author. That assumption in turn means that we are on the lookout for discrepancies between the sense that the narrator will make of the weeks and months that followed the death of her husband

and the sense that the implied Didion will invite her audience to make of that period. On the other hand, if we assume that this passage is nonfiction, then we also assume, as noted above, that the narrating-I is a reliable spokesperson for Didion and, thus, that the sense that the narrator makes of this period is the sense that Didion makes of it.

But is there any way to tell from the evidence of the passage itself whether it is fiction or nonfiction? If we focus only on the language of the text, then I submit that the answer is no. Although the attention to the details about John's death and about Quintana's hospitalization suggests a scrupulousness about extratextual facts that may seem to signal nonfiction, we could also understand that attention as a contribution to the fictional portrait of a detail-oriented character narrator. But if we focus on the language of the text first in conjunction with the tacit assumptions that govern fiction, and second in conjunction with those that govern nonfiction, then I think the answer is a tentative yes. What's more, when we add more passages and do the same comparison, then we need no longer be tentative and can say yes with considerable confidence.

The most salient feature of the passage is its jump from the journalistic reporting ("In outline") of two heartrending events to the more philosophical statement of purpose. But for now let's focus on those two events: the death of the narrator's husband and the life-threatening illness of the couple's only child. (Again, at this point in the thought experiment, the question of whether husband and child are people with an extratextual existence or characters in a novel remains open.) Another salient feature is the way that the passage sets up a clear hierarchy between those events: "the period" that will be the focus of the book begins not with the onset of Quintana's illness but with the moment of John's death at approximately nine o'clock on the evening of December 30, 2003. To put the point even more strongly, the implied Didion and the narrator not only give Quintana's illness secondary status but treat it as necessary exposition for the main event. Furthermore, because the passage treats Quintana's illness this way, Didion's audience can infer either that on October 4, 2004, Quintana is still alive—and no longer in critical condition—or that the narrator has some serious ethical deficiencies. If Quintana had died, then there are strong ethical and aesthetic reasons for a reliable narrator to include that event as part of the outline.

The ethical reasons become apparent once we consider the readerly judgments that would follow from not including it: the narrator would appear to be incredibly callous. But nothing else in the passage suggests such callousness, so this line of thinking seems unfruitful. The aesthetic reasons for including the death can be put more positively; that event would give greater force and significance to the task the narrator sets for herself and explicitly articulates here: coming to terms with the period in which the two events would have occurred and reflecting on that set of difficult issues. On balance, then, the appropriate inference, regardless of whether the narrative is fictional or nonfictional, is that on October 4, 2004, Quintana is still alive.

Now let us consider the passage in relation to the tacit assumptions underlying the reading of fiction. From this perspective, Didion's treatment of Quintana seems at best an unwise use of her novelist's freedom and a worst a huge mistake. If *The Year of Magical Thinking* is a novel about a woman's effort to come to terms with the sudden death of her husband after almost forty years of marriage, then it ought to stay focused on her loss and her efforts to cope with that loss. Giving the character narrator a daughter with a life-threatening illness blurs the novel's focus by introducing a second global instability, one that also makes the narrative seem excessive in the tribulations it visits upon its protagonist. Most editors, it's fair to say, would advise Didion the novelist to "lose the daughter." Alternatively, if Didion insisted on keeping the daughter in the novel, then Didion ought to have the courage and the aesthetic sense to kill her off before October 4, 2004. Such an event would allow the novel to broaden its focus to the character narrator's double loss and to her correspondingly more extensive meditation on death, illness, marriage, parenthood, and mourning. But of course this strategy would require revising this passage by making the daughter's death part of the outline. Read as fiction, the current passage, with its backgrounding of the daughter's illness and its implication that the daughter's condition has improved by October 4, seems to be deeply flawed.

If we approach the passage as nonfiction, however, then Didion's decision to include Quintana's illness shifts from a matter of whether to a matter of how—and the choice of how is very effective. Nonfiction's ethical imperative to be responsible to extratextual events means that Didion needs to include Quintana's situation. This constraint also means that if Quintana has improved by October 4, then the narrative needs to reflect that extratextual reality. At the same time, the ethical imperative leaves Didion free to determine whether to foreground or background Quintana's illness. And Didion's decision to background it makes good sense: John's death, unlike the adult Quintana's illness and improvement, brings about a permanent change in Didion's life, and he had been her partner for almost forty years. Furthermore, the decision gives Didion a clear focus for the narrative to follow. Quintana's illness can be, as it is in this passage, an important part of that narrative, something that influences Didion's experiences and her reflections, but it will always function in relation to her effort to come to terms with John's death.

It is worth noting that, having made these decisions about how to be responsible to the extratextual facts about Quintana, Didion did not have to go back and revise the narrative when, in the summer of 2005, shortly before *The Year of Magical Thinking* was published, Quintana passed away. As we come to the end of our thought experiment, we have good reasons to conclude once again that our tacit assumptions about fiction and nonfiction lead us to respond in markedly different ways to the same textual phenomena.

The reason I say that we can give a tentative but not a definitive yes to the question of whether we can conclude on the basis of this passage that the book is nonfiction is that it's still possible to imagine a plausible trajectory for a fictional narrative that would follow from this passage. That trajectory would resolve the potential problem of competition between the two instabilities by tying them together. More specifically, the solution would be to have the resolution of the instability about the daughter pave the way for the working through of the character narrator's mourning and melancholia. Although this solution might very well lead to a cloyingly sentimental narrative, its existence means that our initial "yes" must be tentative. When, however, we read the rest of the narrative and discover more about Quintana's experiences, we can make that yes a definitive one.

Didion focuses on the instabilities of Quintana's health in chapters 8 through 12 of the narrative, a segment during which Didion oversees Quintana's treatment at UCLA Medical Center after she suffers a subdural hematoma. Quintana's experiences and Didion's response as loving, worried mother who is still dealing with the aftereffects of John's death take center stage in chapters 8 and 9. But chapter 10 returns the focus to John's death and its consequences for Didion, as she describes what she calls the "vortex effect" (107), that is, the way that a small thing can trigger a set of memories of her life with John or her life with John and Quintana that ultimately leads her back to her grief over John's loss and her anxiety about Quintana. Chapter 11 recounts the flight that returns Quintana to New York, and then chapter 12 abruptly resolves the instabilities about her illness as Didion effects a transition back to a focus on her own situation.

Here are the first two sentences of chapter 12: "The day on which Quintana and I flew east on the Cessna that refueled in the cornfield in Kansas was April 30, 2004. During May and June and the half of July that she spent at the Rusk Institute there was very little I could do for her" (142). That paragraph ends, "She was reaching a point at which she would need once again to be, if she was to recover, on her own." And the next paragraph is a single sentence: "I determined to spend the summer reaching the same point" (143). For the remaining eighty-five pages of the narrative, the adult Quintana appears only once, when Didion mentions that she attended Christmas dinner.

If *The Year of Magical Thinking* were fiction, then again we'd conclude that Didion had failed to exercise her novelistic freedom wisely. Rather than following the plausible trajectory we projected from the earlier passage, she gives us one that raises questions about her ability to construct a coherent plot: why give this character so much prominence, create so much readerly interest in the instability about her illness, and then essentially drop her out of the narrative? Again, any good editor would advise Didion the novelist either to eliminate the character or do a lot more with her.

If, however, we approach the narrative as nonfiction, then Didion's handling makes good ethical and aesthetic sense. She is observing the constraints of the extratextual reality when she says that there was very little she could do for Quintana at this point, and her handling is consistent with her decision to keep Quintana's experience subordinated to her efforts to come to terms with her grief about losing John. More than that, she identifies the link between the events of Quintana's life and the events of her own in her resolution to devote her summer to the same general project as Quintana. Thus, textual phenomena that would be a sign of Didion's aesthetic deficiencies if she were writing fiction are actually signs of her aesthetic skill and of her ethically responsible approach to the constraints of the genre.

Again, I do not claim that *Pride and Prejudice* and *The Year of Magical Thinking* represent all fictions and nonfictions, but I do claim that they are representative of two large classes of narrative. I claim further that the analysis of these two cases supports the position that for the standard novel and the standard literary memoir, there are inextricable connections between (non) fictional status, audiences' responses to textual dynamics, and authors' exercise of freedom and constraint in the construction of those textual dynamics.

In chapter 9, I shall return to *The Year of Magical Thinking* and to the significance of the generic frames of fiction and nonfiction for author-audience interactions, though there my focus will be on the interaction between narratorial dynamics and readerly dynamics, as I take up what I call deficient narration, that is, telling in which the actual audience finds themselves unwilling to endorse the position of the authorial audience.

CHAPTER 4

Engaging the Stubborn

NARRATIVE SPEED AND READERLY JUDGMENTS IN FRANZ KAFKA'S "DAS URTEIL"

I N THIS CHAPTER, I continue to explore issues of probability, though I shift from a focus on generic frames to the phenomenon of an unfillable gap in the plot dynamics of fiction, one that leaves rhetorical readers without any adequate causal explanation for what happens. More specifically, I turn to look at the rhetorical dynamics of what I call "the stubborn," that is, textual recalcitrance that does not yield to interpreters' efforts to master it. The stubborn is simultaneously part of textual dynamics and readerly dynamics: the author shapes the textual phenomena to resist interpretation and the authorial audience integrates that resistance into the larger trajectory of its responses in the progression. The stubborn is distinct from "the difficult," textual phenomena that initially appear recalcitrant but are designed to yield to interpreters' efforts to comprehend them. (The difficult is the primary domain of literary criticism.) The stubborn is also different from "the erroneous," textual recalcitrance that works against the author's overall design.[1] (I will discuss a significant subcategory of the erroneous in chapter 9, when I examine what I call deficient narration.) Here I shall focus on Franz Kafka's deployment of stubbornness at the climax of his powerful and strange short story "Das Urteil" (1916), specifically Georg Bendemann's acceptance of his father's judgment

---

1. I first lay out these distinctions in chapter 10 of *Narrative as Rhetoric*. For related work on textual recalcitrance, see the creative criticism in Wright. For related work on recalcitrance that does not yield, see the exceptionally fine books by Weinstein and Abbott.

that he should drown himself, and then draw on that interpretive work to further develop my rhetorical poetics. In particular, I will offer some specific points about the interrelations of narrative speed, narrative judgments, and surprise endings.

I choose "Das Urteil" as my case study for three reasons. First, Kafka is justifiably famous for both the difficulty and the power of his narratives, and, thus, his work provides a valuable site for exploring effective uses of the stubborn. Although I do not view "Das Urteil" as representing the quintessence of Kafka's narrative practice, it is a significant milestone in his career. "Das Urteil" is widely acknowledged to be, in Frederick Karl's words, "the first of [Kafka's] mature works" (434), and Kafka himself regarded the eight-hour writing session on the night of September 22–23, 1912, that ended with his completion of the story as one of the formative experiences in his development as a writer. Second, the story has received extensive, insightful comments from critics, thus relieving me of the burden of producing an original reading of the story and allowing me to focus on the rhetorical dynamics that follow from its stubbornness. Third, "Das Urteil" invites attention to worthwhile issues about narrative progression and about readerly judgments. With respect to progression, the issues are narrative speed and surprise endings. With respect to judgment, the issues are about the interactions of interpretive and ethical judgments of the characters and their actions and the ethics of Kafka's storytelling itself. Ultimately, though, my focus is on how Kafka's handling of the stubbornness at the climax of the story guides the audience's interpretive, affective, ethical, and aesthetic experience of it. I begin by elaborating on a few points I make about narrative progression and narrative judgments in the introduction.

Narrative judgments are crucial components of readerly dynamics. Those dynamics depend upon two main readerly activities: observing and judging. (In this respect, narrative is different from lyric, which invites rhetorical readers to participate in rather than judge a speaker's emotions or attitudes. For more on these points, see my *Experiencing Fiction*.) As observers, we perceive the characters of the narrative as both external to ourselves and distinct from their implied authors. Consequently, we make interpretive and ethical judgments about them, their situations, and their choices. Furthermore, our interpretive and ethical judgments are integral to our affective responses as well as to our desires concerning future events. In addition, this trajectory of judgment and response is intertwined with another kind of judgment we make, an aesthetic judgment about the overall quality of our experience, both as it is happening and once it is complete. Finally, because readerly dynamics involve interpretive, ethical, and aesthetic judgments that develop over time, and thus can themselves be revised, the readerly side of progression often involves a process of *configuration and reconfiguration,* that is, a process of (a) forming a hypothesis about the trajectory of the narrative and how its parts contribute to that trajectory and then (b) revising that hypothesis in light of new judgments.

PROGRESSION, SPEED, AND JUDGMENT IN "DAS URTEIL"

Since there has been so much good commentary on the story, I will work from a helpful summary by Henry Sussman of what that commentary has established and suggest how a rhetorical approach can extend and refine this baseline understanding. In a section on "The Aesthetics of Confusion" within a broader essay on Kafka's aesthetics, Sussman writes:

> Onto Georg Bendemann's best-case scenario of his role in his family, his forthcoming marriage, his business success, and his empathy for his friend, Kafka seamlessly splices, within the continuity of narrative, his father's very different account of the events and arenas in Georg's "life." The "hinge," or graft between the counter-narratives, is a fulcrum for a confusion existing at least *in potentia* for the duration of Kafka's fiction. (135)

From the perspective of rhetorical theory, Sussman's overview of the story is fine as far as it goes, but it does not go far enough. Indeed, because it posits a standoff between Georg's best-case scenario and Herr Bendemann's counter-narrative, it ends up flattening the story out, sacrificing its strangeness to an account of confusion as unresolvable ambiguity. Focusing on progression and judgment leads to a revision of Sussman's account that seeks to preserve strangeness in three main ways: (a) by giving the speed of the narrative its due, (b) by distinguishing more clearly between what is determinate in the story and what remains in an unfillable interpretive gap, and (c) by accounting for the consequences of that gap for readerly dynamics. The results of this analysis will lead in turn to a consideration, first, of the traffic going the other way— that is, of how Kafka's story complicates some ideas of rhetorical theory—and then, second, of the ethics of Kafka's telling.

I begin with an overall sketch of the textual dynamics, in which I see three recognizably distinct stages. Stage one consists of Georg Bendemann sitting at his writing desk and reflecting on his relation with the unnamed friend to whom he has just written a letter. Stage two consists of Georg's conflictual conversation with his father, culminating in his father's condemning him to death by drowning. Stage three consists of Georg's acceptance of and immediate capitulation to his father's judgment. Thus, Kafka begins with a stage in which Georg is alone, then moves to one where he interacts with his father, and then back to one where he is alone.

In addition to highlighting this movement, identifying the three stages also helps us recognize the relation between the story's strangeness and its narrative speed, and indeed looking at that relation can help lead us to a richer understanding of narrative speed. By narrative speed, I mean the pace of the authorial audience's experience as rooted in the interaction of instabilities and complications on the one hand, and readerly judgments on the other. From this perspective, "Das Urteil" begins at a leisurely pace in stage one, rapidly accelerates in stages two and three, and then slows down again in the final sentences. Let us take a closer look, first at the overall trajectory and then at each of the parts.

The first stage is leisurely in spite of its revealing two instabilities, because the first, about Georg's relation to his friend, appears to get resolved within this first stage, and because the second, a more significant one, involving dissonance between Georg's ethical character and his own understanding of that ethical character, does not get complicated until stage two.

Furthermore, the interpretive and ethical judgments evolve slowly in this first stage, in part as a result of Kafka's handling of temporality. Kafka introduces his audience to Georg just after he has finished his letter, and then, after taking us into Georg's consciousness for several paragraphs—almost a third of the whole story—reveals that Georg has been sitting at the desk for an indefinitely long time. In the space between the two statements describing Georg at his desk, Kafka's narrator does not call attention to time passing in the Narrative Now, but rather engages in a narration about the past, reviewing Georg's perceptions of his friend, his own contrasting situation, and the contents of the letter itself. While this material introduces the dissonance between Georg's judgment of himself and the judgment Kafka guides his audience to make, the movement to the past rather than significantly forward in the Narrative Now works as a brake on the story's pace. Kafka's strategy allows for the gradual evolution of our judgments about Georg even as it defers any complication of the instability until the review of the past is complete.

Once Georg goes to talk with his father, however, the pace of the narrative accelerates rapidly because (a) the instabilities get complicated with each line of dialogue, and (b) each new complication requires new interpretive and ethical judgments. As a result, Kafka's readers are likely to have difficulty handling the accelerated pace. At the end of the second stage, the speed shifts into yet a higher gear, as the progression takes a sharp and sudden turn to its climax in Herr Bendemann's judgment of Georg. The breakneck pace continues as the story hurtles on to the third stage, Georg's surprising acceptance of the judgment. Just as important, when Herr Bendemann delivers his judgment at the end of stage two, the authorial audience's struggle to keep up with the necessary interpretive and ethical judgments can meet with only partial success because Kafka builds into that moment a major interpretive gap, one that stubbornly refuses to be filled. Consequently, Kafka's audience follows Georg in his headlong rush to the river with only partial comprehension of the reasons for his behavior, something that further contributes to the story's speed: events are happening faster than the audience can comprehend them.

Once Georg is on the verge of drowning himself, Kafka slows the pace again by focusing on his last actions and last words, allowing the audience to take in the deliberateness of Georg's act. This slowing down does not allow the audience to close the interpretive gap, but instead it emphasizes the radical change the story has represented and the strangeness associated with that change. Among other things, the final sentence of the story, "In diesem Augenblick ging über die Brücke ein geradezu unendlicher Verkehr" (52) ["At that moment, the traffic going over the bridge was nothing short of infinite" (12)[2]], by introducing for the first time a narrative perspective other than Georg's, underlines that strangeness by way of contrast between what has just happened and the everyday quality of what it describes.

This general sketch of the story's progression identifies much of its power and strangeness as resulting from its combining shifts in speed with the unfillable gap at the end of stage two and the beginning of stage three. If the claim holds up, then Kafka has discovered something remarkable: a way to make a significant interpretive gap surrounding the climax of a narrative enhance rather than detract from an audience's interpretive, ethical, and aesthetic experience. In other words, though the climactic events do not finally yield to our efforts to comprehend them, their recalcitrance enhances the story's power. Let us turn now to a longer—and slower—look at the story's progression as a way to better comprehend how Kafka achieves this effect.

Because Kafka uses analepsis so extensively in stage one, a major function of Georg's eight paragraphs of reflections is exposition, and that exposition reveals him, according to his own judgments, to be making his way in the world very well indeed. Although his mother died two years previously, he has become the dominant force in the increasingly successful family business, and he has recently become engaged to Frieda Brandenfeld, "einem Mädchen aus wohlhabender Familie" (42) ["a young woman from a well-to-do family" (5)]. Indeed, the only apparent problem in Georg's life that emerges from

---

2. English translation here and throughout this chapter taken from Corngold, *Kafka: Selected Stories.*

these reflections is his inability to speak openly and honestly to his childhood friend. But Georg himself, in order to please Frieda, decides to write to the friend, and thus, as noted above, that instability appears to get resolved.

Nevertheless, Kafka's handling of the narration brilliantly reveals that underneath this superficial instability is a more substantial one, involving Georg's relation to himself. As many critics have pointed out, Kafka uses Georg's perspective to show that while Georg appears to make reasonable judgments about the difference between his situation and that of his friend, those judgments are ultimately self-serving. John M. Ellis offers a perceptive summary of this effect: "the superficial impression of the breadth of [Georg's] human sympathy for his friend is overshadowed by a contrary impression of narrowness in Georg's judgments of value, for judgments of his friend's life are made rigidly on the basis of Georg's values" (78). Ellis's subsequent general summary is over the top, but it effectively captures both the instability within Georg and the discrepancy between his self-judgments and those Kafka guides his audience to make. "There is, after all, something destructive in Georg's 'considerateness' towards his friend; it seems to provide the opportunity for an orgy of denigration of him, a very full series of imaginings of his helplessness, wretchedness and even disgrace which are very congenial and flattering to Georg" (79).[3]

This dimension of the first stage of the progression becomes more prominent when we reflect on its revelations about Georg's investment in this correspondence. He speaks to Frieda about their "besondere Korrespondenz-verhältnis" (42) [the "special relationship of correspondence between them" (5)], when all the evidence indicates that their correspondence in recent years has been anything but special. Georg writes only about "bedeutungslose Vorfälle" (42) ["insignificant events" (5)], while his friend expressed his sympathy about the death of Georg's mother "mit . . . Trockenheit" (41) ["with dryness" (4)]. More significantly, after finishing the letter, Georg sits at his desk lost in thought for a long time. Kafka invites his audience to make the interpretive judgment that the correspondence is fulfilling some purpose for Georg beyond the maintenance of the friendship itself. That purpose, to put it most sympathetically, is the shoring up of his own self-esteem as he is poised to take his next step into adulthood with his marriage to Frieda. But even that sympathetic account does not deny the ethical deficiency of Georg's using the correspondence in this way. Thus, by the end of the first stage of the

---

3. For additional—and very insightful—commentary on Ellis's reading, see Pascal 27–31. More generally, Pascal is a very fine reader of Kafka, and his larger conclusion about "Das Urteil," though arrived at via a different route, is similar to mine: the story leaves us with "a baffling and painful puzzle" (30).

progression, Kafka opens up a substantial distance between Georg's interpretive and ethical judgments and those of his authorial audience.

As the progression moves into the second stage and picks up speed, Kafka guides his audience to see that Georg's approach to his father is similar to his way of thinking about his friend. That is, Kafka shows Georg to be acting in a way that Georg regards as showing legitimate concern for his father, even as Kafka guides his audience to recognize that Georg is ultimately self-serving and condescending. Here, too, Georg's approach initially appears to serve him well, as he blunts his father's skepticism about the existence of his friend by saying that his father is much more important and by helping him get undressed and then carrying him to the bed and covering him up. However, once Herr Bendemann rises from the bed and escalates his verbal assault on Georg, a new element enters the progression. Georg loses not only the upper hand in the conflict but also full control over his own agency.

After his father makes his strongest accusations—namely, that because Frieda lifted her skirts, Georg decided to betray his friend, profane his mother's memory, and put his father in bed—the narrator reports: "Vor einer langen Weile hatte er sich fest entschlossen, alles vollkommen genau zu beobachten, damit er nicht irgendwie auf Umwegen, von hinten her, von oben herab überrascht werden könne. Jetzt erinnerte er sich wieder an den längst vergessenen Entschluß und vergaß in" (50) ["A long time ago he had firmly decided to observe everything very exactly so as to avoid being taken by surprise in some devious way, from behind or from above. Now he remembered that long-forgotten decision once again and forgot it" (10)]. This pattern of a disparity between Georg's intentions and his actual agency continues, as he blurts out his insult of his father—"Komödiant!" (50) ["Play actor!" (10)]— and as his efforts to mock his father ironically turn into a confirmation of his father's accusations.

Kafka invites his audience to make two related interpretive judgments. First, as Herr Bendemann attacks Georg's conception of his relationship with his friend, Georg begins to lose the sense of self shored up by that conception. Second, as this sense of self gets broken down, Georg begins to feel guilty, though the exact nature and extent of that guilt is not yet clear. Significantly, just before Herr Bendemann's judgment, Georg accuses his father of lying in wait for him—"Du hast mir also aufgelauert!" (52) ["And so you've been lying in ambush for me!" (12)]—but the accusation implicitly reveals both his powerlessness and his guilt. Before I consider the audience's ethical judgments of Georg here, I want to turn to the audience's interpretive and ethical judgments of Herr Bendemann and his judgments.

Kafka claimed that he was thinking of Freud in writing the story, and, indeed, much of the father-son dynamic can be explained as an Oedipal struggle (see, for example, Hughes). But from the rhetorical perspective, what is more significant is that, even as Kafka gradually increases his audience's distance from Georg's interpretive and ethical judgments, he keeps his audience even more distant from most of Herr Bendemann's. Once Herr Bendemann stands on the bed and goes on the attack, he reveals himself to be not a loving but a jealous and vengeful father. In addition, as Russell Berman perceptively points out, Herr Bendemann contradicts himself. He contends, first, that Georg has no friend in St. Petersburg and then later that Georg and the friend have been in constant correspondence. Herr Bendemann attacks Georg both for wanting to marry and for delaying the marriage. Finally, he berates Georg for both his childishness and his ambitions with the business and with his marriage. The resulting interpretive and ethical distance between Herr Bendemann and Kafka's audience is compounded by Kafka's restricting the focalization to Georg, so that we never see Herr Bendemann from the inside. At the same time, Kafka effectively uses the dialogue to show that Herr Bendemann does have what Sussman calls a counter-narrative to Georg's account of his life and to suggest that two of his motives are to rebel against Georg's neglect of him and to shake Georg out of his complacent self-satisfaction.

Nevertheless, when Herr Bendemann renders his ultimate judgment of Georg, Kafka does not give his audience enough guidance to make a clear interpretive judgment of Herr Bendemann's motives or of the judgment's basis in Georg's behavior. Why should this father, who claims to love his son, condemn that son to death? Not even the accusations the father makes warrant such a harsh judgment. The psychoanalytic explanation, that Herr Bendemann is a version of Laius striking back against Oedipus, strikes me as insufficiently responsive not only to the strangeness of the story but also to the particular form that the striking back takes. From Herr Bendemann's/Laius's perspective, wouldn't it be too easy for Georg/Oedipus to reject the judgment? Is there some other knowledge that either Herr Bendemann or Georg has, that Kafka's audience does not, that makes the judgment appropriate? In short, why this judgment, and then why Georg's acceptance of it? These questions hover over this moment in the progression, and because they remain unanswerable, Kafka introduces a permanent gap in the narrative.

Let me clarify the claim I am making about the nature of this interpretive gap and thus clarify what I mean by textual stubbornness. This gap is significantly different, for example, from the one that exists regarding Herr Bendemann's fate after he delivers the judgment. That gap—specifically, whether Georg's hearing him crash onto the bed is a sign of temporary collapse or of death—is an issue about whether one event or another occurs in the fabula, and it is a gap that functions to underline the compulsion Georg feels to act on his father's judgment. Georg hears the crash but is too intent on taking his own life even to wonder what the crash signifies. In other words, Kafka's decision to leave this gap in the textual dynamics contributes to the effectiveness of his audience's interpretive and ethical judgments of Georg and thus to the story's progression as a whole. The gap is not an instance of stubbornness because we can adequately interpret it: there are only two possibilities, and though they are substantially different, their consequences for our understanding of the protagonist's action are not. By contrast, the gap surrounding Herr Bendemann's judgment on Georg is not a gap in the fabula—the event occurs—*but a gap in readerly dynamics that leaves Kafka's audience in a position of being unable to fully interpret the judgment.* Furthermore, that inability in turn means that the audience cannot make a clear and satisfactory ethical judgment of Herr Bendemann, of his judgment, or of Georg in his accepting of it. This gap is an instance of stubbornness because we cannot comprehend the event within the logic of the progression to this point, and yet the event remains crucial to that progression.

One way in which Kafka maintains stubbornness is to block a conventional judgment that Georg is overreacting to his father's condemnation by showing Georg regaining his agency, even as the pace of the progression slows. Although, as Ronald Speirs has noted, Georg is initially driven out of the house by an impersonal force referred to only by *es* (it), once he is hanging from the bridge, his agency returns. Georg thinks about when he should drop, and he utters his declaration of love for both of his parents. The slower pace, the return of Georg's agency, the affirmation of his love for his parents—all these elements underline the point that he accepts the judgment, and that conscious acceptance unsettles our ethical judgment of Georg. Rhetorical readers can conclude neither that he should nor should not have accepted the father's judgment, even as the story puts pressure on its audience to judge Georg's decision.

At the same time, the interpretive gap and Georg's acceptance of his father's judgment have another significant effect on the readerly dynamics, specifically on the audience's engagements with the story's mimetic component, on the one hand, and its thematic and synthetic components, on the other. Although Ellis rightly points out that even the first paragraph of the story does not fully conform to the tenets of straight realism, the dominant signals of the first stage of the progression are those that activate the authorial audience's interest in its mimetic component, and the story rewards our efforts to read such things as the psychology of the characters in mimetic terms.

But one consequence of the textual stubbornness is to move the story from a straight mimetic account to one in which the thematic and the synthetic become more prominent. The gap encourages interpreters to read the story as a parable rather than a psychological study. In such readings, Georg and Herr Bendemann function as types whose interactions are comprehensible less by reference to the plausible psychological behavior of autonomous individuals than by reference to Kafka's working out of the relations among certain ideas.

From the rhetorical perspective, however, this interpretive move to put greater emphasis on the thematic and the synthetic components of the narrative does not resolve the story's textual stubbornness. Instead, it is the textual stubbornness itself that allows for the proliferation of such readings. "Das Urteil" is a parable of guilt that includes elements of father-son struggles going back to Oedipus. It is a story about the power of patriarchy. It is a story about both the necessity and the inevitable imperfections of its title word *judgment*. And it is many other things as well. These thematic readings can be very insightful, and, indeed, I have learned from many of them. But to the extent that they claim to close the interpretive gap at the climax of the story, they overreach. Even if we say that "Das Urteil" belongs to the genre of the parable and that parables are often enigmatic, we cannot convert the stubbornness of Kafka's story into a more conventional textual difficulty because the location of the unbridgeable gap at the climax of the story moves it beyond the enigmatic to the inscrutable. All of these considerations have consequences for our aesthetic judgments of the story, but I will defer that discussion until after I look at how Kafka's shaping of "Das Urteil" contributes to the project of rhetorical poetics.

FROM "DAS URTEIL" TO ISSUES IN RHETORICAL POETICS

Traffic in this direction stops at four stations: at the first, one of the ten principles of rhetorical theory I sketched in the introduction gets substantially reinforced; at the second, rhetorical theory is able to offer some new generalizations about narrative speed; at the third, rhetorical theory is able to say something new about progressions with surprise endings; and at the fourth, rhetorical theory adds to its understanding of textual stubbornness.

Station one. Rhetorical theory works in an a posteriori fashion. Although, as this book demonstrates, the theory has constructed—and continues to construct—a large warehouse of terms and concepts, it regards them not as forming preset molds into which narratives will inevitably fit—or must be made to fit—but rather as available tools for opening up the workings of individual narratives. "Das Urteil" reinforces this lesson because it does not fit any predetermined rhetorical mode, and, indeed, the challenge it presents to the rhetorical critic is to uncover its logic while also preserving its strangeness.

At the same time, as the previous chapters also demonstrate, rhetorical theory is not averse to offering generalizations after it has done its a posteriori work on individual narratives. To eschew generalization altogether is, in effect, to be antitheoretical. It is also to suggest that what one learns from the analysis of one narrative cannot apply to the analysis of another. The delicate matter, of course, is to engage in appropriate generalization, to develop theoretical conclusions that help us work on new narratives without leading us to take what R. S. Crane once called the High Priori Road.

Station two. Attending to speed in "Das Urteil" helps rhetorical theory extend the work of Jan Baetens and Katherine Hume, who have offered a helpful overview of narrative speed as involving both textual and readerly components. On the textual side, Baetens and Hume identify speed effects as occurring at the story level (mentions and descriptions of speed); at the discourse level (effects fall along a spectrum from fast to slow, with elliptical syntax near one end and pauses in the narration of events in favor of description at the other);[4] and at the narration level (by which they mean performances of speed in the typography or in the oral delivery of the text). On the readerly side, they work with the distinctions among implied reader (authorial audience), narratee, and empirical reader (flesh-and-blood or actual audience). Baetens and Hume note that the first two audiences are encoded in the text, while the third operates independently of textual encoding. They also make the astute observation that encoded speed is "never just determined by what is being read here and now, but also by what has just been read and by what one is expecting to read immediately afterwards" (352). In this sense, as Baetens and Hume point out, speed is connected to the larger concept of textual rhythm.

Rhetorical theory is primarily interested in encoded speed, and it endorses Baetens and Hume's point about the relation between speed and rhythm. But as the analysis of "Das Urteil" suggests, rhetorical theory can offer greater precision about the interaction between textual and readerly components of speed through its attention to the dynamics of progression and especially the role of interpretive and ethical judgments—and the strategic placement of an interpretive gap. In other words, what Kafka's story teaches us is that a narrative can accelerate its pace, not simply by increasing the pace of the complication of instabilities, but also by accompanying that acceleration with an

---

4. Baetens and Hume actually locate pauses for description at the story level, but that seems counterintuitive to me.

increasing number of interpretive and ethical judgments—and with a requirement that the audience jump over a space in which one would normally expect to make such judgments. Indeed, as I have indicated above, this combination of accelerated judgments with the strategic gap is central to both the story's power and its strangeness.

Station three. In my discussion of Edith Wharton's "Roman Fever" (1934) in chapter 4 of *Experiencing Fiction,* I have made what I regarded as an appropriate generalization by proposing that effective surprise endings meet three conditions. The surprise must (a) lead to a plausible reconfiguration of the narrative; (b) be prepared for—that is, in retrospect, be part of—a recognizable pattern; and (c) in some way enhance the overall effect of the narrative. Narratives in which the surprise depends upon characters acting in accord with traits that they have not previously exhibited, narratives that include absolutely no clues to the surprise (for example, many versions of the "it was only a dream" ending), and narratives in which the surprise, though congruent and prepared for, is an elaborate contrivance rather than a necessary part of a larger purpose—all either fall flat or come across as ethical or aesthetic cheats.

Wharton's "Roman Fever" meets all of these conditions with consummate skill. The story ends with Grace Ansley's surprising revelation to her rival Alida Slade that the father of Grace's admirable daughter Barbara is not her own husband, but Alida's husband, Delphin. The revelation causes both Alida and Wharton's audience to reconfigure their understanding of what happened in Rome twenty-five years previously, when Alida developed a scheme to have Grace contract tuberculosis and so be unavailable as a possible love interest for her future husband. Alida's scheme was to forge Delphin's signature to a note asking Grace to meet him after dark in the Colosseum. Thus, it is only with this final revelation that Alida realizes how the scheme actually brought about the tryst that led to Grace's conception of Barbara. The surprise fits with the previous progression because it does not contradict but rather rounds out our understanding of Grace's character, and it effectively concludes their conversation that has in some way been a reenactment of the rivalry that they engaged in twenty-five years previously. The surprise has been prepared for in numerous ways, including the disclosure of seemingly incidental information about Barbara and the narrator calling attention to odd emphases or silences in Grace's half of the conversation. And the surprise enhances the story by showing how its present-tense conversation not only reenacts the rivalry but also concludes it in a similar way: Alida has been trying to establish her superiority over Grace only to discover once again that her efforts have actually helped Grace to get the better of her.

Kafka's "Das Urteil" teaches rhetorical theory something new, because its surprise ending works in a remarkably different way, but no less effectively, than that of "Roman Fever." The stubbornness associated with the moment of judgment means both that the surprise is not fully congruent with the rest of the progression and that it is not prepared for in the way that the surprise of "Roman Fever" is. Nevertheless, as we have seen, the surprise significantly enhances the story's strange power and appeal. What "Das Urteil" teaches, then, is that the neat reversals and coherent reconfigurations that characterize "Roman Fever," Ambrose Bierce's "An Occurrence at Owl Creek Bridge" (1890), Ian McEwan's *Atonement* (2001), and other effective stories with surprising endings are not an absolute necessity for all narratives built on the principle of surprise. To put the lesson in more positive terms, "Das Urteil" shows that a limited stubbornness, even—or better, especially—when associated with a climactic moment in the progression, can significantly enhance the power of a story, even as that stubbornness points to a different kind of purpose from the ones we find in the stories that meet my three conditions. Rather than getting its power from a tighter and deeper understanding of the actions we have just read about, Kafka's story gets its power by keeping things open and broadening our explorations into the ethical and psychological dynamics—and thematic meanings—of the events we have just read about. In other words, the value added by the surprise is not that it takes us deeper into the mimetic situation, but rather that it invites us to relate the story to an ever widening range of issues and contexts.

Station four. The lesson here, then, is about stubbornness itself. In my previous explorations of this phenomenon, I have focused on the recalcitrance involved in our adequate interpretation of characters such as Toni Morrison's Beloved in *Beloved* (1987) (see chapter 10 of *Narrative as Rhetoric*). Later in this book, I will consider another recalcitrant character, the eponymous protagonist of Joseph Conrad's *Lord Jim*. In an analysis of Robert Frost's "Home Burial" (1916) in *Experiencing Fiction,* I have also considered the stubbornness that results when an author does not take sides in an ethical disagreement between two sympathetic characters who operate from fundamentally different principles. The case of Kafka's practice in "Das Urteil" encourages me to propose the broad generalization that any element of a narrative is potentially available for the productive functions of the stubborn.[5]

---

5. As these examples indicate, textual stubbornness is a feature available across genres and across works of different lengths. Although I believe, as my attention to narrative speed indicates, that the brevity of the short story form aids and abets the effectiveness of the stubbornness of "Das Urteil," I do not see any necessary general connection between brevity and stubbornness. Indeed, since stubbornness is textual recalcitrance that will not yield to our inter-

AESTHETICS AND ETHICS

As I turn toward the conclusion of this chapter, the traffic of my discussion is ready to move back in the other direction and consider the consequences of my analysis for our aesthetic judgments of "Das Urteil." Given what I've said so far, I realize that I have spoiled any possible surprise. The story is a remarkable aesthetic achievement, one whose speed, limited stubbornness, and consequent openness offer a strange and unsettling experience whose value is indisputable, even if—or because—it is not easy to pin down. To put this another way, "Das Urteil" is a formally innovative story that suggests new possibilities for storytelling itself. It is no wonder that Kafka regarded his composition of the story as marking a significant phase in his development as a writer. In addition, the story's formal innovation is productive precisely because it brings its audience face to face with, among other things, the uncanny elements of father-son relationships and the unsettling nature of guilt, love, and individual agency.

Finally, I turn to consider the ethics of Kafka's telling as revealed in the trajectory of the implied author–authorial audience relationship across the progression. The implied Kafka is at once a subtle guide and a formidable figure who keeps his distance. Furthermore, by leaving the unfillable gap at a key point in that trajectory, he becomes a figure who is as interested in unsettling his audience as he is in guiding it—or perhaps better, interested in guiding us to the point where he can unsettle us most profoundly. But it is also clear that he wants to unsettle us because he believes it will be for own good. I, for one, am willing to conclude that he's right.

---

pretive efforts and since reading always involves interpretation, stubbornness is potentially a feature of any text. But from an authorial perspective, the difference between constructing a textual recalcitrance that won't yield to interpretation and having that recalcitrance function to contribute to the power of one's design is huge.

CHAPTER 5

Estranging Unreliability, Bonding Unreliability, and the Ethics of *Lolita*

W ITH THIS CHAPTER, I move away from discussions of probability and begin a discussion of interrelations among authors, character narrators, and audiences that will continue for the rest of the book— sometimes as the main focus of a chapter and sometimes as a subsidiary focus. These chapters build on work I have previously done, especially in *Living to Tell about It*, a study of what the subtitle designates as "a rhetoric and ethics of character narration," and I will bring in aspects of that previous work as it becomes relevant here. My overarching goal is to extend that work so that I can offer something close to a comprehensive rhetorical poetics of character narration, and I offer a sketch of the results in chapter 12. In this chapter, I develop the general point that authors can and do use the same resources in remarkably different ways in order to achieve different ends, by considering the wide range of interpretive, affective, and ethical consequences that can follow from unreliable narration. I start with the challenge of coming to terms with the ethics of *Lolita*.

WAYNE C. BOOTH, UNRELIABLE NARRATION, AND THE ETHICS OF *LOLITA*

> Can we really be surprised that readers have overlooked Nabokov's ironies in *Lolita*, when Humbert Humbert is given full and unlimited

control of the rhetorical resources? . . . One of the major delights of this delightful, profound book is that of watching Humbert *almost* make a case for himself. But Nabokov has insured that many, perhaps most, of his readers will be unsuccessful, in that they will identify Humbert with the author more than Nabokov intends. (390–91)
—WAYNE C. BOOTH, *THE RHETORIC OF FICTION*, CHAPTER 13

I should have distinguished more clearly between the conclusions that were derived from rhetorical inquiry and those that were simply my unargued personal commitments.

   . . . And sometimes, especially in chapter thirteen, I seem to forget just how difficult it is to do justice to ethical complexities, in our reading experience, in our study of rhetorical problems, and in our thought about the relative values of particular art works in constituting and criticizing selves and societies. (418–19)
—WAYNE C. BOOTH, AFTERWORD, *THE RHETORIC OF FICTION*, SECOND EDITION

You can always count on a murderer for a fancy prose style. (9)
—VLADIMIR NABOKOV, *LOLITA*

In 1961, when Wayne C. Booth published *The Rhetoric of Fiction,* what we now think of as classical narratology had not yet emerged, and the dominant literary theory was the New Criticism. The New Critics famously regarded canonical literary works as verbal icons or well-wrought urns and just as famously ruled that interpretations based on responses of individual readers were guilty of the Affective Fallacy. In this climate, Booth's chapter 13 on "The Morality of Impersonal Narration,"[1] the chapter that includes his commentary on *Lolita,* was a radical statement, because it viewed fictional narratives not as autonomous objects but as acts of communication whose aesthetic qualities were intertwined with their ethical effects on individual readers. Given the hegemony of the New Criticism, it is not surprising that Booth's chapter encountered a lot of resistance from its initial readers or that its remarks about *Lolita* were a flashpoint for that resistance. Even from a twenty-first-century perspective that values ethical criticism—in part because of Booth's 1988 *The Company We Keep*—his 1961 comments invite objections. How can Booth both acknowledge that Nabokov has marked Humbert as an unreli-

---

   1. By "impersonal," Booth means narration that separates the person of the implied author from the source of the narrative information; thus, for Booth, both internal focalization and character narration are impersonal.

able narrator and complain about the morality of *Lolita?* Nabokov should not be impugned for his readers' failures, should he? And isn't Booth here and throughout chapter 13 working with a narrow, moralistic view of the art of fiction?

In his afterword to the second edition in 1983, Booth does not say anything further about *Lolita,* but he does make two general responses to the objections generated by chapter 13. (1) He defends his concerns with the relation between technique and morality as fully consistent with his conception of fiction as rhetorical action. And, (2) he admits two problems with the execution of his argument. As my second epigraph indicates, these are (a) mixing his personal beliefs into his analyses and (b) underestimating the difficulties of ethical criticism. I think Booth is on target in both of these general responses, but I also think that his commentary on *Lolita* is more a sign of his underestimating the difficulties of ethical criticism than of his mixing his personal beliefs into that commentary. Although Booth finds Nabokov's novel to be "delightful" and "profound," his comments also make it clear that he finds nothing "delightful" in the narrative's main action, Humbert's violation of Dolores.

With these considerations in mind, I undertake in this chapter the task of doing better justice to the difficult problem of the relation between technique and ethics in *Lolita.* Given the rhetorical paradigm's emphasis on authors and audience, I initially approach that task not by diving back into the text of the novel but by considering two especially notable groups of actual audience members—and by not castigating either group or Nabokov. The first group is the one that most troubles Booth, those who are taken in by Humbert's artful narration. The second is a group that is, I believe, more common today than it was in 1961, and I have encountered some of its members in my teaching. This group is determined not to be taken in by Humbert and thus resists all of his rhetorical appeals, including those that arise from his self-condemnations at the end of his narrative. Accounting for these two sets of responses will also mean situating these two groups in relation to Nabokov's authorial audience, which in turn means looking at the causes of the response of each group in Nabokov's construction of the novel.

Keeping this focus on audience in mind, I propose a spectrum of readerly effects of unreliable narration that extends from *estranging unreliability* at one end to *bonding unreliability* at the other. By estranging unreliability, I mean unreliable narration that underlines or increases the interpretive, affective, and/or ethical distance between the narrator and the authorial audience. By bonding unreliability, I mean unreliable narration that reduces the interpretive, affective, and/or ethical distance between the narrator and the authorial audience. My hypothesis is that Nabokov's specific and complicated deployment of these two kinds of unreliability, especially in part 1 of *Lolita,* provides the grounds for our understanding of the relations between his authorial audience and the two sets of flesh-and-blood readers I have described above. But before I explore this hypothesis, I want to place the distinction between estranging and bonding unreliability in the context of the account of unreliable narration I have offered in *Living to Tell about It.*

ESTRANGING AND BONDING UNRELIABILITY WITHIN A RHETORICAL APPROACH TO NARRATION

Unreliable narration, like character narration more generally, is a mode of indirect communication. The implied author communicates with his or her audience by means of the voice of another speaker addressing another audience. Put another way, we have one text, two speakers (one explicit, one implicit), two audiences, and at least two purposes. This model predicts nothing about the relation between implied author and narrator in any given instance of character narration, but instead imagines a very wide spectrum of possible relations. It does make the descriptive claim that narrators and audiences interact along three axes of communication that correspond to a narrator's three main functions: reporting (along the axis of information about characters and events), interpreting (along the axis of understanding/perception of what is being reported), and evaluating (along the axis of values).

For now, I will just identify the two ends of the spectrum of character narrator-audience relations. At one end is what I call mask narration, a rhetorical act in which the implied author uses the character narrator as a spokesperson for ideas that she fully endorses. Indeed, the implied author employs the mask of the character narrator as a means to increase the appeal and persuasiveness of the ideas expressed.[2] At the other end of this spectrum is narration that is unreliable along more than one of the three main axes of communication. Such narration along the axis of characters and events is misreporting or underreporting; along the axis of understanding/perception, it is misreading or misinterpreting/underreading or underinterpreting; along the axis of values, it is misregarding or misevaluating/underregarding or underevaluating.

---

2. My concept of mask narration is indebted to Ralph Rader's concept of the "mask lyric" developed in his essay "The Dramatic Monologue and Related Lyric Forms." One important difference between the poet-speaker relationship in mask lyric and the implied author-narrator relationship in mask narration is that the poet has the option of using the mask to try out ideas that he or she does not endorse.

In most work on unreliable narration since Booth's coining of the term in 1961, theorists and critics have focused on this second end of the spectrum. Think of the common examples of unreliable narrators: Ford Madox Ford's Dowell in *The Good Soldier*, Ring Lardner's Whitey in "Haircut," William Faulkner's Jason in *The Sound and the Fury*, Henry James's governess in one reading of *The Turn of the Screw*, Ian McEwan's Jack in *The Cement Garden*. There are good reasons for this focus: using one text to convey substantial gaps between a narrator's reports, interpretations, or evaluations and those of the implied author is no mean feat—nor is being able to account for the dynamics of that feat, as the history of theoretical quarrels about unreliability would suggest.[3]

But when we shift to the rhetorical principle that unreliable narration is a resource that authors can use in different ways on different occasions for different purposes, we become more cognizant of the wide range of its possible effects on readerly response. The distinction between bonding and estranging unreliability helps to identify that range.

The terms *estranging* and *bonding* refer to the *consequences of the unreliability for the relations between the narrator and the authorial audience.* In estranging unreliability, the discrepancies between the narrator's reports, interpretations, or evaluations and those of the authorial audience leave these two participants in the communicative exchange distant from one another—in a word, estranged. Or to put it another way, in estranging unreliability, the authorial audience recognizes that adopting the narrator's perspective would mean moving far away from the implied author's, and in that sense, the adoption would be a net loss for the author-audience relationship. When Lardner's Whitey says that Jim Kendall was "kind of rough, but a good fella at heart," he is misreading and misregarding. As rhetorical readers substitute a much harsher view of Jim, they also increase their ethical and interpretive distance from Whitey.

In bonding unreliability, the discrepancies between the implied author's and the narrator's reports, interpretations, or evaluations have the paradoxical result of reducing the interpretive, affective, or ethical distance between the narrator and the authorial audience. In other words, although the authorial audience recognizes the narrator's unreliability, that unreliability includes some communication that the implied author—and thus the authorial audience—endorses. When Stevens writes at the end of *The Remains of the Day* that "in bantering lies the key to human warmth" (Ishiguro 245), he is underregarding because he does not see that human warmth depends on much more

3. For a sample of these debates, see especially Cohn, Ansgar Nünning, Vera Nünning, Hansen, Olson, Petterson, Zerweck, and Phelan (*Living to Tell*).

than bantering. Nevertheless, the statement shows that Stevens has learned something in the course of the narrative, has moved closer to Ishiguro's ethical beliefs about the importance of affect in human relationships than during his first unenthusiastic responses to Mr. Faraday's bantering. As Stevens moves in this direction, rhetorical readers move toward him both ethically and affectively.

Again, as the emphasis on consequences suggests, this distinction between estranging and bonding unreliability is based on the rhetorical *effect* of the given unreliability on the authorial audience. The taxonomy of six types of unreliability I mention above (misreporting, misreading, misregarding, underreporting, underreading, underregarding) arises not from an analysis of effects but from an analysis of two main variables of the communicative exchange among implied author, narrator, and authorial audience: (a) the axis of communication along which the unreliability occurs and (b) whether the particular communication indicates that the authorial audience needs to reject the narrator's perspective or supplement it. The distinction between estranging and bonding unreliability cuts across the taxonomy of six types. More simply, any one of the six types can function as estranging unreliability or as bonding unreliability.

Applying Phelan's Shaver (see the preface) yields the results that the most important theoretical interventions so far are (a) the distinction between bonding and estranging unreliability and (b) the claim that the effects of unreliability vary across a wide spectrum. However, since most previous work has been on what I call estranging unreliability, I want to focus now on the diverse ways authors deploy bonding unreliability by identifying six of its subtypes. As I do, I shall consider whether each subtype is more likely to occur along one of the three axes of communication than the other two, and, thus, the kind of distance that each type is likely to reduce. This catalog of subtypes is illustrative rather than exhaustive, and, again, its purpose is to further clarify the concept and to show why it matters. More generally, I hope the catalog adds a significant dimension to our understanding of how authors and audiences interact through the resource of unreliable narration.

SIX SUBTYPES OF BONDING UNRELIABILITY: LOCAL AND GLOBAL EFFECTS

The first subtype takes advantage of the single text with two tellers, two audiences, and two purposes by rendering the narrator's communication *literally unreliable but metaphorically reliable*. It most typically occurs along the axes of facts/events and understanding/perception, and it has the potential to reduce the perceptual, ethical, and affective distance between narrator and authorial audience. Consider this passage from Ken Kesey's *One Flew over the Cuckoo's Nest,* in which Chief Bromden describes Nurse Ratched's ability to control the passing of time in the psychiatric ward.

> The Big Nurse is able to set the wall clock at whatever speed she wants by just turning one of those dials in the steel door; she takes a notion to hurry things up, she turns the speed up, and those hands whip around that disk like spokes in a wheel. . . . [E]verybody is driven like mad to keep up with that passing of fake time; awful scramble of shaves and breakfasts and appointments and lunches and medications and ten minutes of night so you barely get your eyes closed before the dorm light's screaming at you to get up and start the scramble again, go like a sonofabitch this way, going through the full schedule of a day maybe twenty times an hour, till the Big Nurse sees everybody is right up to the breaking point, and she slacks off on the throttle, eases off the pace on that clock-dial, like some kid been fooling with the moving-picture projection machine and got tired watching the film run at ten times its natural speed, got bored with all that silly scampering and insect squeak of talk and turned it back to normal.
>
> She's given to turning up the speed this way on days like, say, when you got somebody to visit you or when the VFW brings down a smoker show from Portland—times like that, times you'd like to hold and have stretch out. That's when she speeds things up.
>
> But generally it's the other way, the slow way. She'll turn that dial to a dead stop and freeze the sun there on the screen so it don't move a scant hair for weeks, so not a leaf on a tree nor a blade of grass in the pasture shimmers. The clock hands hang at two minutes to three and she's liable to let them hang there till we rust. (70–71)

The Chief is clearly misreporting here, as we can infer from many signals, including the internal contradictions of the passage. To take just two of the most egregious, the patients cannot sleep for ten minutes twenty times in the space of an hour, let alone eat three meals twenty times in the space of an hour. Nor can they survive without sleep and food for weeks. As typically happens with misreporting, this case of it is accompanied by another kind of unreliability, misreading. The Chief attributes to Nurse Ratched a power over the impersonal phenomenon of time, a power that she of course does not literally have. Both the misreporting and the misreading contribute to our understanding of the Chief's psychological problems, the reasons why he is himself a patient in this psychiatric hospital: he suffers from paranoia and extremely low self-esteem. These conditions, which stem from his experience of watching the white world turn his once strong father into an ineffectual alcoholic, have led him to pretend to be deaf.

While the implied Kesey guides his audience to these inferences about the Chief's unreliability, he also guides that audience to other inferences that lead us to recognize that the Chief nevertheless captures some underlying truths about life on the ward and about Nurse Ratched's role in that life. First, the Chief's narration effectively conveys the sense that the ward is so set apart from the world outside its walls that it might as well have its own system of time, and how, within that system, the subjective experience of time's pace can vary radically from day to day. Second, the Chief's narration indicates that Nurse Ratched has a remarkable degree of power, and, in combination with his reports of her manipulations of patients in group meetings and in many of her other interactions, this narration leads Kesey's audience to share the Chief's ethical evaluation of her. The Chief's analogy between Nurse Ratched and the bored kid at the projection machine is particularly telling. In the Chief's view, Nurse Ratched's motive for easing off "the pace on that clock-dial" has nothing to do with helping the patients and everything to do with her own control of them. She eases off only when she perceives that they're at the breaking point, and she does so not out of concern for them but in the same spirit as a child who gets bored by the once-exciting spectacle of watching a movie projector running at high speed.

More generally, in the Chief's view, Nurse Ratched's control of time on the ward is part of her larger role in the Combine, the Chief's term for all the societal forces that work to enforce a passive conformity on individuals. The Chief identifies the ward as a factory for the Combine, a place to fix those who are resisting the forces of conformity, and he sees Nurse Ratched as the ever-efficient, ever-dedicated manager of that factory. Again, the implied Kesey invites his audience to recognize that the Chief is literally unreliable (there is no Combine) in his understanding but metaphorically reliable in his reporting and reading (the ward does function to enforce conformity—at the price of masculinity, among other things), and reliable in his evaluation (Nurse Ratched's manipulations are all in the service of undermining the patients' self-confidence and self-esteem). *The overall effect of the Chief's narration is that the authorial audience interprets his paranoia as a condition that gives him privileged access to significant metaphorical truths about the narrative world and a corresponding ability to render accurate ethical evaluations of its inhabitants.* To put this point in other terms, the Chief is unreliable in his reports about time on the ward and in his reading of Nurse Ratched's power, but the metaphorical perceptual truths behind that literal unreliability reinforce the reliability of his evaluations of her. This effect contributes substantially to rhetorical readers' sympathy for the Chief and to their desire that his situation—and that of his fellow patients—will improve.

These effects in turn contribute significantly to the larger affective and ethical effects that arise from and influence the textual dynamics. The Chief tells his narratee about McMurphy's power to disrupt the Nurse's efficient manipulation of the patients and control of the ward, but the Chief also reports that McMurphy comes to realize that, as someone who has been committed to the hospital, continuing to exercise his power means running the risk of never being able to leave. The implied Kesey also makes it clear that the best hope for the patients to improve and be able to function on their own is to have McMurphy continue his disruptions and thereby show them that they are not as powerless as they believe. Thus, the implied Kesey puts his rhetorical readers in the unusual position of desiring the sympathetic protagonist to make choices that are likely to lead to his downfall. Rhetorical readers' bonding with the Chief is crucial to the effectiveness of these dynamics: the more sympathetic the audience feels toward him, the more they desire McMurphy to stay on his destructive course, even as they register the risks he takes. And the more the implied Kesey evokes that desire in his audience, the more he commits to satisfying it.

Similarly, the Chief's actions at the end of the narrative, after McMurphy has thoroughly exposed Nurse Ratched as a fallible, manipulative woman and has been lobotomized for his efforts, are crucial to the effectiveness of the novel's ending. The Chief exercises both his own judgments and his newly recovered physical strength, first, to mercifully end McMurphy's life, and second, to triumphantly break out of the hospital. Just as significantly, the Chief's narration of these events is without paranoia and utterly reliable: "I was only sure of one thing: he wouldn't have left something like that sit there in the day room with his name tacked on it for twenty or thirty years so the Big Nurse could use it as an example of what can happen if you buck the system" (270). The bonding unreliability, in other words, gives way to bonding reliability as Kesey brings his progression to its bittersweet endpoint.

Furthermore, this analysis provides a useful ground upon which rhetorical readers can assess Kesey's communications and the ethical positions they ask the authorial audience to occupy. To what extent is the implied Kesey's choice of Nurse Ratched as the representative—indeed, the embodiment—of the Combine a sign of his own unthinking misogyny? To what extent does such misogyny—or unthinking sexism—influence his representation of gender, including his ideas of masculinity and femininity, throughout the novel?

Furthermore, how can one reconcile Kesey's awareness of how whites mistreated Indians in the American Northwest with his apparent trading in stereotypes in the way he uses the Chief's narration to represent the African American orderlies on the ward? More generally, how do one's answers to these questions influence the overall ethical assessment of the novel? If one finds—as I do—significant deficiencies in the novel's ethical positioning of its authorial audience, how much does that undermine one's overall assessment of the novel? I will not offer a definitive answer to these questions, because I believe that different rhetorical readers can find good reasons for markedly different answers, but I would propose that the discussion should take into account both the positive and negative aspects of Kesey's positioning of the authorial audience through the bonding unreliability.

The second, third, and fourth common subtypes of bonding unreliability are well illustrated by passages in Mark Twain's *Adventures of Huckleberry Finn,* so I will consider them together and then make a few remarks on their global effects.[4] The second subtype is what I call *playful comparison* between implied author and narrator. In this technique, the implied author humorously and good-naturedly uses unreliable narration to call attention to similarities or contrasts between himself as teller and the narrator as teller. Depending on how the implied author develops the relation between himself and the narrator, playful comparison can have either estranging or bonding effects. If, for example, the implied author has the narrator overestimate his abilities as a storyteller, we most likely have estranging unreliability. The first paragraph of Twain's novel provides an excellent example of playful comparison with bonding effects.

> You don't know about me, without you have read a book by the name of "The Adventures of Tom Sawyer," but that ain't no matter. That book was made by Mr. Mark Twain, and he told the truth, mainly. There was things which he stretched, but mainly he told the truth. That is nothing. I never seen anybody but lied, one time or another, without it was Aunt Polly, or the widow, or maybe Mary. Aunt Polly—Tom's Aunt Polly, she is—and Mary, and the Widow Douglas, is all told about in that book—which is mostly a true book, with some stretchers, as I said before. (32)

Huck is a reliable reporter about *The Adventures of Tom Sawyer* here, but the question of reliability gets more interesting when we consider his roles as reader and regarder. On the one hand, Huck is a clear authority on that

---

4. This discussion of Huck's narration has some overlaps with the discussion Peter J. Rabinowitz and I offer in *Narrative Theory* (Herman, et al.).

reporting, and so in the authorial audience we have a strong warrant for taking his interpreting and evaluating as reliable. If anyone knows whether *Tom Sawyer* contains stretchers, Huck is the guy. On the other hand, if I do take Huck as fully reliable, then the implied Twain would be guiding me to find some ethical deficiency, however minor, in his writing of *Tom Sawyer*. The way out of this amusing dilemma is not far to seek: Huck's narration here involves mildly unreliable reading and regarding that arises from the implied Twain's play with the relation between the mimetic and the synthetic components of Huck's character. For the authorial audience, Huck is as synthetic (or, if you prefer, invented) as any of the events in *Tom Sawyer*, and so the distinction between truth and stretchers that he makes within that synthetic fiction (or invention) does not hold. The implied Twain is not inviting his authorial audience to go back to *Tom Sawyer* and search for the stretchers, because they wouldn't be able to find them.

Furthermore, the authorial audience recognizes that Huck can accuse Twain of telling stretchers—and condone such telling—only because Twain licenses him to. To put all this another way, the playful comparison involves Twain's deployment of metalepsis: he allows himself to appear on the same diegetic level as Huck (transforming himself from the author of a fiction to the journalist/biographer/historian who investigated Tom's life and then wrote a book about it), while relying on his audience to recognize (a) that he retains his identity as creator of that diegetic level and (b) that, as creator, he gives Huck license to find fault with his diegetic equal. By giving Huck both this license to accuse him of telling stretchers and the ability to be magnanimous about those failings, the implied Twain makes Huck both mildly unreliable and immensely appealing. The result is a first paragraph that leads the authorial audience to bond strongly, both affectively and ethically, with Huck and with the implied Twain.

The third subtype of bonding unreliability is what, with a nod to Viktor Shklovsky's "Art as Technique," I call *naïve defamiliarization,* and it most often occurs as a kind of unreliable reading. Consider this sentence from the first chapter of *Huck Finn*: "but you had to wait for the widow to tuck down her head and grumble a little over the victuals, though there warn't really anything the matter with them" (33). Huck in his naïveté fails to recognize that what he calls grumbling the Widow Douglas would call saying grace. But the freshness of his perspective allows him to capture the rote, thoughtless quality of the prayer even by someone as sincerely religious as the Widow Douglas. In other words, Huck's naïveté defamiliarizes the act of saying grace and does so in a way that both acknowledges and closes the interpretive and ethical distance between him and the authorial audience.

The fourth subtype is what I call *sincere but misguided self-deprecation*. As the term suggests, this bonding unreliability occurs along the axis of ethics/evaluation, and it depends on the coexistence of two judgments, one about the presence of sincere self-deprecation and the other about why the self-deprecation is misguided. The passages in chapter 31 recounting Huck's decision to go to hell are illuminating examples.

> I knowed very well why [the words of my prayer] wouldn't come. It was because my heart warn't right; it was because I warn't square; it was because I was playing double. I was letting *on* to give up sin, but away inside of me I was holding on to the biggest one of all. I was trying to make my mouth *say* I would do the right thing and the clean thing, and go and write to that nigger's owner and tell where he was; but deep down in me I knowed it was a lie—and He knowed it. You can't pray a lie—I found that out. (200)

Here we have the first steps in Twain's use of sincere but misguided self-deprecation. Huck judges himself to be ethically deficient, while the implied Twain guides his rhetorical readers to judge Huck's inability to act against Jim's interest as a sign that he is acting according to a higher ethical standard.

Huck then writes the letter to Miss Watson, telling her of Jim's location, so that he'll be able to pray for help to stop sinning, and he immediately feels better. But before he prays, he starts thinking about the river trip, and his reliability as reporter, reader, and regarder reinforces the previous bonding unreliability through sincere but misguided self-deprecation:

> And [I] got to thinking over our trip down the river; and I see Jim before me, all the time, in the day, and in the night-time, sometimes moonlight, sometimes storms, and we a floating along, talking, and singing, and laughing. But somehow I couldn't seem to strike no places to harden me against him, but only the other kind . . . and at last I struck the time I saved him by telling the men we had small-pox aboard, and he was so grateful, and said I was the best friend old Jim ever had in the world, and the *only* one he's got now; and then I happened to look around, and see that paper. (200–201)

Thus, when he makes his decision to tear up that paper and evaluates his action most negatively, rhetorical readers feel their strongest sympathy for him and the greatest ethical approval of his actions.

> "All right, then, I'll *go* to hell"—and tore it up.

> It was awful thoughts, and awful words, but they was said. And I let
> them stay said; and never thought no more about reforming. I shoved the
> whole thing out of my head; and said I would take up wickedness again,
> which was in my line, being brung up to it, and the other warn't. (201)

With this climactic self-deprecation, the bonding unreliability, begun in the
first paragraph, reaches its apex. While Huck is sure that he's damned, Twain's
rhetorical readers are even more certain that he is saved. These judgments
depend on inferring both that Huck is absolutely sincere in his view of himself
and that he is misevaluating the ethics of his choice.

Attention to Twain's use of different subtypes of bonding unreliability also
sheds light on the controversy about the ending of *Huckleberry Finn*. Although
Twain continues to employ bonding unreliability through Huck's naïve defa-
miliarizations of Tom Sawyer's elaborate schemes, Twain does not continue
with the pattern of bonding through sincere self-deprecation. Instead, Huck
passively accepts most of Tom's schemes and their casual cruelty toward Jim.
In other words, Twain employs bonding unreliability for Huck as misreader,
but he does not employ it in relation to Huck as an ethical evaluator. Thus,
the unreliability during the Evasion both maintains and closes perceptual distance, but with respect to Huck's treatment of Jim, it does not close any significant ethical distance. Indeed, Huck's failure to evaluate the ethical problems
with Tom's treatment of Jim provides such a sharp contrast to the bonding
effect of the sincere but misguided self-deprecation in chapter 31 that it provides good grounds for the complaints of many readers, rhetorical and otherwise, that the Evasion is a serious flaw in the novel's design. I will return to
this point when I discuss deficient narration in the next chapter.

The fifth subtype of bonding unreliability is what I call *partial progress
toward the norm*. This subtype typically occurs along either the axis of ethics/
evaluation or along that of understanding/perception. Stevens's comment that
"in bantering lies the key to human warmth" is one example of this subtype.
Another is this passage from Hemingway's *A Farewell to Arms*.

> That was what you did. You died. You did not know what it was about. You
> never had time to learn. They threw you in and told you the rules and the
> first time they caught you off base they killed you. Or they killed you gra-
> tuitously like Aymo. Or gave you the syphilis like Rinaldi. But they killed
> you in the end. You could count on that. Stay around and they would kill
> you. (327)

One of the implied Hemingway's positions in this novel is that the world is an inherently destructive place and the best response to the knowledge of that destructiveness is to create something positive to counter it, starting with taking pride in one's dignity. Frederic's narration here shows that he has made considerable progress in his understanding of the world's destructiveness from the days when he was convinced that even the war "seemed no more dangerous to me myself than war in the movies" (37). But the tone of complaint shows that he has not yet moved all the way to the implied Hemingway's view—and understandably so, since he has just learned that his and Catherine's son has died in childbirth. Nevertheless, the dominant effect of the passage is to close the interpretive, ethical, and affective distance between Frederic and the authorial audience, and in that way to mark his genuine progress toward Hemingway's views.

Shortly after this point, Frederic learns that Catherine too has died. His first impulse is to say a romantic good-bye to her, but that effort fails miserably. "It was," he says, "like saying good-bye to a statue" (332). Then somehow he is able to complete the last steps of his movement toward the implied Hemingway's views, and that completion closes the rest of the interpretive, ethical, and affective distance between Frederic and the authorial audience. The understated and controlled quality of his narrative's thoroughly reliable last sentence subtly conveys the closing of the final distance. "After a while I went out and left the hospital and walked back to the hotel in the rain" (332). The sentence appears to be only a report, but rhetorical readers' unfolding responses to Frederic and his experiences—their following Frederic's difficult but gradual movement towards sharing Hemingway's views of the destructive world and how to live in it—leads them to recognize the sentence as conveying much more than the surface description of Frederic's action. The interaction of textual and readerly dynamics here means that the sentence also functions as an ethical statement of Frederic's decision not to be utterly destroyed by Catherine's death but instead to move forward even as he acknowledges his loss.

The sixth subtype is what I call, with a nod to social science research on coping strategies (Pearlin and Schooler), *bonding through optimistic comparison*. It occurs when the narration juxtaposes clearly estranging unreliability to something far less estranging. Just as you and I can better cope with our situations in life, almost no matter how bleak they look, by comparing them with some even less rosy alternative, implied authors can guide audiences to recognize one example of unreliability as "better" than another. Such comparisons within a single narrator's discourse will take us back to "partial progress toward the norm," so I suggest reserving this category for comparisons between narrators within a single narrative. For example, when Faulkner juxtaposes Anse's and Darl's narrations in *As I Lay Dying*, Anse's deficiencies on the axis of ethics make Darl's occasional deficiencies on that axis and on the axis of perception almost endearing. As this example indicates, the flip side of bonding through optimistic comparison is estranging through negative comparison. The juxtaposition between Darl and Anse works not only to enhance our bonding with Darl but also to increase our estrangement from Anse.

ESTRANGING AND BONDING UNRELIABILITY AND THE ETHICS OF *LOLITA*

How, then, can the distinction between estranging and bonding unreliability illuminate the twin phenomena of one set of readers being too easily taken in by Humbert and another set of readers thoroughly resisting him? My hypothesis is that in part 1, Nabokov frequently employs bonding reliability, bonding unreliability, and a "complex coding" of some of Humbert's other narration, a coding in which he gives the narration many marks of bonding unreliability but ultimately marks it as estranging unreliability. For the complex coding to work, its marks of bonding unreliability must be sufficiently persuasive that the authorial audience seriously considers moving closer to Humbert before estranging themselves from him. This combination of bonding reliability, bonding unreliability, and this complicated coding almost guarantees that many actual readers will be taken in by Humbert—and not just because they will miss the marks of the estranging unreliability. Actual readers will also be taken in because once any unreliability is detected, it is easy to conclude that one is wise to the narrator's tricks and therefore will not be taken in by them. Such readers, in effect, stop too soon. They respond to Humbert by saying, "Yes, but," while the implied Nabokov is asking his authorial audience to make one more move, to "You almost got me to say 'Yes, but,' but ultimately I can't say 'yes' at all." Furthermore, the technique of complex coding, with estranging unreliability ultimately privileged, almost guarantees that another set of readers will build up their defenses against all of Humbert's appeals and therefore decide that all his narration, even in part 2, where he appears to be making partial progress toward the authorial norms, is ultimately estranging.

Unlike Chief Bromden, Huck Finn, Stevens, or Frederic Henry, Humbert is a highly self-conscious narrator, though one with limited aesthetic control—as his estranging unreliability indicates. Humbert is very much aware of his agency and purpose as a writer, yet he has a limited ability to achieve the effects and purposes he seeks, since those purposes are ultimately quite different from Nabokov's. One consequence of this difference is that the subtype of bonding through naïve defamiliarization is not available for Nabokov's use. A second consequence is that bonding unreliability through playful comparison is likely to be a very attractive technique. And in fact, Nabokov employs it on the very first page, where Humbert writes, "You can always count on a murderer for a fancy prose style" (9). The playful comparison works to highlight similarities—and an important difference—between Nabokov and Humbert. Both are self-conscious stylists, both intend and enjoy the irony of Humbert's statement, both are making an important disclosure while calling attention to their style. The authorial audience appreciates the playfulness and the skill of both tellers and, in that way, is drawn toward Humbert. But Humbert, unlike Nabokov, is a murderer, and his irony here suggests the authorial audience needs to be wary about his ethical judgments, as his statement plays with the ideas that the murder is less important than the style or that the style is compensation for the murder. To get at more of the effects of the bonding unreliability here, I bring in its larger context.

Humbert's statement is the last sentence of his third paragraph, and it comes after he has been engaging in some remarkable wordsmithing. It is an immediate follow-up to his explanation in the previous sentence that he met Dolores's precursor "about as many years before Lolita was born as my age was that summer" (9). But the comment applies not just to that clever circumlocution but also to the artful first two paragraphs. The first is marked by its lyrical direct address and its carefully crafted parallel structures and alliterations: "Lolita, light of my life, fire of my loins. My sin, my soul." The paragraph is also marked by Humbert's luxurious celebration of the linguistic glory of her name: "Lo-lee-ta: the tip of the tongue taking a trip of three steps down the palate to tap, at three, on the teeth. Lo. Lee. Ta." The second paragraph continues the linguistic play with her name as Humbert runs through its many variations: Lo, Lola, Dolly, Dolores, and back once more to Lolita. "She was Lo, plain Lo, in the morning, standing four feet ten in one sock. She was Lola in slacks. She was Dolly at school. She was Dolores on the dotted line. But in my arms she was always Lolita" (9).

Thus, when Humbert opines that "you can always count on a murderer for a fancy prose style," his jest calls attention not only to the master stylist behind his own fancy telling and, on this measure of style at least, to their similarity; it also calls attention to the link between the style and the keen perceptions about Dolores it conveys. Consequently, one effect of the playful comparison is to align Humbert with the implied Nabokov along the axis of perception. To be sure, as with the "you can always count" statement itself, Nabokov includes in the first few paragraphs some important warning signals against bonding too closely on the ethical axis with Humbert (his narration raises the question of whether his image of Lolita in his arms is the image of a four-foot-ten schoolgirl), but the bonding effects on the axis of perception remain strong. To put these points another way, the implied Nabokov uses the playful comparison so that an element of the novel's aesthetics, Nabokov's stylistic virtuosity, which he allows Humbert to share, disposes rhetorical readers to regard Humbert as a reliable interpreter. This disposition is, of course, subject to change as the narration proceeds, and, especially in light of the warning signals, it does not automatically generate a disposition to regard Humbert as a reliable evaluator. But on the whole, Nabokov's strategy is to encourage rhetorical readers' initial bonding with Humbert.

This bonding is also encouraged by optimistic comparison with the narration of John Ray Jr., whose foreword frames Humbert's narration. The interrelations of reliability and unreliability in Ray's narration are themselves worthy of an extended analysis, but for my purposes, the most relevant feature of his narration is the inconsistency of his style. It varies from a clumsy formality ("the two titles under which the writer of the present note received the strange pages it preambulates"; "this commentator may be excused for repeating" [3, 5]) to a straightforward effectiveness ("he is horrible, he is abject" [5]), to the repetition of platitudes: "'Lolita' should make all of us—parents, social workers, educators—apply ourselves with still greater vigilance and vision to the task of bringing up a better generation in a safer world" (6). The result is a narrator whose perceptions and evaluations Nabokov invites his audience to question, even if he does not give his rhetorical readers enough information to construct clear alternative views. More generally, after serving up three pages of John Ray Jr., Nabokov has made his rhetorical readers more susceptible to the rhetoric of Humbert Humbert, and when Nabokov employs the technique of playful comparison on the first page of Humbert's narration, he encourages his audience to bond with Humbert to a considerable extent.

In much of the rest of the early chapters, however, Nabokov employs his strategy of complex coding. A particularly salient example occurs in chapter 5, as Humbert presents his theory of nymphets.

> Now I wish to introduce the following idea: Between the age limits of nine and fourteen there occur maidens who, to certain bewitched travelers, twice or many times older than they, reveal their true nature which is not human, but nymphic (that is, demoniac); and these chosen creatures I propose to designate as "nymphets."
>
> It will be marked that I substitute time terms for spatial ones. In fact, I would have the reader see "nine" and "fourteen" as the boundaries—the

mirrory beaches and rosy rocks—of an enchanted island haunted by those nymphets of mine and surrounded by a vast, misty sea. Between those age limits, are all girl-children nymphets? Of course not. Otherwise, we who are in the know, we lone voyagers, we nympholepts, would have long gone insane. Neither are good looks any criterion; and vulgarity, or at least what a given community terms so, does not necessarily impair certain mysterious characteristics, the fey grace, the elusive, shifty, soul-shattering, insidious charm that separates the nymphet from such coevals of hers as are incomparably more dependent on the spatial world of the synchronous phenomena than on that intangible island of entranced time where Lolita plays with her likes. (16–17)

Having used the playful comparison to dispose us to accept Humbert's interpretations, the implied Nabokov uses that disposition to his advantage here. The earlier bonding unreliability and Humbert's play with metaphor combine to encourage rhetorical readers to consider whether he is metaphorically reliable. Perhaps Nabokov wants his rhetorical readers to think that the perceptive Humbert is onto something; surely many of us, male and female, have entertained ideas about special subgroups of the opposite sex. Entertaining this possibility also means recognizing that the appeal of Humbert's narration is that it can do more of what it does here, namely, explain the mysteries of this group and the effect its members have on those travelers whom they bewitch. To bond with Humbert here, in other words, would not mean becoming a bewitched traveler but rather seeing the world through such a traveler's eyes.

But Nabokov constructs the narration of Humbert's theory of nymphets so that it is ultimately estranging rather than bonding. In the passage above, the main signal is the utter elusiveness of the qualities, those "certain mysterious characteristics" that make one girl a nymphet and another merely human. Even if "nymphets" are not obvious to the unbewitched, surely this bewitched witness should be able to offer a more precise account of their characteristics than the vague and grandiose designations he offers here. Indeed, the gap between Humbert's lofty rhetoric and the reality of the situation it obscures—his pederasty—exposes Humbert's nymphet defense as ultimately an elaborate rationalization of his lust. Yes, that lust is selective, but Humbert's explanation of that selectivity is ultimately a sham. Nabokov includes even stronger signals of estrangement in the next paragraph.

Furthermore, since the idea of time plays such a magic part in the matter, the student should not be surprised to learn that there must be a gap of several

years, never less than ten I should say, generally thirty or forty, and as many
as ninety in a few known cases, between maiden and man to enable the lat-
ter to come under a nymphet's spell. It is a question of focal adjustment, of a
certain distance that the inner eye thrills to surmount, and a certain contrast
that the mind perceives with a gasp of perverse delight. When I was a child
and she was a child, my little Annabel was no nymphet to me [. . .]. (17)

Here Humbert's theory of nymphets gets thoroughly exposed as a highly
wrought rationalization of his pederasty. By having Humbert emphasize the
difference in age, Nabokov calls attention to the differences in size and power
between "maiden and man." By having Humbert extend the range of the gap
between "maiden and man" to ninety years, Nabokov calls attention to the
implausibility of Humbert's claims. As a result, the idea of the man coming under the spell of the nymphet becomes misreporting, misreading, and
misevaluating, and the overall effect of the passage is to estrange rhetorical
readers from Humbert and from one of the chief planks of his defense in
part 1.

Humbert, of course, continues to try to defend himself in part 1, and
Nabokov allows him intermittent passages of bonding unreliability, though
he also continues the pattern of complex coding. However, as I have argued
in *Living to Tell about It,* from the end of part 1 on, Humbert's own engagement with the task of narrating his experiences with Dolores leads him to see
more clearly the irreparable harm he has done to her. As a result, he eventually
cannot sustain his purpose of exonerating himself, so he stops rationalizing
his behavior and starts taking responsibility for ruining her life. Accompanying these changes is Nabokov's increased use of bonding unreliability through
partial progress toward the authorial norm. The clearest example of this strategy is his statement, "Had I come before myself, I would have given Humbert
at least thirty-five years for rape, and dismissed the rest of the charges" (308).
Humbert, of course, is not accused of rape but rather of the murder of Clare
Quilty. His willingness to dismiss the murder charge shows that he is still an
unreliable evaluator of his own actions. But his willingness to sentence himself
to at least thirty-five years for rape—indeed, his willingness to use the term
rape for the first time—shows how far from the rationalizations about being
bewitched by a nymphet he has traveled. As I try to demonstrate in *Living
to Tell,* Nabokov's ability to plausibly represent Humbert's change from the
beginning of his narration to this end, and to guide his rhetorical readers to
feel moved by his alteration, is a remarkable ethical and aesthetic achievement, even as that achievement has its own dark side.

Nevertheless, if I am right about the complex coding of Humbert's narration in part 1, then the emergence of the two groups of actual audience members I identified earlier—those taken in by Humbert and those who refuse to take even his self-condemnation seriously—is not surprising. Those who get taken in privilege the bonding unreliability over the estranging. Those who refuse to see him as altered in any significant way privilege the estranging unreliability over the bonding. As I perceive Nabokov's communication to his authorial audience, both groups of readers are missing important aspects of Nabokov's complex strategy. In both cases, however, the misreadings have their sources in that strategy itself, in Nabokov's effort to use the resources of estranging and bonding unreliability for his purposes of guiding his readers to a many-layered and evolving set of ethical responses to Humbert.

These conclusions bring us back to the larger questions about the ethics of the telling in *Lolita*. Does it make ethical sense—that is, is it fair—to hold Nabokov accountable for the misreadings of his strategy? By the same token, does it make ethical sense—is it fair—to say he has no ethical accountability other than to say more loudly what all authors can say, "Caveat Lector"? I do not want to answer "yes" to either of these questions, which leads me to think that there is something wrong with the way they are formulated. What's wrong, I think, is that the questions enforce a separation between implied author and actual audience, when the act of rhetorical reading leads to their mutual dependence. In other words, both Nabokov and his readers bear some responsibility for the misreadings, just as both bear some responsibility for the more successful communication. Since Nabokov's experiment with unreliable narration sets up interpretive and ethical traps for readers, Nabokov must bear some responsibility for readers who fall into those traps. But his experiment also challenges readers to recognize those traps and avoid them, and they bear some responsibility if they are not up to the challenge.

More important, however, are the implications of this conclusion for my analysis itself and for my conception of rhetorical poetics. The conclusion implies that if I find these other two groups of readers not fully responsive to Nabokov's communication, I must in turn acknowledge my own readerly fallibility. In practical terms, this acknowledgment means that what I regard as "Nabokov's authorial audience" is itself a hypothesis subject to further testing and revision. This admission does not mean that the authorial audience is only a projection of my readerly interests and desires—*Lolita*, like so many other narratives I have read, contains too much material that does not conform to my interests and desires—but it does mean that authorial audiences and actual audiences can rarely, if ever, be fully and definitively distinguished.

Since rhetorical poetics is interested in the ideal of fully understanding narrative communication as well as the practical details of actual somebodies communicating with actual others, I regard both the analytical separation and the inescapable linkage of authorial and actual audiences as both necessary and beneficial features of approaching narrative as rhetoric.

CHAPTER 6

The How and Why of Backward Narration in Martin Amis's *Time's Arrow*

N THIS CHAPTER, I continue to thicken the rhetorical account of character narration, as I take up Martin Amis's remarkable deployment of "backward narration" (a telling that reverses the direction of time's progression) in his 1991 novel about a Nazi doctor, *Time's Arrow*. By saying that I will thicken my account, I mean that I will not be offering new categories of unreliability so much as extending the work of chapter 5 and my overall approach to character narration in order to unpack the multiple ways Amis deploys the unusual technique. I shall be concerned with the multiple effects that follow from his deployment, including its bonding and estranging consequences, as well as its ethical and aesthetic dimensions.

Because Amis's character narrator experiences and reports time unfolding in reverse chronological order—from death to birth rather than vice versa—the backward narration functions as a global strategy for unreliability. Among other things, reversing time's arrow means undoing the default relations between causes and effects. In general terms, Amis deploys the resource for two purposes: to defamiliarize the atrocities of the Holocaust, a purpose that the approximate forty-five year interval between the events and the occasion of Amis's telling makes more urgent, and to explore the psychology of a perpetrator, a purpose that the interval makes more palatable. But following the principles of rhetorical poetics and looking more closely at Amis's handling of the resource, I identify some other significant aspects of his communication. The most extraordinary feature of Amis's handling of the technique is his construction of what I call "pockets of reliability" within the overall fabric of unreliability. In other words, despite using a technique whose default setting is unreliability, Amis finds a way to build in some passages of reliability that have ripple effects on the ethical, affective, and aesthetic dimensions of the novel's progression. In this and other ways, *Time's Arrow* vividly demonstrates the rhetorical principle that as skillful authors pursue their different purposes, they often shape the resources at their disposal in ways that are simultaneously surprising, ingenious, and effective.

As Susan Suleiman notes in a recent essay, historians and artists working on the Holocaust have recently been giving more attention to the difficult task of comprehending the psychology of the perpetrators. When undertaken by novelists, as Suleiman shows in her insightful analysis of Jonathan Littell's *Les Bienveillantes,* this effort inevitably raises significant ethical and aesthetic issues, ones that are related in some degree to my discussion of probability in fiction and nonfiction in chapter 3. How can the novelist plausibly render the psychology of the perpetrator? How does history constrain the fictional representation of perpetrators, and how does fiction provide some freedom from the constraints of history? What are the ethical and aesthetic consequences of narrative techniques that put the reader in the position of sharing the perpetrator's perspective, even if the novelist marks that perspective as unreliable?

Time's Arrow is an especially intriguing case because Amis foregrounds the psychological state of Odilo Unverdorben (the last name is German for *uncorrupted* or *innocent*) by emphasizing his dissociation of personality and using one side of that personality, a figure I shall, following Seymour Chatman, call Soul, to narrate the action.[1] The dissociation leads to Soul experiencing time backwards, and that in turn radically alters his understanding of events as he gives an account of Unverdorben's life from the moment just before his death to the moments of his earliest consciousness. In my analysis, I offer some general reasons for—and consequences of—Amis's technique, and then, for the bulk of the chapter, undertake a more specific examination of its workings, including a detailed account of how Amis manages the relation between

---

1. Chatman's essay "Backwards" does an excellent job of analyzing the basic mechanism of the backwards narration and discussing its relation to similar techniques. Vice offers another impressive analysis of Amis's technique, one that effectively responds to the charge that Amis is more interested in his narrative technique than in the subject matter of the Holocaust. McGlothlin develops an instructive comparison between *Time's Arrow* and another representation of a perpetrator, Bernhard Schlink's *Der Leser.* Other insightful work on Amis's novel has been done by Diedrick, Harris, Finney, Easterbrook, and Dermot McCarthy, but none of these critics focuses on the ethics and aesthetics of its technique to the extent that I do here.

reliability and unreliability and how he treats Unverdorben's behavior at Auschwitz. My goal is to demonstrate that Amis's technique is not just a clever conceit but part and parcel of an artistic response to the Holocaust that is at once aesthetically innovative and ethically valuable.

THE WHAT AND (SOME OF) THE WHY OF AMIS'S TECHNIQUE

Apart from its detailed workings, Amis's technique of backward narration has two significant and interrelated general effects: (1) It implicitly comments on the skewed—and ethically appalling—logic of National Socialism, the reversal of values that led to the systematic extermination of millions of people. To enter the orbit of National Socialism is to enter a world almost beyond logic, a world aptly described by Primo Levi's concentration camp guard when he said "here there is no why" (*hier ist kein warum*).[2] In order to capture National Socialism's abandonment of reason and ethics, Amis suggests, one needs a radical approach to telling about it. By reversing time's arrow, he reverses a fundamental principle of order. (2) As noted above, this reversal defamiliarizes Amis's audience's perceptions and understandings of every event it describes, from the most mundane (shopping in a grocery store, hailing a taxicab) to the most horrific (the killings at Auschwitz). It requires the audience to correct all the reversals of order and the concomitant misunderstandings of cause and effect, and, in so doing, to see things afresh.

In this respect, Amis's project entails not only rendering the psychology of the perpetrator but also refreshing his audience's perceptions of the Holocaust. To be sure, Amis's technique does yield some diminishing returns—once readers get used to inverting temporal order, the defamiliarization becomes less pronounced. But such a decline also helps to shift the audience's attention from the technique itself to what it is representing. In addition, Amis retains his ability to tap into the defamiliarizing effects of the technique by varying other elements of it—including the situations in which Soul offers a new per-

---

2. The guard's phrase has become a useful shorthand for referring to the inverted logic of the camps, but here is the context in which it occurs:

> Driven by thirst, I eyed a fine icicle outside the window, within hand's reach. I opened the window and broke off the icicle but at once a large, heavy guard prowling outside brutally snatched it away from me. "Warum?" I asked in my poor German. "Hier ist kein warum" (there is no why here), he replied, pushing me inside with a shove.
>
> The explanation is repugnant but simple: in this place everything is forbidden, not for hidden reasons, but because the camp has been created for that purpose. (35)

spective on his own relation to Odilo. Sometimes Soul emphasizes his distance/difference from Odilo, describing what "he" and "I" do, but at others, he acknowledges his union with Odilo, describing what "we" and even sometimes "I" do. I will return to this point when I consider the narration of the events at Auschwitz.

Even as the narration performs these general functions, Amis specifically motivates it through Unverdorben's experience as a doctor in Auschwitz. As Amis explains in the novel's afterword, he had been "considering the idea of telling the story of a man's life backward in time" (167), but it was only after reading Robert Jay Lifton's study *The Nazi Doctors* that he was able to execute the idea. Indeed, Amis notes that "my novel would not and could not have been written without" Lifton's book (167). Lifton argues that the Nazi doctors managed to function in the camps only through a psychological doubling that allowed them to compartmentalize their behavior in such a way that they could both maintain some level of humanity and participate in systematic genocide. One compartment contained their technical skill and task orientation, while another contained the emotional and ethical dimensions of their being. The strong compartmentalization allowed them to function, but it also induced a significant dissociation of personality.

Amis's innovation is to take Lifton's findings and give them another turn of the screw: he gives his protagonist such an extremely dissociated personality that the side of himself tuned in to emotions and ethics experiences time backwards. More specifically, this narrator is aware that he is connected to Unverdorben because he is physically bound to him and because he has access to Unverdorben's feelings and dreams. But he also typically feels separate from Unverdorben because he does not have access to his host's conscious thoughts and does not have any control over his actions. Furthermore, Unverdorben, who is initially called Tod Friendly (friendly death), and then John Young and Hamilton de Souza before we discover his given name, remains wholly unaware of the narrator's presence.

These features of the technique give rise to a progression that moves simultaneously along two different but interrelated tracks: The first involves the instabilities and tensions surrounding Soul's quest to make sense of the life he is suddenly thrown into, a quest that includes his interest in discovering the ethical nature of his host and such things as the closely guarded secret of his host's life. This first track includes the tensions resulting from the global and local unreliability of the backward narration. With respect to readerly dynamics, this track orients Amis's audience in one temporal direction, that of the reverse chronology. The second track of the progression involves the set of instabilities in Unverdorben's life as it follows the usual direction of time's arrow.

With respect to readerly dynamics, following this second track means not only reorienting our temporal direction but also properly configuring the events of Odilo's life as he lives it forward. Thus, what functions for Soul as forward movement in time and an advancing understanding of Unverdorben's developing life simultaneously functions for Amis's audience as backward movement and backstory. Furthermore, as Soul moves in his forward direction, Amis's audience continually seeks to configure the unfolding elements of backstory into a larger coherent narrative of Unverdorben's life. Following the two tracks simultaneously puts a heavy cognitive load on the authorial audience, one that requires extensive and often complex interpretive judgments and, as we shall see, similarly extensive and complex ethical judgments. The audience's aesthetic judgments will depend to a great extent on whether it finds the intense cognitive labor of following the progression to be appropriately rewarded. I am one member of the actual audience who finds ample reward.

Because Soul has access to Unverdorben's feelings, he is not exactly on the outside looking in. Instead, it would be more accurate to say that he is on the inside looking in but doing that looking from the wrong temporal direction. Furthermore, as I noted above, within this basic setup, Amis varies the relationship between Soul and Unverdorben. Sometimes Soul treats Unverdorben as a wholly other being, but at other times as the larger part of himself, and on a few occasions as someone that he has just about fully merged with. In addition, as the discussion so far suggests, Amis constructs a doubled experiencing-I: first, Soul as the experiencer who seeks to make sense of Unverdorben and his actions, and second, Unverdorben as an experiencer containing but also distinct from Soul.

Describing the what and why of the technique also entails analyzing the relation between the mimetic and the synthetic components of the narrative. At first glance, Amis's technique, which is clearly an example of unnatural narration, suggests that Amis wants to plant his stake firmly in the territory of the synthetic. But a closer look reveals that in all other respects, Amis follows the conventions of standard mimesis. The characters in the storyworld, including Odilo, are bound by all the other rules and restrictions on human powers of action, and they all have recognizable human psychologies. In addition, the novel's storyworld has a familiar and documentable history and geography that includes the Nazi death camp at Auschwitz and such historical figures as Josef Mengele and Eduard Wirths.[3] Consequently, Amis's handling of the progression, while it always keeps the synthetic in the foreground, ultimately puts the synthetic at the service of his mimetic and thematic purposes. We can better understand those purposes after a look at the detailed workings of Amis's narration, but I end this section by noting again that the rhetorical perspective cuts across the one offered by unnatural narratology (see chapter 2). It regards the unnatural technique primarily as a means toward ends that in this case are fully compatible with those of natural narratives.

THE HOW AND (MORE OF) THE WHY OF THE TECHNIQUE

Addressing the how of the technique entails (a) identifying the logic under-lying Amis's decision to divide the narration as he does—eight chapters coincide with the eight different temporal points from which Soul offers his retrospective narration[4]—and (b) unpacking the relation between reliable and unreliable narration. It's worth noting that Amis further divides his eight installments of Soul's narration into the three distinct parts of his novel. Part 1, which consists of chapters 1–3, follows Unverdorben's life in the eastern United States after World War II. The first chapter starts at the moment of his death and goes backward approximately six years to recount his time in Wellport, a (fictional) suburb of Boston. The second focuses on his work as a doctor in Wellport and his series of unsatisfying love affairs. The third gives Soul's account of Unverdorben's time in New York, where he is a successful doctor and an active womanizer. Part 2, chapters 4–7, consists of Unverdorben's expe-riences in Europe as an adult. Chapter 4 traces his movements (backward) from the journey by boat across the Atlantic to various stops that bring him to the edge of the experience of Auschwitz. Chapter 5 focuses on Auschwitz. Chapters 6 and 7 focus on the highlights of Unverdorben's pre-Auschwitz life, especially his training as a doctor at Schloss Hartheim, the place where the Nazis first experimented with different modes of mass extermination, and his marriage to a woman named Herta. And part 3 consists only of the short, final chapter 8, which is split between Unverdorben's visit to Auschwitz at age thir-teen and his early experiences at age three.

3. Like Mengele, Wirths was a Nazi doctor at Auschwitz. Lifton, who devotes a chapter to Wirths, succinctly summarizes his role: he "established the camp's system of selections and medicalized killing and supervised the overall process during the two years in which most of the mass murder was accomplished" (384).

4. The retrospection is intermingled with narration from the time of the telling and occa-sionally with simultaneous present-tense narration, such as at the end of section 2, when acting and telling coincide: "I'm on a train now, heading south at evening" (63).

We can understand the logic of Amis's choice to have Soul narrate from discrete temporal moments by considering its effect on the first track of the progression—Soul's efforts to comprehend the situation in which he finds himself, which means trying to comprehend Unverdoben and his actions. As Soul observes Unverdorben early in the narration, he notes that Unverdorben frequently feels shame and fear, that he is unable to have a relationship with a woman that is both durable and satisfying, and that he gets annual letters from "some guy in New York" (16) that report only on the weather. In short, the narration by installment allows Amis to introduce significant tensions about Unverdorben's past and to resolve those tensions very slowly, even as the resolutions of the tensions—as, for example, when we find out that Unverdorben has indeed been a Nazi doctor—increase our understanding of the instabilities along the second track of the progression, the one concerned with Unverdorben's life as lived forward. If Amis were to adopt the alternative approach of having Soul narrate retrospectively from a single point in time, he would need to choose a point near the beginning of Unverdorben's life—perhaps in his adolescence—so that he could give a full account of his experiences from the moment of death back to that temporal point. But then Soul's narration would necessarily be informed by the knowledge he had acquired throughout his adult years, including from his experiences in Auschwitz, and that would effectively eliminate the first track of the progression and its resulting readerly dynamics. Amis's choice of narration by installment allows him to combine Soul's retrospection and his gradual discoveries, which he nevertheless often misinterprets, in an especially compelling way.

By reversing time's arrow, Amis makes unreliability the default condition of the narration, because he asks his audience to recognize that Soul is reporting events in the wrong order and compounding that misreporting with a misreading of the relations between cause and effect. Soul, of course, believes that his reports and readings are on target—his unreliability is unintentional on his part—but Amis gives his audience enough clues to recognize that Soul has things backwards. Rhetorical readers' interpretive judgments are further complicated because, within this dominant fabric of unreliability, Amis inserts what I will call pockets of reliability, and so Amis's audience must frequently negotiate the shifts between the two modes.

A passage from early in the novel indicates how Amis weaves the fabric of unreliability: "A child's breathless wailing calmed by the firm slap of the father's hand, a dead ant revived by the careless press of a passing sole, a wounded finger healed and sealed by the knife's blade: anything like that made me flinch and veer" (26). The passage has an initially—and deliberately—disorienting effect as Soul attributes positive outcomes to small acts of violence.

And although rhetorical readers can readily invert the order of events and reassign cause and effect (the slap causes rather than calms the wailing), Amis also gives those readers pause by concluding the passage with Soul's response to the violence, a response that is more in line with the one rhetorical readers have to their revised understanding of his report. Indeed, the last phrase of the passage illustrates the point that misreporting and misreading may or may not be closely linked with misregarding. In this passage, Soul's flinching at violence is a sign of his reliable regarding.

But now consider Soul's description of Tod Friendly's motivation for going to church on Sunday, where his backward experience of time leads him to simultaneously misreport, misread, and misregard:

> The forgiving look you get from everybody on the way in—Tod seems to need it, the social reassurance. We sit in lines and worship a corpse. But it's clear what Tod's really after. Christ, he's so shameless. He always takes a really big bill from the bowl. (15)

The difference between the two passages is instructive: In the first, Soul is directly reporting his own response, and it is not at all surprising that his narration is reliable on the axis of values. In the second, Soul is judging the experiencing-Unverdorben after having misreported and misread his behavior, and, again, it is not surprising that he misregards Tod as selfish rather than generous. (As the progression develops and reveals more about Tod/Unverdorben's life, the authorial audience reconfigures the generosity as motivated at least in part by guilt, but this reconfiguration does not alter their judgment of Soul's misregarding.)

Not surprisingly, Amis often uses Soul's unreliability for bonding effects on the ethical axis. That is, even when he is misregarding, as in his judgments of Tod's motives for going to church, he employs a set of values that the authorial audience shares. Or to take another example, consider this passage about Soul's experience in New York City:

> This business with the yellow cabs, it surely looks like an unimprovable deal. They're always there when you need one, even in the rain or when the theaters are closing. They pay you up front, no questions asked. They always know where you're going. They're great. No wonder we stand there, for hours on end, waving goodbye, or saluting—saluting this fine service. The streets are full of people with their arms raised, drenched and weary, thanking the yellow cabs. Just the one hitch: they're always taking me places where I don't want to go. (65–66)

Here too Soul misreports and misreads: his inability to recognize the actual order of events in the script for taxi rides leads to his misattributing the relations between cause and effect. His generous praise for the enterprise indicates that he is also misregarding. But all this unreliability makes the passage—and the self who narrates it—endearingly funny. Amis uses Soul's reversal of time as the basis for what his audience understands as essentially naïve narration: the narration captures the events but is clueless about interpreting them. Soul's naïveté defamiliarizes the whole business of using taxicabs in New York, highlighting its difficulties and annoyances ("we stand for hours on end," trying to flag one down) as well as its compensations (the cabs do take their users where they want to go). But most significantly, Soul's enthusiastic misregarding demonstrates a generosity of spirit that is ethically appealing. Consequently, the passage as a whole has a bonding effect, one that increases rhetorical readers' sympathy for him and his quest to have his life make sense.

POCKETS OF RELIABLE NARRATION

Just as important as these passages that are dominated by unreliability are the pockets of reliability. I use the term *pockets* in order to emphasize the point that these instances of reliability are almost always surrounded by the larger fabric of unreliability. Examining these pockets along the three axes of communication will take us deeper into the how of Amis's technique.

(A) The Axis of Ethics. Along this axis, we find numerous such pockets, often occurring when Soul offers ethical judgments that distinguish him from what he understands as the ethically deficient Unverdorben. The following passage from chapter 1 provides the larger context for the one in which Soul comments on his responses to small acts of violence:

> Surprisingly, Tod is known and mocked and otherwise celebrated for his squeamishness. I say surprisingly because I happen to know that Tod *isn't* squeamish. *I'm* squeamish. I'm the squeamish one. Oh, Tod can hack it. His feeling tone—aweless, distant—is quite secure against the daily round in here, the stares of vigil, the smell of altered human flesh. Tod can take all this—whereas I'm harrowed by it. From my point of view, work is an eight-hour panic attack. You can imagine me curled up within, feebly gagging, and trying to avert my eyes. . . . I'm taking on the question of violence, this most difficult question. Intellectually I can just about accept that violence is salutary, that violence is good. But I can find nothing in me that assents to its ugliness. (26; ellipsis original)

The pocket of reliable regarding can be found in Soul's underlying ethical and *aesthetic* judgment that there's something wrong with the pain and corresponding ugliness of violence. Not surprisingly, that reliable regarding creates a bonding effect: Amis, his audience, and the narrating self all share the same values. But Amis complicates this bonding by juxtaposing this reliability with the unreliable report that Tod is not squeamish. If the report were reliable, then Tod would not be celebrated among his coworkers for his squeamishness. The consequence of this unreliability reverberates throughout the whole narrative because it complicates our view of the relations between Soul and Tod/Unverdorben. We realize that the neatness of Soul's frequent dichotomy between those two selves cannot be sustained, since the "other" narrated self actually shares traits and responses that Soul does not acknowledge, either because he cannot recognize them or because doing so would mean that he cannot claim ethical superiority over Tod/Unverdorben. But the larger effect is that we come to see that Unverdorben, the larger being who contains both the narrating self and the narrated self, is neither simply an unfeeling monster nor a sensitive soul who has been corrupted against his will. Instead, we come to see him as someone capable both of having an ethical and aesthetic objection to violence and pain and of being wholly indifferent to them.

The ending of the passage reinforces this point. Soul's view of violence as salutary stems immediately—and forgivably—from the reversal of time's arrow, since from that perspective violent acts seem to heal people. In addition, his view of violence as ugly stems from an apparently inherent sense of the aesthetic. But having now seen that Soul and Tod are not as distinct as Soul believes, rhetorical readers can also see that Tod shares these attitudes. The underlying ethic of the Holocaust, according to Nazi doctrine, was that violence against the Jews was salutary and good, and Amis eventually reveals that Tod/Unverdorben acted in accord with that belief even though he is someone who has an aversion to the ugliness of violence. The larger effect is to humanize Tod/Unverdorben and, in that way, to make his behavior more horrific.

(B) The Axis of Facts and Events. Along this axis, there are two recurring pockets of reliability: (1) While the narrating self consistently misreports *the order* of events, he reliably reports the *events themselves*. Indeed, our ability to recognize his misreporting and misreading and our ability to reconstruct the chronological sequence of events in Unverdorben's life depend on this substrate of reliable reporting. In addition, this reliable reporting allows Amis to establish brief pockets of reliability even within passages of strong misreading and misregarding. (2) Soul reliably reports on his own inner life as well as on the dreams and feelings of Unverdorben. Consider this passage from the end of chapter 3, a point in the story during which Unverdorben, then known as John Young, is working as a doctor in New York:

> Is it a war we are fighting, a war against health, against life and love? My condition is a torn condition. Every day, the dispensing of existence. I see the face of suffering. Its face is fierce and distant and ancient.
>
> There's probably a straightforward explanation for the impossible weariness I feel. A perfectly straightforward explanation. It is a mortal weariness. Maybe I'm tired of being human, if human is what I am. I'm tired of being human. (93)

The immediate impetus for Soul's initial question is his misreading of a doctor's work: with time's arrow reversed, he sees that medical treatment almost always makes people worse—patients who are initially healthy become sick or injured. But his report of his incredible weariness is totally reliable, and that, in turn, leads us to take seriously his hypothesis that he is tired of being human. Since that hypothesis goes beyond the specific condition of being a doctor, our taking it seriously also means generalizing that condition.

Here Amis's use of the first-person plural pronoun before switching to the singular becomes especially significant. The pronoun usage, combined with the absence of any "I-he" comparison such as we have seen in the passage about squeamishness, signals that Soul's weariness is shared by Unverdorben, even if Soul does not understand why. And when we ask why Unverdorben should feel this weariness, we can infer that the answer is to be found in something beyond these experiences in New York, that is, experiences from Unverdorben's yet-to-be-narrated past. He has likely seen the face of worse suffering and perhaps been more responsible for it. That Soul can now register the suffering of others in Unverdorben's apparent campaign against life and love also suggests that at some level, Unverdorben registered such suffering in the past. But Amis's rhetorical readers also infer that his registering the suffering had no consequences for his behavior. The interaction between reliable and unreliable narration here aids Amis in his larger nuanced treatment of the ethical being of the perpetrator: he portrays Unverdorben as a fellow human, highlights the cost of his actions in his dissociation of self, and simultaneously suggests that his weariness now pales beside the actual destruction that he participated in.

(C) **The Axis of Perception and Knowledge.** The reversal of time's arrow means that Soul's unreliability is greatest on this axis, but even here there are two recurring pockets of reliability. The first involves Soul's ability to analyze reliably once he steps back from his assumptions about the direction of time's arrow. Consider this passage from the end of chapter 2. Unverdorben is riding on a train away from one city and toward another, and Soul in his usual fashion gets the direction wrong. But within that framework of misreading, Amis creates a remarkable pocket of reliable reading and regarding:

> It must be New York. That's where we're going: to New York and its stormy weather.
>
> He is traveling toward his secret. Parasite or passenger, I am traveling with him. It will be bad. It will be bad, and not intelligible. But I will know one thing about it (and at least the certainty brings comfort): I *will* know *how* bad the secret is. I will know the nature of the offense. Already I know this. I know that it is to do with trash and shit, and that it is wrong in time. (63)

Because, as we learn on the very next page, his inference about New York is correct, the passage initially establishes his reliability as a reader of the situation. This reliability leads us in turn to take the other interpretations and evaluations, that the secret has to do with trash and shit and that it is wrong in time, as equally reliable. But this reliability exists alongside the standard misreporting of the distinct separation between the two narrated selves, between the experiencing-Soul and the experiencing-Unverdorben, a separation that seems even less warranted here where the narration has shifted to the present tense. Once we focus on that unreliability, we realize that Unverdorben is aware of how bad the secret is—and that in *traveling away from* New York, he is vainly trying to escape it. Indeed, once we reset time's arrow this way, we can see that the passage is revealing that Unverdorben lives with the consciousness of what Primo Levi referred to as "the nature of the offense" (qtd. by Amis 168). This passage has even more weight because Amis uses that phrase as the alternate title for the book (the title page reads *Time's Arrow or The Nature of the Offense*).

The realization that Unverdorben lives with this consciousness in turn sheds a retrospective light on the second track of the progression to this point, that is, the part of Unverdorben's life that has already been narrated—his postwar life in America. The passage helps reveal that he does not deal with his awareness of the nature of the offense very well at all. Although the outer trappings of his life are fine, his inner life is ruled by fear and shame and by various unsuccessful efforts to forget, deny, or overcome these emotions, including his endless pursuit of sexual conquest that only ends up demonstrating his inability to sustain a serious relationship with a woman.

Once again, then, the overall effect of the passage is to lead Amis's audience to a series of complex ethical judgments that initially have both bonding and estranging effects. On the one hand, rhetorical readers can endorse not only Soul's reliable reading but also his willingness to face the secret and learn how bad it is. But on the other hand, the audience infers both that Unverdorben is himself an active agent in what is terrible about the secret (indeed, his agency is connected to its being terrible) and that he has not managed to deal with his behavior in an ethically productive way. The best he can do, it seems, is to dissociate.

The second pocket of reliable narration along the axis of perception and interpretation involves Amis giving Soul the occasional recognition that his temporal orientation is backward. For example, during a passage when Soul is employing the first-person singular as he describes his doctoring in America, he suddenly remarks:

> But wait a minute. The baby *is* crawling, only one or two panting inches at a time—but crawling *forward.* And the mother with the magazine, the glossy pages ticking past her face: she's reading, or skimming, *forward.* Hey! Christ, how long has it been since I . . . ? Anyhow, it's soon over, this lucid interval. (82; ellipsis original)

This intermittent recognition functions as a strong reminder that the split between the two narrated selves requires a huge effort to maintain and is therefore subject to breaking down at just about any point. That Unverdorben is nevertheless able to maintain the split self points, first, to the depth of his guilt and shame, and, second and more powerfully, to the horrible actions that are the source of those feelings.

THE NARRATION OF UNVERDORBEN'S EXPERIENCE AT AUSCHWITZ

Amis's use of Soul's consistent misreading of the relation of cause and effect for bonding effects complicates his task in chapter 5, the central chapter of the novel, because it deals with Unverdorben's experience at Auschwitz. Because Soul experiences time backwards, he must misinterpret Unverdorben's diligent participation in the extermination of the Jews as his heroic efforts toward what Soul calls the "preternatural purpose" (116) of creating a race. Indeed, because of these views, Soul feels that in Auschwitz, life suddenly makes more sense than it has before.[5] If Amis were to narrate the chapter using primarily unreliable narration with bonding effects, he would run the risk of undermining his own ethical authority and, in so doing, seriously mar the quality of the novel. But he varies the narration in significant ways: sometimes he uses the unreliability for estranging effects, and sometimes he employs pockets of reliability to convey his own strongly negative ethical judgments. A closer look at both variations shows how his handling of Soul's narration both defamiliarizes standard perceptions of the Holocaust and effectively uses aesthetics in the service of ethics. Consider how Soul's naïveté works in this passage:

> To prevent needless suffering, the dental work was usually completed while the patients were not yet alive. *The Kapos would go at it, crudely but effectively, with knives or chisels or any tool that came to hand.* Most of the gold we used, of course, came direct from the Reichsbank. But every German present, even the humblest, gave willingly of his own store—I more than any other officer save "Uncle Pepi" himself. I knew my gold had a sacred efficacy. All those years I amassed it, and polished it with my mind: for the Jews' teeth. (121; my emphasis)

Once again we have misreporting, misreading, and misregarding for defamiliarizing effects. As Soul praises the generosity of the German executioners, Amis underlines their greed and their brutality, especially Unverdorben's. Soul's host has distinguished himself among the group by hoarding more of the victims' gold fillings than anyone else. Furthermore, Amis uses the first-person singular here, thus eliminating much of the distance between the narrating-Soul and both narrated selves (experiencing-Soul and experiencing-Unverdorben). Consequently, Amis matches Soul's enthusiasm for this work with Unverdorben's even as he underlines the sharp ethical contrast between their respective reasons for their enthusiasm. In addition, the first person again underlines the point that Soul and Unverdorben are ultimately part of the same person. The larger result is to estrange rhetorical readers from Unverdorben by deepening the horror of his actions and underlining the depth of his dissociation of personality. This estranging effect is frequently repeated throughout chapter 5, as Amis continues to conflate Soul and Unverdorben by means of the first-person singular pronoun.

Amis also uses pockets of reliable reporting to influence our ethical judgments of Unverdorben and of Auschwitz. Consider the second sentence in the passage about the extraction of gold fillings from the victims' teeth: "The

---

5. See Vice for an excellent discussion of Amis's reappropriation of parts of Lifton's study in his representation of Auschwitz.

Kapos would go at it, crudely but effectively, with knives or chisel or any tool that came to hand." Divorced from Soul's understanding of sequence (he mistakenly understands that the knives and chisels are tools for filling cavities), the sentence offers a very reliable report of the perpetrators' behavior, and it functions to enhance the estranging effects of the surrounding unreliability.

Within chapter 5, Amis also uses the pockets of reliability to make a remarkable link between ethics and aesthetics, one that extends the link in the earlier passage about squeamishness. Consider these two passages, which occur within just a few pages of each other in the beginning of chapter 5:

> Ordure, ordure everywhere. Even on my return through the ward, past ulcer and edema, past sleepwalker and sleeptalker, I could feel the hungry suck of it on the soles of my black boots. Outside: everywhere. This stuff, this human stuff, at normal times (and in civilized locales) tastefully confined to the tubes and runnels, subterranean, unseen—this stuff had burst its banks, surging outward and upward onto the floor, the walls, the very ceiling of life. Naturally, I didn't immediately see the logic and justice of it. (117)

> What tells me that this is right? What tells me that all the rest was wrong? Certainly not my aesthetic sense. I would never claim that Auschwitz-Birkenau-Monowitz was good to look at. Or to listen to, or to smell, or to taste, or to touch. There was, among my colleagues there, a general though desultory quest for greater elegance. I can understand that word, and all its yearning: *elegant.* Not for its elegance did I come to love the evening sky above the Vistula, hellish red with the gathering souls. Creation is easy. Also ugly. (119–20)

In the first passage, Amis gives us reliable reporting and juxtaposes it with underreading and underregarding. Auschwitz in its last days—albeit the first days from Soul's perspective—has become overtaken with human excrement, a development that Amis's audience interprets as having a logic and justice entirely different from anything that Soul is able to assign. Indeed, Amis's rhetorical readers interpret the aesthetic horror and ugliness of the camp as a sign of its ethical horror and ugliness, something that Soul is wholly unable to grasp and that Unverdorben is, at this point in his forward experience of time, still able to deny.

In the second passage, the effects depend on Amis's juxtaposition of reliable reading with misreading and misregarding. Soul reliably represents the aesthetic ugliness of Auschwitz, its assault on all five senses, and the hellish quality of the sky above the crematorium, but his misplaced love of that sky underlines for us the horror of the destruction that Unverdorben, in his dissociated state, cannot face. Indeed, Soul's description of the sky underlines not only that dissociation but also Amis's close juxtaposition of reliability and unreliability for defamiliarizing effects. Amis's rhetorical readers readily endorse Soul's reading of the sky as "hellish red" but then suddenly must reject his phrase "with gathering souls" and replace it with its opposite: "with bodies literally going up in smoke."

TWO FINAL POCKETS OF RELIABILITY

Some significant additional effects of the authorial audience's ethical judgments in chapter 5 result from their influence on the readerly dynamics of two final pockets of reliability, one at the very end of chapter 7 and the other in the very last lines of the novel. The first pocket provides a partial resolution to one of the global tensions of the first track of the progression: Soul's question about Unverdorben's ethical being. After reflecting on whether Unverdorben could use violence (which, from Soul's perspective, "mends and heals") in his developing relationship with Herta, Soul says,

> I've come to the conclusion that Odilo Unverdorben, as a moral being, is absolutely unexceptional, liable to do what everybody else does, good or bad, with no limit, once under the cover of numbers. He could never be an exception; he is dependent on the health of his society, needing the sandy smiles of Rolf and Rudolph, of Rüdiger, of Reinhard. (157)

Amis has ensured the reliability of Soul's conclusion not only by making it a culminating point of the progression but also by giving his audience evidence of how well Unverdorben has fit in at Auschwitz. This reliable conclusion in turn functions as Amis's thematic generalization about the perpetrator. Amis has clearly been influenced by Lifton's contention that the Nazi doctors were neither beasts nor demons but human beings who were "neither brilliant nor stupid, neither inherently evil nor particularly ethically sensitive" (4) and who had to engage in some kind of doubling to participate as they did in the genocide. But by using the resources of fictional narrative, and especially those of reliable and unreliable narration, Amis's exploration gives his audience a perspective on the perpetrator that substantially complements Lifton's. Amis defamiliarizes the horror of Auschwitz, enables his rhetorical readers to view it, albeit indirectly (via Soul rather than Odilo), from the perpetrator's perspective, and ably guides his audience's judgments so that they recognize the links among Unverdorben's conformity, his dissociation, and his participation in the genocide. In this way, Amis also paves the way for his actual readers to move from immersion in his fictional world back to our own with a deeper understanding of how the Holocaust could have happened, and how, in particular, some doctors could participate in its genocide. The deeper understanding also works as a reminder that such an event could happen again.

With the final pocket of reliability in the last lines of Soul's narration, Amis gives the narrative one final, powerful turn of the screw. He has shifted to the present tense in order to capture the process of Odilo's becoming ever younger.

> Look! Beyond, before the slope of pine, the lady archers are gathering with their targets and bows. Above, a failing-vision kind of light, with the sky fighting down its nausea. Its many nuances of nausea. When Odilo closes his eyes, I see an arrow fly—but wrongly. Point first. Oh no, but then . . . We're away once more, over the field. Odilo Unverdorben and his eager heart. And I within, who came at the wrong time—either too soon, or after it was all too late. (165; ellipsis original)

Soul reliably reports that the archers shoot their arrows, but he has a moment of unreliable reading, when he interprets their first direction as the wrong one. He soon recovers, though, and reliably notes that time's arrow has now reversed direction, propelling him not toward the oblivion of nonexistence but toward experiencing everything he has just told us about in the opposite order.[6] Unverdorben is not made whole by the reversal of time's arrow, and that fact renders the ending both poignant and horrific. It is poignant because, as Soul says, he will remain within Unverdorben, unable to do anything but observe and report, as he has done throughout this narrative. He is too soon or too late, depending on where one stands in time, but in either case, he is powerless. This new reversal of time's arrow is horrific, because Soul will no longer be able to systematically misread the relation between cause and effect in the events of Unverdorben's life—and because Unverdorben will repeat his participation in the atrocity of the Holocaust. Furthermore, by reversing time's arrow once more at the end of the narrative and implying an eventual return to Auschwitz, Amis suggests something about the continuing effects of the Holocaust as history marches on, about its living on in

---

6. I am indebted to Brian Finney for calling my attention to Amis's move here. Finney describes its effect this way: "the narrative condemns [its readers] to share with the narrator an endless oscillation between past and present, incorporating the past into our sense of modernity" (111).

historical memory, and its lingering effects on all of us who are still trying to come to terms with it.

Looking back on the whole narrative, we can see that Amis, inspired by Lifton's book on Nazi doctors, has found an effective way to confront the ethical and aesthetic challenges of representing the perpetrator. To be sure, his approach is oblique—through Soul, not Odilo himself—and that approach involves significant trade-offs. Amis's rhetorical readers can bond with Soul in a way that they could not with Odilo, but that very bonding reinforces a certain distance from Odilo. That distance, in turn, heightens those readers' negative ethical judgments of Odilo, but it also means that Amis will only partially get inside the psychology of the perpetrator. Consequently, as I hope this analysis has shown, Amis is able to use what may appear as a gimmick—the backwards narration—as a key building block in what becomes for his rhetorical readers a rich ethical and aesthetic experience, even as they remain aware that this experience is ultimately just one partial glimpse into the complexity of the perpetrators and the horror of the Holocaust itself.

CHAPTER 7

"I affirm nothing"

LORD JIM AND THE USES OF TEXTUAL RECALCITRANCE

JIM'S CHARACTER AND EXPERIENCE AS AN INSTANCE OF THE STUBBORN

I N THIS CHAPTER, I return to the phenomenon of textual stubbornness, but this time with a focus less on event and more on character and character narration. Joseph Conrad's participant-observer narrator Marlow wants desperately to gain interpretive mastery over the eponymous protagonist of *Lord Jim,* but, despite both his desire and his considerable efforts, he is unable to achieve that mastery. Furthermore, although Conrad does often communicate to his audience more than Marlow communicates to his narratee, that additional communication does not include information that allows the audience to understand Jim's character as well as it understands Marlow's. Conrad, in other words, has his participant-observer narrator set out on a quest to understand and come to terms with the nature and experiences of his protagonist, but he does not allow that narrator to succeed in the quest or his audience to succeed where the narrator fails. Consequently, Conrad's protagonist remains a stubborn character for Marlow and for the authorial and actual audiences. Since the audience in effect joins Marlow in the quest to plumb the depths of Jim's character, Jim's stubbornness becomes closely tied to the readerly dynamics of the whole progression. Furthermore, that stubbornness becomes crucial to the ethics of both Marlow's telling and Conrad's telling. More generally, then, in this chapter I will take up the interrelations of stubbornness, reliable and unreliable narration, and the ethical dimensions of Conrad's novel. But I begin with the interpretive challenges it presents.

Lord Jim is justly famous for both its artistic achievement and its difficulty. These two qualities of the novel have attracted many astute commentators who have offered significant insights into many of its techniques and strategies (e.g., Watt and Lothe). The novel's difficulty has also meant that critical consensus about some central issues of the novel has never been achieved. Two very astute commentators in the 1980s nicely represent the spectrum along which most critical opinion falls. At one end of the spectrum, J. Hillis Miller argues that the novel is ultimately indeterminate:

> The indeterminacy lies in the multiplicity of possible incompatible explanations given by the novel and in the lack of evidence justifying a choice of one over the others. The reader cannot logically have them all, and yet nothing he is given determines a choice among them. The possibilities, moreover, are not just given side by side as entirely separate hypotheses. They are related to one another in a system of mutual implication and mutual contradiction. Each calls up the others, but it does not make sense to have more than one of them. (40)

At the other end of the spectrum, Ralph Rader sees the novel as determinate but built on a principle of "unambiguous ambiguity," by which he means that Conrad incorporates what Marlow calls "the doubt of the sovereign power enthroned in a fixed standard of conduct" (*Lord Jim* 307) into the representation of Jim's movement toward his eventual fate. In Rader's view, the novel traces Jim's development within the frame of both the fixed standard and the inescapable doubt. Rader argues that Conrad endorses Jim's final decision to take the death of Dain Waris on his own head (in that decision, Jim is living up to the fixed standard) but stops short of making that decision heroic because the doubt about the rightness of that standard persists.

In this chapter, I want to say "Yes, but" to both Miller's and Rader's accounts of the novel, and in so doing, to advance the conversation about the relation between the novel's artistic achievement and its difficulty. Indeed, I want to link those two elements even more tightly than Miller's and Rader's analyses do. If we were to accept fully Miller's view of the ultimate indeterminacy of the novel, we would have to give up—or significantly revise—most of our claims for the novel's artistic achievement. Within Miller's deconstructive view, the novel's achievement is not finally in its representation of Jim's struggles and Marlow's efforts to comprehend them, but rather in the way literary language inevitably immerses its readers into the deconstructive element. On the other hand, if we were to accept fully Rader's view of the ultimate determinacy of the novel, we would be shortchanging the novel's difficulty, its way of using Marlow's narration to underline the way Jim's life resists definitive interpretation. In my view, Conrad's artistic achievement is interwoven with this resistance, because he succeeds in making that resistance serve a larger narrative purpose. Furthermore, that purpose is best described not simply in thematic terms, such as some statement about the fixed standard of conduct, but even more importantly with reference to the affective and ethical consequences of Marlow's—and ultimately Conrad's own—telling about it.

Conrad's use of the stubborn is different from Kafka's because the recalcitrance is not restricted to a pair of events at the end of the narrative, however crucial. Instead, Conrad makes Marlow's unsuccessful effort to master the recalcitrance of Jim's behavior a prominent part of the whole narrative, which, as I noted above, serves as a stand-in for his audience's similar unsuccessful quest.[1] In other words, *Lord Jim* wears its stubbornness on its very long sleeve. But at the same time, *Lord Jim* is more than just Marlow's telling about his unsuccessful effort to master the significance of Jim's experience; it is Conrad's telling about Marlow's telling, which is itself contained within the telling of a noncharacter narrator, a telling that is not stubborn. This nesting of narratives means, among other things, that Conrad's audience views Jim from a broader set of perspectives than Marlow does. I turn now to examine how Conrad maintains Jim's stubbornness within that broader perspective—and how that stubbornness is crucial to the power of his novel.

MARLOW'S NARRATION AS RHETORICAL ACTION

The most striking general feature of *Lord Jim* is the double quality of its progression. It combines, on the textual level, two main sequences of instability-complication-resolution: the first involving Jim as character and the second

---

1. One of Jim's traits of character is, of course, stubbornness, and Conrad not only shows that trait in action but also has Marlow refer to Jim as "stubborn" eight times. In this way, Conrad's representation of Jim's trait is very clear and thus, from the perspective of readerly understanding, qualitatively different from the textual stubbornness surrounding the meaning and significance of Jim's life. In addition, I believe it is good interpretive practice to be cautious, if not entirely suspicious, about hanging major interpretive conclusions on connections that are made primarily on the basis of terminology. (If I'd called the textual recalcitrance I find in *Beloved, The French Lieutenant's Woman,* "Das Urteil," and *Lord Jim* "the intractable" rather than "the stubborn," I might not be writing this note.) With these caveats in mind, I still want to suggest that Conrad invites us to reflect on the similarities and differences between Jim's stubbornness of character and the stubborn recalcitrance of the whole novel.

involving Marlow as narrator who seeks to come to terms with Jim's story. The textual dynamics of Jim's story, though marked by multiple anachronies, follow the standard pattern of instability-complication-resolution: he has dreams of heroism inspired by light holiday literature; he fails to live up to those dreams in his jump from the *Patna,* and suffers as a consequence; he is given another chance in Patusan, where he succeeds for a time, until Brown arrives and reminds him of his past failure; as a result, he misjudges Brown badly, which leads to the death of many Bugis natives, including Dain Waris; and for that misjudgment, Jim pays with his life.

Turning to the progression of Marlow's quest to comprehend Jim, I note first that one of the effects of Conrad's breaking Marlow's narration in two is to emphasize Marlow's ongoing effort. Having told the incomplete story "many times" (24), Marlow feels compelled to tell the most interested listener the rest of the story, and that means, as he says, that he has had to build a complete picture from fragmentary information. Although this act of construction raises the possibility that Marlow can move from the uncertainty he openly acknowledges at the end of the oral narration to some determinate interpretation and evaluation of Jim's life, that possibility is never realized. Instead, for Marlow Jim "passes away under a cloud" (303). (In *The Great Gatsby,* F. Scott Fitzgerald works with the same kind of double progression, but he allows—indeed, needs—Nick Carraway to succeed with his quest to come to terms with Gatsby.)

The readerly dynamics associated with the progression of Jim's story are difficult to specify at this point, because they are so deeply influenced by the textual dynamics of Marlow's progression. For now, what Albert Guérard said long ago will suffice: Marlow's narration generates a dynamic interaction between sympathy and judgment in audience responses to Jim. In addition, in responding to the textual dynamics, Conrad's rhetorical readers cannot help but recognize the pattern of repetitions—both in the oft-noted two-part structure of the novel (divided between the *Patna* incident and the Patusan events) and in Marlow's repeated efforts to comprehend Jim. As the narrative progresses, however, the repetitions add to rather than remove the recalcitrance of Jim's experience to the audience's full understanding, and in that way, add to the novel's ultimate stubbornness.

This outline of the progression allows me to reformulate one of my earlier points: since Conrad constructs Marlow as a figure who undertakes within the world of the novel the same activity that Conrad's audience undertakes outside that world, rhetorical readers must perform a double decoding. They must puzzle through Marlow's puzzling over Jim in order to reach their own decisions about the meaning and significance of Jim's story. For this reason, in what follows, I will focus much more on Marlow than on Jim, considering both Marlow's narration as a rhetorical action and his specific execution of that action (both of which are contained within Conrad's rhetorical action).

The noncharacter narrator of the early chapters introduces Marlow's narration with two salient comments: (1) "And later on, many times, in distant parts of the world, Marlow showed himself willing to remember Jim, to remember him at length, in detail and audibly" (24). (2) "And with the very first word uttered Marlow's body, extended at rest in the seat, would become very still, as though his spirit had winged its way back into the lapse of time and were speaking through his lips from the past" (25). Taken together, these two comments reveal not only Marlow's great interest in Jim's story (why else tell it many times in detail all around the world?) but also his effort to enter once again into the time of the action—his effort, in other words, to reimagine and even reexperience the events of Jim's life. But the larger consequences of these comments become clear only at the end of the oral narrative, when Conrad has Marlow comment on what he makes of Jim and then has the noncharacter narrator return to describe the immediate aftermath of Marlow's telling. Let us take a closer look.

It is worth noting that the noncharacter narrator's telling does not involve any stubbornness. His narration, though holding back information about "the fact" that keeps the adult Jim "a seaman in exile from the sea" (4), offers an otherwise clear view of Jim's character as flawed and limited, overly affected by his reading of light holiday literature, not able to handle the harsher demands of the sea. Strikingly, however, this narrator's view does not make Conrad's audience infer that Marlow's uncertainties about Jim are a result of special pleading. Instead, because Conrad makes Marlow so earnest and scrupulous in his effort to come to terms with Jim and because Marlow narrates events that are much more complicated than those narrated by the noncharacter narrator, Marlow's view of Jim ultimately has more weight for Conrad's audience.

Here is Marlow at the end of his oral tale describing and reflecting on his last look at Jim:

> He was white from head to foot, and remained persistently visible with the stronghold of the night at his back, the sea at his feet, the opportunity by his side—still veiled. What do you say? Was it still veiled? I don't know. For me that white figure in the stillness of coast and sea seemed to stand at the heart of a vast enigma. [. . .] And, suddenly, I lost him. . . . (244)

In light of the noncharacter narrator's descriptions of Marlow as he begins the oral narrative, the two most prominent sentences here are the two in the present tense. "What do you say?" and "I don't know." Despite Marlow's deep interest in Jim and despite Marlow's many efforts to reimagine and reexperience the events of Jim's story, he is not yet able to come to terms with Jim's life. The reference to the "still veiled" opportunity by Jim's side not only identifies Jewel but also recalls Marlow's earlier report that, as Jim first entered Patusan, "his opportunity sat veiled by his side like an Eastern bride waiting to be uncovered by the hand of the master" (177). His uncertainty about whether the opportunity is still veiled and his direct address to his audience constitute a confession that he is unable to render a clear interpretation of the meaning of Jim's success in Patusan. Moreover, accompanying Marlow's interpretive hesitation is his inability to render a clear ethical judgment about Jim. If Jim's jump from the *Patna,* whatever the mitigating circumstances, is an ethical failure that calls into question the whole ideal of conduct upon which Marlow's life has been based, does Jim's current success constitute an appropriate atonement, however partial, for that failure? Is it enough to restore Marlow's firm belief in the ideal and that those like him are fit to live up to it? At this stage, the best Marlow can answer is "I don't know."

Furthermore, Conrad has not given his rhetorical readers sufficient grounds to answer the questions any better than Marlow can. Although Conrad does not make Marlow a wholly reliable narrator—I shall shortly examine some instances of his unreliability—he does not do anything to undermine Marlow's conclusion that Jim existed at the heart of an enigma. As Conrad has Marlow end his oral narration, he also solidifies the stubbornness surrounding Jim.

At the same time, however, Conrad uses Marlow's direct address to his narratees as a way to highlight rhetorical readers' active engagement in trying to interpret and evaluate Jim's success in Patusan. When Marlow asks his assembled audience, "What do you think?," Conrad's audience can't help but feel that he is simultaneously directing the question at them. In addition, with the commentary of the noncharacter narrator about Marlow's narratees at the beginning of chapter 36, Conrad extends an invitation to his audience that Marlow is unaware of:

> With these words Marlow had ended his narrative, and his audience had broken up forthwith, under his abstract, pensive gaze. Men drifted off the verandah in pairs or alone without loss of time, without offering a remark, as if the last image of that incomplete story, its incompleteness itself, and the very tone of the speaker, had made discussion vain and comment impossible. Each of them seemed to carry away his own impression, to carry it away with him like a secret [. . .]. (245)

Since Marlow's narratees are barely characterized, they function as figures for Conrad's readers. Consequently, the report that each narratee has his own secret impression not only implies that many are able to decide upon interpretations and evaluations of Jim's story but also authorizes Conrad's individual readers to reach their own decisions.

That this invitation is just an extension of Marlow's "What do you think?" also reveals an important element of the ethics of the telling by both Marlow and Conrad. Marlow, despite his own conclusion that Jim stands at the heart of an enigma, remains open to the idea that his listeners can and should have other thoughts. Conrad goes further and invites his audience to have those other thoughts—though it is just as important that he does not yet articulate specific alternatives. At the same time, because the narrative is, as the noncharacter narrator says, "incomplete," any answers Conrad's readers might give at this stage will be provisional. Nevertheless, as Conrad breaks Marlow's narration in two here, he simultaneously calls attention to the stubborn quality of his representation of Jim and to his invitation to his audience to get beyond that stubbornness by rendering their own interpretations and ethical judgments of him. Before I consider how Marlow's written narrative builds on these effects, I want to offer a more detailed analysis of where the progression stands at the end of Marlow's oral narration.

By breaking Marlow's narration in two at the point of Marlow's last meeting with Jim, Conrad marks a distinct intermediate stage in both tracks of his progression, as we can see by examining the interactions in chapters 34 and 35 among Conrad, Marlow, and Conrad's audience. The key element of that interaction is the combination of authority, unreliability, and limitation that Conrad gives to Marlow. When Conrad has Marlow report that his enigmatic friend has become Lord Jim and brought peace and stability to both Patusan and his own life, Conrad's rhetorical readers take the report and interpretation as fully reliable and recognize that the complications of Jim's progression have now reached a point of temporary stasis. At the same time, Conrad invites his readers to recognize more clearly and fully than Marlow does that Jim's progression is "incomplete." Conrad's rhetorical readers cannot yet see Jim as having mastered his fate because Jim himself will only go as far as saying that he was "satisfied . . . nearly" (236) and because Jim has not yet had to confront the past whose return had always previously made him flee. Thus, when Marlow interprets Jim's situation in Patusan as evidence that he has mastered his fate, Conrad invites his rhetorical readers to regard the interpretation as unreliable because it is too hasty, more motivated by Marlow's desire than by the larger narrative logic. Indeed, Marlow's own concluding comments show that he himself moves away from this interpretation.

Similarly, when Marlow remarks that because Jim regards himself as "satisfied . . . nearly," "it did not matter who suspected him, who trusted him, who loved him, who hated him—especially as it was Cornelius who hated him" (236), Conrad's audience cannot trust Marlow's interpretation. They cannot trust it because it, too, stems from Marlow's own desire for Jim's success, because Cornelius, however defeated he currently seems, is still an enemy who comes from the world from which Jim has fled. Conrad's rhetorical readers also cannot trust Marlow's interpretation because his formulation of it sets in motion the operation of what I'll call the Rule of Hubris, namely, that a character's unquestioning confidence about a happy future is a sure sign that the future will not be so happy.

The other significant instability that remains in Jim's progression involves his relationship with Jewel. Although they live and work together with mutual devotion and love, and although both Jim and Marlow assure her that Jim will never leave, Jewel's fear cannot be assuaged. Conrad links this instability with the one about the possible return of Jim's past not only to make such a return more likely but also to raise the stakes of his response to it. What will be at stake now is not just his own fate but also that of the woman he loves. At this intermediate stage in the narrative, then, because of Marlow's treatment of Jim in his roles as both character and narrator, Conrad's audience comes to share Marlow's hope and desire that Jim will ultimately master—and be satisfied with—his fate, even as the pattern of action and Marlow's own occasional unreliability cue the audience to expect that their hope and desire will not be fulfilled.

MARLOW'S NARRATION AND FAREWELL IN THE WRITTEN NARRATIVE

As *Lord Jim* makes the transition from Marlow's oral to his written narrative, Conrad introduces one specific interpretation and evaluation of Jim's life—that made by the privileged man. I will return to the details of the privileged man's view of Jim later, but for now I want to focus on Marlow's prefatory comments about his own final view of Jim:

> I affirm nothing. Perhaps you may pronounce—after you've read. There is much truth—after all—in the common expression "under a cloud." It is impossible to see him clearly—especially as it is through the eyes of others that we take our last look at him . . . ; there shall be nothing more [from him]; there shall be no message, unless such as each of us can interpret for

himself from the language of facts, that are so often more enigmatic than the craftiest arrangement of words. (246–47)

These comments constitute a startling move in the track of the progression involving Marlow's efforts to understand Jim and the audience's configuration of those efforts. Marlow's "I affirm nothing" significantly changes Conrad's rhetorical readers' relation to Marlow's narrative: rather than being immersed in following his efforts to understand Jim, these readers now know the outcome of those efforts. Consequently, readerly interest shifts from *whether* Marlow will finally be able to come to terms with Jim to *why* he will be unable to. At the same time, Conrad uses Marlow's "perhaps you may pronounce" to reiterate his own invitation to his audience to reach conclusions beyond Marlow's. This time, however, the invitation comes with explicit attention to the difficulty, though not the ultimate stubbornness, of the evidence: "perhaps" we rhetorical readers may pronounce, but only if we can interpret the enigma contained within the language of facts. Marlow's concluding comments link up with these prefatory ones, but before turning to them, I want to look more closely at some differences between his oral and his written narration and what these differences reveal about why he is unable to come to terms with Jim.

In Marlow's oral narration, he is frequently featured as a character—and not just because he recounts his many interactions with Jim. When he brings in the perspectives of other characters such as Brierly, Jones, Chester, and the French Lieutenant, he typically focuses on his interactions with those characters and his responses to their opinions and ideas. This method is central to Conrad's establishing the double progression of Jim's story and to tracing Marlow's quest to understand Jim and his story. In the written portion of the narrative, Conrad largely confines Marlow's role as character to his cover letter to the privileged gentleman, where he describes his visit to Stein's house and his interactions with Tamb' Itam, Jewel, the Bugis trader who took them to Stein's, and Stein himself. These descriptions both establish a tension of unequal knowledge between Marlow and Conrad's rhetorical readers (who know that Jim has died but not how or why) and foreground several outcomes of Jim's death: its negative effects on Stein, Jewel's conviction that Jim has betrayed her, and the mystery that still surrounds Jim in the eyes of Tamb' Itam and the Bugis trader. These too are matters I will return to; for now, I want to keep my focus on the way Marlow's role as character gets greatly diminished in the longer narrative he writes.

Another of Marlow's prefatory remarks is that "my information was fragmentary, but I've fitted the pieces together, and there is enough of them to make an intelligible picture" (249). This situation opens the door for him to continue his habits in the oral narrative, that is, narrating his interactions with the characters who gave him the fragmentary information as he also tells Jim's tale. Instead, however, he keeps the focus on Jim and Brown. When Marlow does refer to his encounter with Brown, he almost never records how he responded at the time to what Brown told him. As a result, the function of these returns to that scene is not to involve Marlow the character in the events but rather to have Brown serve as commentator on the picture that Marlow the narrator is putting together.

Here is a report that occurs early in the written narrative, shortly after Brown's arrival in Patusan, and immediately after Marlow tells the narratee that Kassim, accompanying Cornelius on a visit to Brown, has brought food for Brown and his men: "The three drew aside for a conference. Brown's men, recovering their confidence, were slapping each other on the back, and cast knowing glances at their captain while they busied themselves with preparations for cooking" (266).

This report is another example of implausibly knowledgeable narration of the kind Fitzgerald employs in *The Great Gatsby* and that I examined in chapter 2. Conrad employs the Rules of Duration and Self-Assurance along with the Meta-Rule of Value Added to disguise the fact Marlow must have invented what he reports. Brown is the only possible source for this information about his men, but he has left them to confer with Kassim and Cornelius. That Brown's drawing aside takes him out of their eyesight is suggested by Conrad's choice of the phrase "cast knowing glances at their captain" rather than, say, "exchanged knowing glances with" him. This passage indicates that as Marlow pieces his fragmentary information together, Conrad not only continues to make him a reliable reporter but also extends his authority to matters that he does not have any sources for. Moreover, extending Marlow's authority in this way provides Added Value: Marlow's narration here helps flesh out his portrait of Brown as someone who, though currently in a bad situation, nevertheless inspires considerable confidence in his men and who is therefore more resourceful and more dangerous than anyone Jim has had to deal with in Patusan.

Marlow's remark about piecing together fragmentary information and this example of his reporting beyond what his sources have told him also underline his active work in reconstructing Jim's story. And the extent of that work is given further support by what Conrad's rhetorical readers can infer about the interval between Marlow's meeting with Brown and his sending the written narrative to the privileged man. Marlow meets Brown "eight months" (251) after getting his initial fragments of the story from Tamb' Itam, Jewel, and the Bugis trader at Stein's, meetings that occur shortly after Jim's death.

His cover letter to the privileged man comments that the final events of Jim's life occurred "in the year of grace before last" (249), that is, not in the previous year but the one before that. Since up to two years may have passed since Jim's death, and Marlow met Brown about nine months after that death, it seems fair to conclude that it took Marlow approximately a year to compose his narrative. That is certainly time enough for him to use the new information about Jim to come to a determinate interpretation and judgment of him. Consequently, at this stage, Marlow's statement that "I affirm nothing" seems more rather than less puzzling.

Let us turn to a passage of Marlow's narration in which he does render interpretations and evaluations. I choose one from chapter 40, shortly after his report, based on Brown's testimony itself, that while waiting for Jim and negotiating with Kassim, Brown felt "the lust for battle" (269):

> No doubt the natural senseless ferocity which is the basis of such a character was exasperated by failure, ill-luck, and the recent privations, as well as by the desperate position in which he found himself; but what was most remarkable of all was this, that while he planned treacherous alliances, had already settled in his own mind the fate of the white man, and intrigued in an overbearing, offhand manner with Kassim, one could perceive that what he had really desired, almost in spite of himself, was to play havoc with that jungle town which had defied him, to see it strewn over with corpses and enveloped in flames. Listening to his pitiless, panting voice, I could imagine how he must have looked at it from the hillock, peopling it with images of murder and rapine. (269–70)

Marlow is interpreting Brown here because he is going beyond anything Brown told him directly. And Marlow is evaluating here because those interpretations are inextricably connected to his ethical assessment of both Brown's character (its natural senseless ferocity) and his desire (his imaginative peopling of his surroundings with "images of murder and rapine"). In a sense, this passage shows Marlow doing at the level of interpretation and evaluation what he does at the level of reporting in the previous passage: he leaps beyond the information provided by Brown to his own conclusions about what is driving Brown and about what Brown most desires. And again, although Conrad could have used the evidence of Marlow's leap as a sign that rhetorical readers should not fully trust his interpretation and evaluation, Conrad does nothing in the passage to cast doubt on them, and then he dramatically confirms them by Brown's later actions. In short, the interpretation and evaluation are reliable, authoritative, and significant. Indeed, I can find no instances of Marlow being an unreliable interpreter or evaluator in this section of the narrative.

But now consider another passage of Marlow's interpretation, this one occurring in Chapter 43, after his report that most of the Bugis agreed to Jim's proposal to let Brown go free because they "believed Tuan Jim." "In this simple form of assent to his will lies the whole gist of the situation; their creed, his truth; and the testimony to that faithfulness which made him in his own eyes the equal of the impeccable men who never fall out of the ranks" (287).

Initially, Marlow's interpretation is both reliable and authoritative, as he sums up the "whole gist" of Jim's situation in Patusan, but as Marlow moves toward interpreting the larger significance of Jim's "faithfulness," he actually switches from interpreting to reporting, as he veers away from offering his own view of Jim's faithfulness and instead giving Jim's. Given Marlow's broad authority as reporter and as interpreter of Brown and of the motives of the Bugis members of the Council, his limitation as interpreter of Jim stands out—though the passage itself does not help us come any closer to understanding the gap between his narratorial powers with everyone else and his narratorial powers with Jim. I turn for a possible answer to the novel's ending, especially Marlow's concluding reflections and reports.

Marlow reliably reports Jim's arrival at the end of his progression, his following through on his promise to take responsibility for the dire consequences of his misjudgment of Brown. But once again, Marlow is unable to make the move from reliable reporting to determinate interpreting and evaluating:

> And that's the end. He passes away under a cloud, inscrutable at heart, forgotten, unforgiven, and excessively romantic. Not in the wildest days of his boyish visions could he have seen the alluring shape of such an extraordinary success! For it may very well be that in the short moment of his last proud and unflinching glance, he had beheld the face of that opportunity which, like an Eastern bride, had come veiled to his side.
>
> But we can see him, an obscure conqueror of fame, tearing himself out of the arms of a jealous love at the sign, at the call of his exalted egoism. He goes away from a living woman to celebrate his pitiless wedding with a shadowy ideal of conduct. Is he satisfied—quite, now, I wonder? We ought to know. He is one of us—and have I not stood up once, like an evoked ghost, to answer for his eternal constancy? Was I so very wrong after all? Now, he is no more, there are days when the reality of his existence comes to me with an immense, with an overwhelming force; and yet upon my honour there are moments too when he passes from my eyes like a disembodied spirit astray

amongst the passions of this earth, ready to surrender himself faithfully to the claim of his own world of shades.

Who knows? He is gone, inscrutable at heart, and the poor girl is leading a sort of soundless, inert life in Stein's house. Stein has aged greatly of late. He feels it himself, and says often that he is "preparing to leave all this; preparing to leave, . . ." while he waves his hand sadly at his butterflies. (303–4; ellipsis in original)

The first effect of this farewell is to give the greatest possible emphasis to Jim's ultimate stubbornness: not only Marlow but "we"—his narratees and Conrad's readers—ought to know whether Jim was satisfied, whether he was eternally constant, whether he is an ongoing immense force or just a shadowy presence who never fully emerges into light. But we don't because he remains inscrutable at heart. This emphasis on the stubbornness sheds some retrospective light on the discrepancy between Marlow's narratorial powers with regard to Brown and everyone else, on the one hand, and with regard to Jim, on the other. Marlow "affirms nothing" because his own identification with Jim means that by his own code of ethics, he must be as scrupulous as possible in interpreting and evaluating him. In a sense, Marlow's own commitment to an ethics of telling leaves him unable to overcome Jim's stubbornness.

Although Marlow cannot reach any determinate judgment, his farewell does implicitly rule out some other interpretations and evaluations, especially the one offered by the privileged man at the end of the oral narrative. Marlow writes in his cover letter,

I remember well you would not admit he had mastered his fate. You prophesied for him the disaster of weariness and of disgust with acquired honour, with the self-appointed task, with the love sprung from pity and youth [. . .]. You said also [. . .] that "giving your life up to them" (*them* meaning all of mankind with skins brown, yellow, or black in colour) "was like selling your soul to a brute." (246)

Marlow's farewell eliminates this response as a viable option not only because the privileged man's prophecy does not come true, but also because neither Marlow nor Conrad shares his blatant racism. Indeed, if Marlow shared that attitude, he could not entertain the possibility that in his final acts Jim achieves a satisfactory heroism. In this connection, it is worth noting that the farewell's simultaneous emphases on the textual stubbornness surrounding Jim and on the inadequacy of the privileged man's view of him also explain why Conrad does not return to the frame provided by the noncharacter narrator. Such a return would diminish both effects because Marlow's uncertainty would surely allow the privileged man to maintain his basic position.

More importantly, the conclusion of Marlow's letter to the privileged man functions as a highly effective way for Conrad to complete his rhetorical action because of its affective and ethical consequences. Although Conrad does not provide any textual basis for rhetorical readers to convert Jim from an instance of the stubborn to an instance of the difficult, he does push those readers beyond Marlow's formulations because Conrad uses those formulations as one means to enhance the affective power of the ending, even as they underline the narrative's ultimate stubbornness. To put this point another way, although Conrad's narrative does not allow rhetorical readers to settle on a final interpretation and evaluation of Jim, that very uncertainty contributes to the sense that in his death, something—and someone—significant has gone out of the world, and this sense makes his death deeply moving. The uncertainty contributes to this effect because it means that readers can enter into the disparate views of Jim held by all who knew him well, and, thus, can recognize the wide-ranging consequences of his death on the lives of those people. Conrad constructs Marlow's last paragraph to call attention to Jim's effects on Jewel and on Stein.

It is striking that here, at the end, the emphasis is not on Jewel's anger and outrage but on what these emotions have previously covered over: her sorrow and emptiness now that Jim has gone out of her life. It is also striking that Jim has such a powerful effect on Stein, who has previously been represented as capable of rising above any situation. And above all, Conrad insists that his audience pay attention to Jim's powerful effect on Marlow, to the way that Jim's story has turned Marlow, first, into a version of the Ancient Mariner, and then into an active and imaginative historian who, because he still remains uncertain, remains in the grip of Jim's inscrutability.

Indeed, it is in the realm of the affective that Conrad creates the greatest gap between Marlow's conclusions and those of rhetorical readers, because those readers see both Marlow and Jim within the larger frame of Conrad's construction. For Marlow, Jim and his life are above all inscrutable; for Conrad's audience, Jim and his life are not just inscrutable but also very moving. The affective power of the ending keeps Conrad's audience, like Marlow, fascinated by Jim, but also, I submit, even more tempted than Marlow to solve the riddle of Jim's character. And while Conrad does use Marlow's direct address and his many rhetorical questions to invite his audience to keep seeking their own answers, he also trusts that audience not to settle on any determinate answer. In other words, the ethics of his own telling, an ethics he invites his rhetorical readers to share, involve a commitment to a kind of negative capability: he unequivocally makes the case that Jim's life is worthy of Marlow's and of rhetorical readers' quest for its meaning without allowing Marlow or his audience to complete that quest by arriving at any definitive formulation. Individual rhetorical readers, like many of the characters in the novel, may find themselves reaching conclusions about Jim, converting his stubbornness into difficulty. Indeed, if, as Albert Guérard suggests, each of us has a *Patna* incident in our lives, then we may find ourselves needing to come to some determinate judgment about Jim and, indeed, about Marlow's inability to reach such a judgment. Nevertheless, precisely because Conrad ends by underlining Jim's stubbornness, rhetorical readers are likely to find that any determinate interpretive and ethical judgments that they make of Jim will be subject to revision as their own lives progress.

Attending to the affective and ethical consequences of Jim's stubbornness also sheds light on the overall completion of the progression. These consequences help us explain why the ending, despite its qualities of indeterminacy and open-endedness, remains aesthetically satisfying. The affective power points to Conrad's ability to combine the resolution of the action in Jim's track of the progression with the lack of resolution in Marlow's narrative quest to produce an emotionally appropriate conclusion. Conrad's handling of the ethics of both Marlow's telling and his own telling enhances rhetorical readers' ethical engagement and ethical admiration for the open-endedness. In achieving these effects, Conrad has also demonstrated in his own way something that Kafka also demonstrated in his: foregrounding the stubbornness of a major element of a narrative can paradoxically enhance its power.

CHAPTER 8

Toni Morrison's Determinate Ambiguity in "Recitatif"

I N THIS CHAPTER, I continue to explore the ways in which authors can
use the resources of character narration and ambiguity in order to achieve
their communicative purposes. As I consider Toni Morrison's purposes in
her remarkable short story, "Recitatif," I move from the multiple, competing
meanings of stubbornness about event and character in "Das Urteil" and *Lord
Jim* to the determinate ambiguity of an either/or interpretive judgment about
a teller (and its ripple effects) in Morrison's powerful exploration of race, class,
gender, (dis)ability, and women's friendship. At the same time, I broaden the
theoretical discussion by taking up the relation between the project of rhetorical poetics and some lines of research in cognitive narrative theory.[1]

Indeed, as a rhetorical narrative theorist interested in the flourishing sub-
field of cognitive narrative theory, I have been struck by a significant and
surprising gap in narrative studies. Rhetorical and cognitive narrative theory share several fundamental commitments and interests, but for the most
part, rhetorical theorists and cognitive theorists have engaged in parallel play

---

1. Of course, feminist narrative theory, which emphasizes the imbrication of narrative
with the identity issues foregrounded in Morrison's story, would be another highly relevant
approach to pair with the rhetorical theory. But I also think that the lines of differentiation
between the rhetorical and feminist ways of looking at "Recitatif" would not be that strong.
To put it another way, my rhetorical reading, while not identical to a feminist reading, is not
merely compatible with, but to a large extent is informed by, such a reading.

rather than productive collaboration. On those occasions when they have engaged with each other's work, they have emphasized differences and disagreements more than what they share and how they might join forces.[2] To counter this line of discussion, I would like to demonstrate one way that the two approaches can effectively collaborate as I take up the task of interpreting "Recitatif." Morrison invents joint protagonists, Twyla and Roberta, of different races (one white, one black) and has Twyla tell the tale. Twyla's narration makes it clear that the two characters know each other's race and that their racial difference strongly influences their relationship, but Twyla never explicitly identifies herself or Roberta by race. In addition, Morrison frustrates her audience's ability to use other cultural markers as a way to assign racial identities to her co-protagonists. As the critical conversation to this point demonstrates, the very salience of Morrison's withholding of her characters' racial identity for the story's thematic explorations of race, class, and disability[3] can lead us to overlook other striking aspects of Morrison's design, including her handling of other aspects of the character narration and her management of the overall progression. As I analyze these elements of Morrison's story, I shall draw on Lisa Zunshine's insights about metarepresentation, Alan Palmer's work on social minds, and various concepts I have developed in this book. At the same time, I shall remain open to the ways in which Morrison's use of her resources may require some refinements to these theoretical constructs. In my conclusion I shall briefly reflect on my way of bringing cognitive and rhetorical theory together. I begin by elaborating on reasons why rhetorical and cognitive narrative theory should be theoretical allies.

The approaches share at least two important principles and one important mode of inquiry. **Principle 1:** Narrative is a purposeful communicative exchange between authors and readers. This book has been an exercise in

---

2. See the exchange between Alan Palmer and me (Palmer, "Attributions," and Phelan, "Cognitive Narratology") and the one between David Herman, on the cognitive side, and Peter J. Rabinowitz and me, on the rhetorical side, in Herman et al., *Narrative Theory: Core Concepts and Critical Debates* (where both approaches are also juxtaposed to a feminist approach, advanced by Robyn Warhol, and an antimimetic approach, advanced by Brian Richardson). These exchanges are respectful, but the participants focus on where they diverge. For recent essays that emphasize the compatibility of rhetorical and cognitive approaches, see Rabinowitz and Bancroft ("Euclid") and Rabinowitz ("Cognitive Flavor").

3. Elizabeth Abel's excellent "Black Writing, White Reading: Race and the Politics of Feminist Interpretation" highlights this feature of the story, and many subsequent essays explore its thematic consequences. See especially Marie Knoflíčková and David Goldstein-Shirley. Howard Sklar takes up the worthwhile question whether the disabled Maggie functions as what David Mitchell and Sharon Snyder call a "narrative prosthesis," that is, the use of a disabled character (and negative stereotypes associated with the disability) as a device by which a narrative accomplishes its effects. See their *Narrative Prosthesis: Disability and the Dependencies of Discourse*. I will return to this issue later in the chapter.

developing the consequences of the principle. Although I am not aware of any cognitive theorist explicitly endorsing this larger vision of narrative, cognitive theory does assume that there is a mind behind the text and that interpreters attempt to read that mind (often by reading the minds of characters). David Herman argues that the interpretation of narrative needs to be built on the assumption that "stories are irreducibly grounded in intentional systems" ("Intentional" 240). Lisa Zunshine contends that even post-structuralist proclamations about the death of the author and the birth of the reader implicitly assign some agent as the begetter of the communication and thus indicate "the tenaciousness with which we cling to the idea that there must be some source (e.g., an author, a reader, multiple authors, multiple readers) behind a narrative" (*Why* 67). In other words, regardless of where we locate the source, we assign it an authorial function.

Principle 2: One important task of narrative theory is to offer insights into the general conditions and mechanisms governing that exchange between authors and readers. At this stage in the progression of this book, I worry that I'm annoying my readers with repetitions of this point. To take just one illustration from cognitive theory, Palmer analyzes differences between internalist and externalist views of consciousness as part of his effort to explain the ways authors construct and readers understand fictional minds (*Social Minds* 39–42). More generally, both rhetorical and cognitive theorists often seek to transform tacit understandings that underlie our experience as writers and readers into articulate knowledge that in turn can enrich our appreciation of those experiences.

Common Mode of Inquiry: Both approaches conduct interpretations in order to demonstrate how individual narratives deploy those general conditions and mechanisms and, where appropriate, to show how those deployments can lead to revisions in our understanding of those general conditions and mechanisms. To take an example beyond this book, Peter J. Rabinowitz's efforts to understand the details of different kinds of passing in Nella Larsen's *Passing* led him to propose the initially counterintuitive idea that some narratives have multiple authorial audiences ("Betraying"). Zunshine's efforts to analyze source monitoring in the genre of the detective story led her to offer a much more nuanced view of the dictum that detective plots and romance plots don't mix. To be sure, narrative theorists with different projects from those of rhetorical and cognitive theorists also engage in this mode of inquiry, so my claim is not that rhetoricians and cognitivists are unique in this practice. Instead, my claim is that this shared practice provides another reason why the two groups should be looking to each other's work more than they have so far. Indeed, in light of what the approaches have in common, we ought to pause and consider why there has not yet been much collaboration.

I identify four main reasons: (1) As cognitive narratology has emerged over the last two decades or so, it has understandably been focused on how it is *distinct* from other approaches to narrative, especially what Herman has dubbed classical narratology.[4] (2) Cognitive theory's chief way of establishing that distinctiveness has been to focus on the consequences of various findings of cognitive studies—findings ranging from research on Theory of Mind to Daniel Dennett's philosophical work on consciousness—for the way we understand narratives themselves. In other words, the work moves from cognitive studies to generalizations about narrative and then to testing and exemplification in relation to individual narratives. Those moves neither require nor encourage engagement with rhetorical theory. (3) Rhetorical theory, as the previous chapters in this book indicate, has been concerned with revising and extending work in its tradition in order to establish its own distinctiveness among other approaches. Indeed, the contributions that Rabinowitz and I make to *Narrative Theory: Core Concepts and Critical Debates* primarily seek to stake out rhetorical theory's place in the landscape of contemporary narrative studies. (4) Narrative theorists have been emphasizing the point that their field now contains multiple approaches, and this emphasis has worked against efforts to integrate those approaches.

I acknowledge at the outset that a single inquiry cannot demonstrate all the ways in which the projects of rhetorical poetics and cognitive narratology may productively collaborate. My modest goal, then, is to carry out one such collaboration, and my immodest hope is that it will spur other researchers both to respond to it and to explore other ways of bringing the projects together.

METAREPRESENTATION, CHARACTER NARRATION, AND THE ETHICS OF MORRISON'S TELLING

Since Morrison's decision to withhold the racial identity of Twyla and Roberta is central to understanding her communication, I begin with it. In terms

---

4. While Herman's distinction between classical and postclassical narratologies has provided a useful shorthand for discussing the history of the field, it has had the unfortunate side effect of suggesting that the narratology of the French structuralists of the 1960s and 1970s is the fountain from which all subsequent narrative theory flows. Among other things, this view either omits or discounts the Aristotelian tradition out of which contemporary rhetorical theory has grown.

FIGURE 8.1. Duck or rabbit? Source: Jastrow, J. (1899). The mind's eye. *Popular Science Monthly*, 54, 299–312.

of the story's progression, the withholding functions as a global tension of unequal knowledge that is never resolved. Both Morrison and Twyla know the characters' racial identities, but neither reveals them. Twyla's withholding is inadvertent: she assumes that her narratee knows her race and therefore knows Roberta's as well. Morrison's withholding, by contrast, is deliberate, and it invites questions about the ethics of her telling. Why shouldn't we regard her relation to her audience as the high-culture equivalent of a Mean Girl taunting someone with chants of "I know something you don't know"? A close look at the nature and effects of Morrison's withholding in conjunction with Zunshine's work on metarepresentation (from *Why We Read Fiction*) and with another consideration of Wittgenstein's duck/rabbit figure (figure 8.1) will aid our vision. In this figure, the artist provides signals that can be construed as forming the image of a duck or of a rabbit, but our perceptual apparatus does not allow us to perceive it as both *at the same time*. Furthermore, the artist does not provide any signal that if we could only see better or deeper, we could determine that the image was actually that of a duck or that of a rabbit. In other words, just as character-character dialogue is not just an element of story or of discourse but of both (see the discussion in chapter 1), this figure is not just a duck and not just a rabbit but rather a duck/rabbit. Morrison's ambiguity is significantly different from that of the figure, because she signals that (a) Twyla and Roberta are either black or white, not black/white (duck or rabbit, not duck/rabbit); (b) they know each other's race and therefore so does she; and (c) she shapes the story so that her audience cannot know which one is which.[5]

As Zunshine explains, *metarepresentation* is a term referring to our cognitive ability to keep track of the sources of information. Thus, an act of metarepresentation has two parts, one concerned with the source of the information and one concerned with the content of the information. The first sentence of this paragraph provides a handy example: it provides a content (the definition) and a source for that content (Zunshine). Your understanding of my sentence adds an additional source: "Phelan writes that Zunshine says that metarepresentation is . . ." When we monitor sources as well as content, we remain open to the possibility that the content is unreliable or otherwise limited, as the expression "consider the source" indicates. When we lose track of sources, we are susceptible to mistaking lies, distortions, and other unreliable messages for accurate reports, interpretations, or evaluations. Zunshine impressively shows how a focus on source-tracking can illuminate our experience of unreliable narrators (her main examples are Richardson's Robert Lovelace and Nabokov's Humbert Humbert) and of detective stories.

As a rhetorician, however, I am struck by Zunshine's relatively weak commitment to the (implied) author as the ultimate source of fictional communication. By a weak commitment, I mean that Zunshine recognizes this point in theory but does not give much weight to it in her interpretive practice. In her discussions of *Clarissa* and *Lolita,* Zunshine focuses not on the choices made by Richardson and Nabokov but rather on the character narrators' own failures in monitoring themselves as sources and their consequences for readerly decisions about unreliability. In this way, Zunshine effectively treats unreliable narration as if it works primarily along a single communicative track running

---

5. One might take the duck/rabbit figure as a closer analogue to "Recitatif" by contending that Morrison simultaneously constructs Twyla and Roberta as white and as black. In this view, rather than creating a single storyworld and impeding her audience's access to one of its crucial features, Morrison simultaneously creates two distinct storyworlds and thus two distinct narratives: in one Twyla is white and Roberta black and in the other their racial identities are reversed. One could make the analogy even tighter by contending that Morrison makes it impossible for us to determine whether there is one storyworld or two. I find some merit in both hypotheses but ultimately find them less compelling than the view that Morrison constructs a single storyworld and denies our access to part of it. This view corresponds more closely to most readers' experience. In addition, the hypothesis about two storyworlds foregrounds the synthetic component of Morrison's characters and her storyworld and thus emphasizes their fictionality, when every other feature of the narrative points to Morrison's interest in minimizing the difference between her storyworld and the actual world—and the realities of its racial politics.

from narrator to reader. Zunshine's summary of her analysis illustrates this point:

> [Some narratives with unreliable narrators] portray protagonists who fail, on some level, to keep track of themselves as sources of their representations of their own and other people's minds, and, by doing so, they force the reader into a situation in which she herself becomes unsure of the relative truth-value of any representation contained in such a narrative. (*Why* 124)

Not surprisingly, I want to adapt Zunshine's work by strongly committing to the (implied) author as the ultimate source of narrative communication. I would then revise Zunshine's summary statement this way:

> Implied authors of narratives often employ character narrators who fail, on some level, to keep track of themselves as sources of their representations of their own and other people's minds. By depicting these failures, these implied authors typically signal to their audiences that these character narrators are unreliable, though the exact nature and degree of that unreliability will vary from case to case.

The practical advantages of this adaptation become clear when we turn to the metarepresentation in "Recitatif"—even as Morrison's determinate ambiguity adds at least two additional turns of the communicative screw governing character narration. First, by withholding Twyla's racial identity, the implied Morrison gives us one text that simultaneously has three tellers and three purposes. The withholding means that we must give each sentence of Twyla's narration and each line of dialogue from Twyla and from Roberta a triple reading: one that assigns the content to a white speaker, a second that assigns that content to a black speaker, and an all-encompassing third that assigns both readings to the implied Morrison and asks what effects she creates through the juxtaposition of the first two readings.

The specific effects of the triple sourcing vary along a broad spectrum. At one end, the implied Morrison uses the first two readings to generate substantially different understandings of Twyla's narration, differences that highlight links between an audience's assumption about a speaker's race and the meaning of her utterances. At the other end, the implied Morrison uses the first two readings to show that some situations transcend race. As an example of the first set of effects, consider Twyla's confession about not knowing how black-white relations were "in those days" (the 1960s) when Roberta snubbed her after they met at the Howard Johnson's where Twyla was working:

But I didn't know. I thought it was just the opposite. Busloads of blacks and whites came into Howard Johnson's together. They roamed together then: students, musicians, lovers, protestors. You got to see everything at Howard Johnson's and blacks were very friendly with whites in those days. (255)

In both of the first two readings, the passage is an example of unreliable interpretation based in naïveté. Morrison expects her rhetorical readers to recognize that what Twyla observed at Howard Johnson's hardly reflects the state of race relations in the United States in the 1960s. Indeed, Morrison's depiction of the meeting between Twyla and Roberta functions as evidence of Twyla's unreliable interpretation. Rather than being happy to see each other for the first time since they were together at the orphanage, they are wary of each other, and Roberta is particularly unwilling to show affection in the presence of her two friends who are of her same race. If Twyla is white, then the unreliability reflects her white privilege: it is easy for her to think that blacks and whites were so friendly because she did not have to experience the pervasive effects of white racism. But if Twyla is black, then the naïveté reflects both her personal good fortune in not having felt those effects and her lack of awareness of what so many who shared her skin color had to endure. Morrison's meta-communication is about how deeply race sometimes matters.

Now consider Twyla's report of her feelings about Roberta leaving St. Bonaventure's: "I thought I would die in that room of four beds without her and I knew Bozo had plans to move some other dumped kid in there with me" (248). Here the first two readings produce the same effect. Whether this narration is from a white girl speaking about the effects of losing her black friend or vice versa, it powerfully conveys the speaker's regret about her friend's departure and her feeling of being left behind. Morrison's meta-communication is not that race is irrelevant in this situation but that Twyla and Roberta have forged a genuine friendship across their racial divide and thus that the divide does not have to be unbridgeable. As the narrative continues, however, Morrison invites her audience to be aware that it is easier for Twyla and Roberta to bridge that divide when they are children and when they are in the confined space of the orphanage.

The actual audience's need to engage in this triple source-tracking leads to the second turn of the communicative screw: Morrison makes her readers aware of the various ways in which we make identifications of race on the basis of markers of class and culture—including, as Elizabeth Abel astutely points out, ways rooted in our individual racial identities. For example, Roberta's knowledge of Jimi Hendrix and Twyla's ignorance of him will incline many white readers to assume, as Abel did, that Roberta is black and Twyla is white, until someone points out, as Abel's black friend Lula Fragd did, that Hendrix was more popular with whites than blacks. Similarly, many black readers might assume, as Fragd did, that Roberta's anti-bussing stance and her affluence mark her as white, until they learn, as Abel did from Morrison herself, that Morrison gives Roberta's husband a position with IBM because that company had a program for recruiting black executives in the 1970s (Morrison does not regard this information as indicating that Roberta is black but rather as helping to keep the question of her race open) (Abel 470–77).

We can now answer the question about the ethics of Morrison's telling. Morrison is far from the high-culture equivalent of a Mean Girl because the effects of her withholding are to engage her audience more fully in this process of unpacking the multiple, inescapable, and yet unstable markers we use to assign race and class in American culture. This engagement makes the reading experience not fruitless and frustrating but revealing and rewarding.

NARRATIVE PROGRESSION, SOCIAL MINDS, AND A PROBABLE IMPLAUSIBILITY IN "RECITATIF"

As I noted above, Palmer distinguishes between internalist and externalist perspectives on the mind, with the internalist perspective emphasizing "those aspects that are inner, introspective, private, solitary, individual, psychological, mysterious, and detached" and the externalist emphasizing "those aspects that are outer, active, public, social, behavioral, evident, embodied, and engaged" (*Social Minds* 39). Palmer notes that the perspectives are complementary, not competing, but also contends that previous work on fictional minds has been far more influenced by the internalist perspective than the externalist. He sets out to redress the balance, paying special attention to representations of "social minds" characterized by "intermental thought," that is, "joint, group, shared, or collective" cognition (41). Palmer maintains that the representation of social minds "looms large as a technique and as a subject matter" in the history of the novel. Significantly, from the perspective of rhetorical theory, Palmer goes on to add that "techniques and subject matters are parts of novels, not purposes of them. They are means rather than ends. What matters, ultimately, is the purpose to which a particular sort of consciousness representation is put" (63).[6]

---

6. Full disclosure: Palmer included these qualifications in response to my reader's report on the manuscript of *Social Minds*. Here's the relevant passage from my report: "It seems to me that the representation of consciousness looms large as a technique and as a subject matter in all the novels Palmer discusses but techniques and subject matters are parts of novels not

Morrison's use of social minds in "Recitatif" nicely exemplifies this last point. Much of her story traces the formation, the fragility, the breakdown, and possible re-formation of the social mind shared by Twyla and Roberta. But for Morrison, that tracing is one means toward her larger purposes, which include (1) at the thematic level, heightening her audience's awareness of the myriad personal and cultural factors that influence the trajectory of Twyla and Roberta's efforts to bridge their racial divide; (2) at the mimetic level, guiding her audience's ethical judgments and affective responses so that we desire their success and understand their failures and can take genuine satisfaction in the story's bittersweet ending; and (3) at the aesthetic level, constructing a narrative that rewards attention not only to the nuances of the relationships between the characters but also to those between herself and her audience. In this section, then, I will draw on Palmer's work for insights into some aspects of Morrison's construction of the progression, especially its beginning and ending, but I shall also consider one aspect of the character narration that is crucial for the progression and seems to me best understood from the perspective of rhetorical theory.

Morrison builds the plot dynamics around a global instability and its complications: Twyla and Roberta's struggle to relate across their racial difference, a struggle complicated by their relationships to their neglectful mothers and to Maggie, the disabled cook at the orphanage where they meet, and by broader cultural issues affecting race relations in the United States from the 1950s to the early 1980s. (Strikingly, Twyla's and Roberta's fathers are never mentioned and do not function as absent presences.)

Morrison divides the story into five parts. In the first, set in the 1950s at St. Bonaventure's, the girls are eight years old and they bond. In the second, set in the 1960s at the Howard Johnson's where Twyla works, they cannot bridge their divides. In the third, set in the early 1970s in a suburban shopping center, they are in their late twenties;[7] at first they effortlessly reconnect, but conflict-

---

purposes of them, means rather than ends. Palmer doesn't have to agree with this position, but I do think it would be helpful if he addressed it." I stipulated that Palmer didn't have to agree because I didn't want to impose my views on Palmer. I do regard Palmer's agreement as an additional warrant for the project of this chapter.

7. Twyla says that when they meet as married women, "twenty years" have passed since they were at the orphanage and "twelve years" have passed since they met at Howard Johnson's. Since they are eight when they're at St. Bonny's, they would be sixteen and twenty-eight at these subsequent meetings. But Twyla implies that she has to drive to Howard Johnson's ("Kind of a long ride" [249]), and Roberta is on her way from New York to "the coast" with two male friends, and thus they seem to be closer to twenty than to sixteen. If they are twenty, then the "twelve years" would capture the interval between their time at St. Bonny's and their meeting at Howard Johnson's rather than the interval between the two later meetings. (I can't help but note that this is the second time I'm finding fault with Morrison's time-tracking. For the first, see my

ing memories about Maggie during their time at the orphanage limit their bond. In the fourth, set later in the 1970s, primarily outside a school at the center of a bussing controversy, they are thirty-somethings on opposite sides in the controversy. And in the fifth, set primarily in a coffee shop, they are in their forties and move back toward each other.

Morrison begins to develop the global instability in the story's first two paragraphs.

> My mother danced all night and Roberta's was sick. That's why we were taken to St. Bonny's. . . . There were four to a room, and when Roberta and me came, there was a shortage of state kids, so we were the only ones assigned to 406 and could go from bed to bed if we wanted to. And we wanted to, too. We changed beds every night and for the whole four months we were there we never picked one out as our own permanent bed.
>
> It didn't start out that way. The minute I walked in and the Big Bozo introduced us, I got sick to my stomach. It was one thing to be taken out of your own bed early in the morning—it was something else to be stuck in a strange place with a girl from a whole other race. And Mary, that's my mother, she was right. Every now and then she would stop dancing long enough to tell me something important and one of the things she said was that they never washed their hair and they smelled funny. Roberta sure did. Smell funny, I mean. So when the Big Bozo (nobody ever called her Mrs. Itkin, just like nobody ever said St. Bonaventure)—when she said, "Twyla, this is Roberta. Roberta, this is Twyla. Make each other welcome." I said, "My mother won't like you putting me in here." (243)

The first two sentences introduce the instability of the girls having absent mothers, and the second paragraph ties that instability to the relationship between the girls: Twyla's response to Roberta's racial difference stems from her having assimilated her mother's racist attitude. But since Twyla does not directly voice her racist judgment, Roberta does not take serious offense. Indeed, as the first paragraph indicates, the two girls do bond sufficiently to become a "we" and to function as a social mind: they act together (going from bed to bed) and they desire together ("we wanted to"). By juxtaposing the two paragraphs, Morrison shows that what threatens the ongoing functioning of their social mind is less the basic instincts of the two girls than the ways those instincts get distorted by other forces.

---

discussion of the temporal problems in the opening pages of *Beloved* in *Experiencing Fiction* [59]. Whether I'm a good close reader or just a pedant is a judgment I leave to my audience.)

Twyla and Roberta bond more fully in response to the hostile behavior of the adolescent girls, who, as I'll discuss below, function as a rival social mind. At the same time, Morrison shows the fragility of Twyla and Roberta's intermental unit, especially when their mothers get involved. When their mothers come to visit for Easter (time of hope and change), Twyla is so happy at receiving Mary's initial expressions of love that she "forgot about Roberta" (247). But after Roberta's mother offers a racist and classist rejection of Mary (and Twyla)—she looks them over and without saying a word grabs Roberta and walks away—Twyla takes on Roberta's mother's negative view. Prior to this interaction, Twyla minimizes the things about Mary that she doesn't like because she feels loved. But in the wake of Roberta's mother's snub, all Twyla can focus on are Mary's limitations; indeed, she has murderous thoughts: "I could have killed her" (248).

Morrison's triple sourcing here highlights the differences in rhetorical readers' understanding of the scene as they assign different racial identities to the characters. If Roberta and her mother are white, then Twyla's response primarily shows how white racism influences her sense of her and her mother's racial inferiority. If Roberta and her mother are black, then Twyla's response primarily shows her sense of her and her mother's class inferiority.

Furthermore, in noting the difference between her meager lunch of mashed jelly beans and Roberta's ample one, Twyla herself falls into racist thinking: "Things are not right. The wrong food is always with the wrong people" (248). By having Twyla imply that she should have Roberta's lunch and Roberta hers, Morrison not only underlines her thematic point about the contagious nature of racist thinking but also shows how easily Twyla and Roberta's intermental unit can dissolve. But their bond is not so fragile that it breaks, and after the visit, Roberta and Twyla reestablish it through their mutual mind-reading. Roberta, aware that Mary did not bring lunch, gives Twyla "a stack of grahams" when the visit is over, and Twyla reads the motives behind the gift: "I think she was sorry that her mother would not shake my mother's hand. And I liked that and I liked the fact that she didn't say a word about Mary's groaning all the way through the service and not bringing any lunch" (248).

Morrison uses Twyla's narration about the older girls to show a contrasting social mind in operation, one whose hostility brings Twyla and Roberta closer together (though they stop short of sharing their fears):

> They were put-out girls, scared runaways most of them. Poor little girls who fought their uncles off but looked tough to us, and mean. . . . [S]ometimes they caught us watching them in the orchard where they played radios and

danced with each other. They'd light out after us and pull our hair or twist our arms. We were scared of them, Roberta and me, but neither of us wanted the other one to know it. So we got a good list of dirty names we could shout back when we ran from them through the orchard. (244)

Even as the passage overtly emphasizes hostility and fear, Morrison's use of the iterative covertly indicates that Twyla and Roberta are also attracted to these girls. Despite their fear, they repeatedly return to the orchard to watch the "gar girls" dance (the nickname itself—Roberta's distortion of "gargoyles," which are simultaneously grotesque and appealing—reinforces their mixed feelings).

This approach/avoidance conflict also plays out in Twyla and Roberta's ethically deficient response to the older girls' treatment of Maggie, the old, "sandy-colored" "kitchen woman with legs like parentheses," who could not speak and who wore a "stupid little hat—a kid's hat with ear flaps" (245). Twyla reports that when Maggie fell while walking across the orchard, "the big girls laughed at her. We should have helped her up, I know, but we were scared of those girls with lipstick and eyebrow pencil" (245). Morrison uses Twyla's focus on the "lipstick and eyebrow pencil" in conjunction with her description of Maggie's "stupid little hat" to convey Twyla and Roberta's underlying attraction to the older girls and their implicit alignment with them rather than Maggie.

Morrison more strongly indicates that attraction by showing that Twyla and Roberta imitate the gar girls' meanness to Maggie. With one voice they call her "Dummy! Dummy!" and "Bow legs! Bow legs!" (245). In aligning themselves with the gar girls, Twyla and Roberta embrace their effort to elevate themselves by denigrating Maggie, whose disability makes her an easy target. Morrison has Twyla follow up her report of this name-calling with narration from her perspective at the time of the telling: "I think she could hear and didn't let on. And it shames me *even now* to think there was somebody in there after all who heard us call her those names and couldn't tell on us" (245; my emphasis). I highlight the phrase "even now" because it implies that Twyla felt shame even then. At the same time, Morrison uses the presence and power of the social mind of the gar girls to mitigate her audience's negative ethical judgment of these eight-year-olds.

In parts 2 through 4, Morrison shows how the cultural pressures of Twyla's and Roberta's individual situations and their shame about how they treated Maggie prevent them from reestablishing their bond. In part 3, Roberta contends that Maggie didn't fall in the orchard but was pushed by the gar girls—a situation that makes their failure to help her more ethically deficient. In part

4, Roberta insists that Maggie was black and that they joined with the adolescents in kicking Maggie when she was down.

Twyla is vulnerable to Roberta's accusations precisely because the two of them had been an intermental unit. Roberta in effect says, "I know what you did because I know what I did and you and I were a single unit." Twyla is also vulnerable because of her shame. In addition, rhetorical readers' triple source-tracking leads them to consider the consequences of Roberta's insistence that Maggie was black. If Twyla is white, then her kicking a black woman is a sign of her racism. And if Twyla is black, then her kicking is evidence of some self-hatred. Twyla's angry, defensive response—she calls Roberta "liar!," which leads Roberta to hurl the accusation back at her—shows both that the accusation stings and that their former dyad has almost completely come apart. Furthermore, Morrison guides her rhetorical readers to recognize the complex ways in which Maggie figures in the relationship between the two women. On the one hand, they share the negative judgment of their former behavior toward Maggie, but on the other, they reduce Maggie to a counter in their own conflict.

At the end of part 4, however, Morrison has Twyla reflect on Roberta's memories and accusations. After concluding that she cannot be sure about Maggie's race, Twyla goes on and achieves a remarkable epiphany:

> It dawned on me that the truth was already there, and Roberta knew it. I didn't kick her; I didn't join in with the gar girls and kick that lady, but I sure did want to. We watched and never tried to help her and never called for help. Maggie was my dancing mother. Deaf, I thought, and dumb. Nobody inside. Nobody who would hear you if you cried in the night. Nobody who could tell you anything important that you could use. Rocking, dancing, swaying as she walked. And when the gar girls pushed her down, and started roughhousing, I knew she wouldn't scream, couldn't—just like me—and I was glad about that. (259–60)

Twyla can know that Roberta already knows the truth because of their experience as a social mind. But the rest of the passage highlights Twyla's internalist perspective, her individual mind, and her realization that Maggie was a stand-in for her mother.

In addition, the triple source-tracking works like this: if Twyla is black, then the source of her identification with Maggie's powerlessness is her race, her class, and her gender; if Twyla is white, then the source of her identification is her class and her gender. Morrison's meta-communication is about the similarities among racial, class, ability, and gender bias. At the same time,

Morrison guides her rhetorical readers to recognize that Twyla's epiphany is itself limited because it uses Maggie as what Mitchell and Snyder call a narrative prosthesis. Twyla has made Maggie the key to her epiphany about her own feelings of powerlessness and resentment, but she has failed to give Maggie her own distinctive selfhood. If Morrison were to fully endorse Twyla's epiphany, then she too would also be using Maggie as a narrative prosthesis, but her canny awareness of the complex interactions of identity markers, an awareness that underlies all of "Recitatif," is ample warrant that she withholds a full endorsement.

In part 5, Morrison gives Roberta a speech that strongly echoes this passage as it reveals Roberta's own internalist perspective on Maggie. Roberta admits that although she really did think Maggie was black, she now cannot be sure. And she goes on:

> And because she couldn't talk—well, you know, I thought she was crazy. She'd been brought up in an institution like my mother was and like I thought I would be too. And you were right. We didn't kick her. It was the gar girls. Only them. But, well, I wanted to. I really wanted them to hurt her. I said we did it, too. You and me, but that's not true. . . . It was just that I wanted to do it so bad that day—wanting to is doing it. (261)

Roberta's perspective parallels but does not merge with Twyla's, and that parallel emphasizes both their similarity (each displaced her feelings about her mother onto Maggie) and their separateness (each came to the recognition of her feelings on her own). Roberta's withdrawal of her accusation and Twyla's recognition of the parallel prepares the way for the story's ending, in which they take steps back toward re-forming their intermental unit. But before I examine those steps, I want to examine a curious feature of the passage communicating Twyla's epiphany.

There is a revealing glitch in that passage, but, like the instances of impossibilities and implausibilities that I examined in chapter 2, it is one that most readers are not likely to notice—or to be bothered by when it is pointed out. The implausibility here is a logico-temporal one that becomes visible once we notice that Twyla has now, without comment, replaced her earlier report that "Maggie fell down" with the account that the gar girls pushed Maggie down and then kicked her. Since Twyla the character comes to accept this account before Twyla the narrator begins telling, and since Twyla the narrator is a retrospective non-self-conscious narrator, Twyla the narrator ought never to have reported that Maggie fell.[8] Morrison's use of the present tense at the time of reporting only magnifies the implausibility: "I think it was the day before Maggie fell down . . ." (246). Twyla the narrator should either give her perspective at the time of the telling or her perspective at the time of the action—or indicate how her perspective has altered over time. Here she purports to be giving her perspective at the time of the telling ("I think"), but it turns out that she is actually giving a perspective she adopted at some unspecified point between the time of the action (when she witnessed what happened) and the time of the telling (when she accepts what she witnessed). Why are actual readers likely not to notice this implausibility, and why does Morrison need it?

Readers are not likely to notice the glitch primarily because Morrison relies on the Rule of Temporal Decoding along with the Meta-Rules of Dominant Focus and of Value Added. More specifically, when Morrison's audience comes upon Twyla's initial report that Maggie fell, they do not know that Twyla is distorting what she knows. Moreover, when Twyla silently shifts to the new account, Morrison has directed her audience's focus to the content of Twyla's epiphany about the relation between her mother and Maggie. In other words, Morrison has directed her audience's attention away from one aspect of source-tracking (does the source tell a consistent story?) to some crucial content of that story.

As for the Value Added Meta-Rule, Morrison needs the implausibility because it is crucial to the way she constructs the progression. Both the textual and readerly dynamics derive much of their power from the way Morrison constructs Twyla's epiphany as the story's first (and limited) climax. If Morrison let Twyla's narration be guided by a strict temporal and mimetic logic, she would have had Twyla report something like the following: "I think it was the day before Maggie got pushed down and kicked by the older girls, while Roberta and I watched, wanting to join in because we each saw our mothers in Maggie—I think it was that day that we found out our mothers were coming to visit." Such a passage would show Morrison sacrificing effective storytelling on the altar of mimetic logic, because it would spoil not only the climactic nature of the epiphany but also the readerly suspense surrounding Twyla's and Roberta's contested claims about what happened to Maggie in the orchard. No reader would want Morrison to make that trade, and therefore no rhetorical theorist would either.

After Roberta's confession, Twyla reaches out to her and Roberta responds once more:

---

8. She also ought not to have reported that fear of the gar girls kept her and Roberta from helping, since fear is only part of the story. For the sake of clarity, however, I will focus just on her report of the event itself.

"Did I tell you? My mother, she never did stop dancing."

"Yes. You told me. And mine, she never got well." Roberta lifted her hands from the tabletop and covered her face with her palms. When she took them away she really was crying. "Oh shit, Twyla. Shit, shit, shit. What the hell happened to Maggie?" (261)

The close juxtaposition of Twyla's epiphany and Roberta's confession and then this final interchange show that the two women have taken steps toward forming a new, more mature dyad. By repeating what they already know about their mothers, they each reaffirm their shared vulnerability. Then Roberta's moment of what Zunshine calls embodied transparency (*Getting Inside* 21–25)—Roberta's tears, her swearing, and her final question give Twyla (and Morrison's audience) clear access to her anguish and regret—has the potential to take them to the next step. Roberta is willing to show even more vulnerability as she seeks guidance from Twyla in a way that she has never done before.

Morrison adds to the significance of Roberta's embodied transparency by implicitly contrasting it with her attempt to hide her mental state at the end of the scene in Howard Johnson's. Twyla responds to Roberta's disrespect by asking about her mother, and Roberta lies by saying "Fine" with a "grin [that] cracked her whole face" (250). Furthermore, Morrison builds multiple layers into Roberta's final question. It is—finally—a genuine question about Maggie because Roberta can think of her as someone with her own distinct identity. But it is also a question about their mothers, about why they could not take care of their children. And, given the way Maggie has come to be so significant to their dyad, it is a question about what happened to their friendship, a question that invites a commitment to improve it.

Still, Morrison does not take them beyond these first few steps, and, given their fraught history as well as the way the story has emphasized the multiple factors beyond themselves that influence that history, the ending raises more questions than it resolves. How does Twyla respond to Roberta now and in the future? Will Twyla share her epiphany with Roberta or keep it to herself? Will the women perhaps succeed in reestablishing their social mind, if only for a short time? Is this moment the closest they will ever get? Such is the difficulty of the divide that they are trying to bridge that Morrison's decision to leave these questions open seems just right.

A FINAL REFLECTION: while I staunchly believe that combining the cognitive and rhetorical approaches has offered insights into "Recitatif" that neither approach could have offered alone, I also realize that I have deployed cognitive theory as a very helpful Robin to my rhetorical Batman. I have done so not because I think cognitive theory must always be the junior partner in any collaboration with rhetorical theory but because the issues and problems I identified in "Recitatif" seemed to respond best to such a relationship. I have no doubt that my identification of those issues and problems was influenced by my rhetorical commitment. But this recognition also leads me to expect that cognitive theorists—or rhetorical theorists!—will identify issues and problems in narrative texts that respond best to relationships in which cognitive theory plays the role of Batman and rhetorical theory the role of Robin.[9] And as rhetorical and cognitive theorists continue to engage with each other's work, I expect that on some occasions they will form a social mind whose separate parts cannot be so easily distinguished.

---

9. See Rabinowitz, "Toward a Theory of Cognitive Flavor" for an example.

CHAPTER 9

Conversational and Authorial Disclosure in Dialogue Narrative

GEORGE HIGGINS'S *THE FRIENDS OF EDDIE COYLE* AND JOHN O'HARA'S "APPEARANCES"

> Reading is not a spectator sport . . . it is a participatory event.
> —GEORGE V. HIGGINS, *ON WRITING* (109)

THIS CHAPTER moves from the focus on character narrators to one on characters as the somebodies who tell. It picks up the discussion in chapter 1 about the way authors use character-character dialogue as both events and modes of telling in order to accomplish their purposes. It also expands the discussion in chapter 2 of how readerly dynamics influence textual dynamics. Returning to my example from chapter 1, George V. Higgins's *The Friends of Eddie Coyle,* and then turning to John O'Hara's intriguing short story "Appearances," I further develop the distinction between *conversational disclosure* (what characters communicate to each other in a scene of dialogue) and *authorial disclosure* (what authors communicate to their audiences through the conversational disclosures). In addition, I highlight a resource that follows from that distinction, *authorial disclosure across conversations* (what authors communicate to their audiences by means of the links between and among the scenes of dialogue). Authorial disclosures across conversations are the core features of the art of the dialogue novel. They are crucial not only to the dynamics of character-audience relationships (do characters know more than audiences or vice versa? and what follows ethically and affectively from these epistemological relationships?) but also to the activity of the authorial and actual audiences. It is authorial disclosure across conversations that transforms the experience of reading dialogue-narrative, in the words of my epigraph, from a spectator sport to a participatory event. At the same time, authorial disclosures across conversations are another site where the role of the unfolding responses of the audience influence the developing construction of a narrative. Authors rely on the inferences their audiences make on the basis of earlier scenes of dialogue in their construction of subsequent scenes. In other words, the underlying logic of the construction of a later scene resides in (a) the details of the character-character relationship in interaction with the specific occasion of the dialogue, (b) the author's assessment of what the audience has inferred from previous conversations, and (c) the author's assessment of what the audience needs to infer from this new scene.

Both Higgins and O'Hara follow one typical trajectory of authorial disclosure across conversations: characters initially know more than the audience, then audiences catch up and there is considerable overlap in their relevant knowledge of the key events and issues of the narrative, and by the end, the audience knows much more about those events and issues than any one character. This pattern also allows the implied author to engage the audience in epistemological questions of just how much and how firmly they—and the characters—know. In other words, the pattern invites both interpretive challenges for the audience and play with degrees of ambiguity. At the same time, in employing this pattern, the implied author can use the unfolding readerly dynamics—the authorial audience's responses to both the shifts in knowledge and to the developing affective and ethical dimensions of the progression—to inform their construction of the later authorial disclosures. In addition, how the implied author handles this trajectory of revelation has a major effect on the ethics of the telling. My analysis of the two narratives shall focus on demonstrating the different ways Higgins and O'Hara deploy the pattern and the larger consequences of each one's deployment for the implied author–authorial audience relationships in their narratives.

CONVERSATIONAL AND AUTHORIAL DISCLOSURES IN *THE FRIENDS OF EDDIE COYLE*

As noted in chapter 1, *The Friends of Eddie Coyle* consists of thirty chapters, each devoted to a scene of dialogue (or a small set of such scenes) presented in chronological order. Higgins typically restricts his narrator to the tasks of delivering basic exposition, identifying speakers, and reporting key events in a straightforward, matter-of-fact manner. He refrains from using the narrator to make connections across scenes or to do more than minimal interpretation of the events. As a result, the task of discerning the trajectory and coherence of the larger narrative falls to Higgins's audience. To be sure, Higgins gives rhetorical readers a great deal of *indirect* guidance, and here I shall expand on my analysis in chapter 1 by focusing on two of his main methods, each associated with a different central character. In the first method, deployed in the presentation of Eddie Coyle, the authorial and conversational disclosures combine to reveal an increasingly clear view of the character and his situation, and rhetorical readers need to relate those disclosures to the developing progression. In the second method, deployed in the presentation of Eddie's so-called friend, the saloon keeper Dillon, the conversational disclosures initially dominate the authorial disclosures and misdirect Higgins's audience's understanding of the character and his role in the progression. Only gradually do the authorial disclosures overtake and subsume the initial conversational disclosures, and when they do, they lead Higgins's rhetorical readers to some substantial reconfigurations of the progression. But before I move to detailed analysis of these two methods, I need to provide two additional contexts: (a) Higgins's reputation for composing authentic dialogue and (b) a broader theoretical discussion of communication through dialogue.

HIGGINS'S DIALOGUE

Although literary critics have not paid much attention to *Eddie Coyle*, other crime novelists hold Higgins's narrative and its dialogue in high esteem. (A search with the key words "*Higgins*" and "*The Friends of Eddie Coyle*" in the MLA International Bibliography in February 2017 turns up only four entries, two by me, one of which is an earlier version of this analysis.)[1] As I mentioned in chapter 1, Denis Lehane calls *Eddie Coyle* "the game-changing crime novel of the last fifty years" (vii), and Elmore Leonard goes so far as to declare it the "best crime novel ever written," one that "makes *The Maltese Falcon* read like Nancy Drew" (vii). Both Leonard and Lehane also single out Higgins's dialogue as crucial to the novel's success. Leonard, after noting the "authenticity" of Higgins's dialogue, employs the principle that imitation is the highest form of flattery: "Five years after *Eddie Coyle*, a *New York Times* review of one of my books said that I 'often cannot resist a set piece—a lowbrow aria with a crazy kind of scatological poetry of its own—in the Higgins manner.' And that's how you learn, by imitating" (vii). Lehane simply indulges in good old-fashioned hyperbole:

---

1. William Vesterman offers many astute observations about the style of Higgins's dialogue as well as some insightful observations on the opening chapter. Peter Wolfe's *Havoc in the Hub* offers an intelligent overview of Higgins's corpus. His chapter on *Eddie Coyle* is compatible with my argument, but his focus is primarily thematic. The other essay by me is a companion piece to this analysis ("Voice, Tone").

Ah, the dialogue. It takes up a good eighty percent of the novel, and you wouldn't mind if it took up the full hundred. No one, before or since, has ever written dialogue this scabrous, this hysterically funny, this pungently authentic—not Elmore Leonard, . . . not Richard Price, not even George V. Higgins himself [. . .]. Open any page of this book and you will find vast riches of the spoken word. . . . In most novels, talk is the salt and plot is the meal. In *The Friends of Eddie Coyle,* talk *is* the meal. It's also the plot, the characters, the action, the whole shebang. (ix–x)

I wholeheartedly agree that Higgins's dialogue deserves plaudits. Indeed, like Vladimir Nabokov's style in *Lolita,* it provides an excellent example of a well-crafted part of a narrative that offers substantial aesthetic pleasure independent of its contributions to the evolving progression. This pleasure arises from the very display of such colorful speech, from the Bakhtinian heteroglossia within and across conversations, and more generally from Higgins's performance as the composer of it all, including the "lowbrow arias." Different readers will have their own favorite passages. Here are just a few of mine: Eddie's telling the gun dealer Jackie Brown in the very first chapter what it was like to get his fingers slammed in a drawer, an aria that ends with "Ever hear bones breaking? Just like a man snapping a shingle. Hurts like a bastard" (5). Eddie's metaphor to describe the magazine of a gun: "Got a mouth on her like the Sumner Tunnel" (21). Jackie Brown's line, "This life's hard, but it's harder if you're stupid" (78). And this exchange between Eddie and Dave Foley, an enforcement agent for the U.S. Treasury: Eddie talks about buying skis to take on his trip to New Hampshire for his sentencing hearing after his conviction for transporting stolen whiskey. Eddie: "I figure as long as I got to go up there I might as well make a weekend out of it, you know? Think we'll have snow by then?" Foley: "I think we're getting some right now" (12). The dialogue is often so arresting that it is easy to get stuck on the idea of its "authenticity," but I shall resist that impulse here as I focus on how Higgins uses it to communicate with his audience.

DIALOGUE AND THE DIALOGUE NOVEL; OR CONVERSATION AS NARRATION

In *Living to Tell about It,* I argue that character narration is an art of indirection, one in which an implied author designs a single text to fulfill the different communicative purposes of at least two tellers (implied author and character narrator) addressing at least two audiences (narratee and authorial audience). As I noted in chapter 1, character-character dialogue is an even more complex art of indirection than character narration, since it entails additional speakers with different purposes (implied author and at least two characters), and since the implied author *must simultaneously motivate each character's speech within its mimetic context and within that of his or her own communicative purpose.*[2] Furthermore, sometimes that mimetic context means that the characters themselves will seek to disguise their purposes or otherwise attempt to deceive their interlocutors. In the exchange between Eddie Coyle and Dave Foley about skis and snow, Higgins motivates Eddie's speech in his desire to persuade Foley that he regards the sentencing hearing as no big deal, and Higgins motivates Foley's in his interest in letting Eddie know that he sees through the act. At the same time, Higgins communicates to his audience that Eddie has a lot of anxiety about the hearing and that Foley not only has the upper hand in their exchange but also has no hesitation about reminding Eddie of that fact. Strikingly, however, Higgins depicts Dillon as better able to disguise his conversational purposes, and consequently, both Foley and Higgins's rhetorical readers initially remain in the dark about them.

Just as narrators perform three main tasks—*reporting* about characters, settings, and events; *interpreting* those reports; and *evaluating* them—so too do characters, though sometimes authors will package these communications to their audiences with characters' more pointed exchanges with their interlocutors. To put this point another way, sometimes in dialogue the reporting, interpreting, and evaluating will be direct and at others it will be indirect. Eddie Coyle launches into his aria about getting the bones in his hand broken as a way to impress upon Jackie Brown the importance of obtaining guns that can't be traced, but Higgins also uses it to communicate to his rhetorical readers two additional points: (a) Eddie already has one strike against him with the higher-ups in the mob, and (b) however much Eddie acts superior with Jackie, he is ultimately a small cog on a bigger wheel, a cog that cannot afford another malfunction. Jackie's line about this life being hard is both an interpretation and an evaluation that reveals his own commitment to the values of toughness and intelligence. Over the course of the narrative, Higgins communicates his general endorsement of Jackie's statement—though Higgins has a broader view of "this life." In addition, Higgins also indicates, in one of his many ironic strokes, that Jackie has himself been stupid for boasting to Eddie about his deal to sell machine guns and then later letting Eddie see the guns themselves.

---

2. I am describing the default situation. Of course authors can deviate from the default for particular purposes, and in such cases, the effects of the authorial disclosure will depend in part on the audience's recognition of the deviation.

This discussion of dialogue as in part an art of indirection has already begun to illuminate the distinction between conversational disclosure and authorial disclosure. This distinction enables us not only to identify the two tracks of communication in any dialogue but also to analyze the relationship between those tracks. This relationship can vary widely, from minimal distance (in cases where the implied author uses a character as a reliable spokesperson for his views) to maximal distance (in cases where the implied author communicates messages that run counter to the facts, interpretations, and ethical evaluations the characters deliver in the dialogue). Implied authors have multiple ways of signaling their distance: they can place clues in the conversation itself, and they can establish particular characters as unreliable reporters, interpreters, or evaluators so that whenever they speak, the audience's default assumption is that there's something off-kilter about their communication. In addition, as noted above, implied authors frequently use a series of conversational disclosures as the basis for authorial disclosure in a new dialogue: in other words, in any given dialogue, the authorial disclosure may exceed the conversational disclosure as a result of knowledge that the implied author and audience share and that the participants in the conversation do not. As a novel progresses, this kind of authorial disclosure across conversations is likely to increase precisely because the author has more previous conversations to draw upon.

As noted above, conversational disclosure itself is often far from straightforward. Strikingly, Higgins himself is on the record praising the dialogue in "Appearances" because O'Hara does not make the motives of his characters transparent (*On Writing* 120–21). Conversational disclosure will exceed authorial disclosure when the mimetic context makes it clear that one or more of the characters possesses knowledge that the implied author has not (or not yet) disclosed to his audience. For example, in chapter 3 of *Eddie Coyle,* Eddie asks his interlocutor, identified here only as "the second man" but later revealed to be Jimmy Scalisi, where he'd like to pick up the guns Eddie will supply him. Eddie: "Same place?" Scalisi: "I think that's going to be a little out of my way tomorrow" (23). Both Eddie and Scalisi know which place they're referring to, but Higgins does not bother to invent a way to tell his audience. For Higgins, that specific information is less important than the fact that Scalisi can't get there and so makes a plan for them to leave messages for each other at Dillon's bar—and in that way bring them within Dillon's orbit. In cases of authorial disclosure across conversations, the implied author relies on the audience to track the relationships between and among conversations (convergences, complementarities, divergences, contradictions, and so on) and to draw the appropriate inferences. For example, in chapter 23 of *Eddie Coyle,* when Dave

Foley tells Dillon, "I don't really know very much about [Coyle's New Hampshire] case" (148), Higgins relies on his audience's prior knowledge of Foley's discussions with Coyle to communicate something very different, namely, that Foley does not trust Dillon enough to share his knowledge.

Once we attend to the relationships between authorial disclosure and conversational disclosure in *Eddie Coyle,* we can recognize that Higgins's skill with the dialogue is at least as much about his management of those relationships as it is with his ability to make the dialogue sound "authentic." It is this skill, I suggest, that Lehane is responding to in his hyperbolic claim that in *Eddie Coyle* the dialogue is "the whole shebang."

TEXTUAL DYNAMICS IN *EDDIE COYLE*

Although Eddie is the protagonist, the textual dynamics indicate that Higgins is constructing a network novel. That is, Eddie's fate is inextricably tied to events, including the flow of information, and judgments by people in two larger networks in which he participates: (a) the Boston crime network, involving gun dealers, bank robbers, some other small-time players like himself, the initially enigmatic Dillon, and ultimately the head of the regional Mafia, and (b) the New England law enforcement network, involving U.S. Treasury agents like Foley, the Boston police, the Massachusetts State Police, and the district attorney in New Hampshire. In addition, the very structure of the telling—the thirty discrete scenes of dialogue—can be understood as a network of disclosure that reinforces the novel's interest in networks and the flow of information within and across them. The textual dynamics show that although different characters have different degrees of knowledge about the links in the larger networks, no single character has a comprehensive knowledge of those links, something that has major consequences for Eddie, as a sketch of the plot dynamics will reveal.

In the first three chapters, Higgins shows Eddie making three deals: one with Jackie Brown to buy some guns, one with Foley to inform on Jackie, and one with Jimmy Scalisi to sell the guns at a nice profit. By the end of the third chapter, Higgins has clearly established Eddie's character and shown his connections to the two different networks, with the crime network itself having two distinct branches. By the end of the third chapter, Higgins has launched the progression by intertwining Eddie's three deals and indicating that Eddie's facing jail time is one global instability and the question of whether he can walk the tightrope between the different networks is another. The ensuing chapters trace multiple complications. Jimmy Scalisi uses the guns he gets from Eddie for a series of well-executed bank robberies. Meanwhile, Dillon has his own meetings with Foley at which he reveals that Eddie and Scalisi have been working together on some unspecified activities. Although Eddie does inform on Jackie, the New Hampshire prosecutor tells Foley that's not sufficient to keep Eddie out of jail. Eddie thus has to decide whether to inform on Scalisi, and he goes so far as to set up a meeting with Foley. But before they can meet, Scalisi and his crew get caught because they have been informed on by Scalisi's girlfriend, Wanda, who wants payback for Scalisi's disrespectful treatment of her. In the gunplay accompanying the arrest, the protégé of the Mafia boss gets killed, and the boss wants his own payback. The word circulates through the mob that Eddie must have made the deal he'd only been contemplating. Therefore, the boss hires Dillon to eliminate Eddie, a job Dillon skillfully executes. In the final chapter, as I noted in my discussion in chapter 1, a prosecutor and a defense lawyer discuss Jackie's case and his probable fate as someone who will be in and out of the official legal system repeatedly in the coming years.

HIGGINS AND EDDIE; OR, AUTHORIAL AND CONVERSATIONAL DISCLOSURE IN CHAPTER 2

I turn now to readerly dynamics by examining Higgins's first method of providing indirect guidance to his audience's efforts to configure the narrative. I will look most closely at the conversation between Eddie and Foley at the end of chapter 2, but it will be helpful first to reconstruct the context provided by chapter 1. Since Eddie is turning to Jackie for the first time, his deal immediately places Eddie in a new network involving Jackie, his suppliers, and Jackie's other customers. Although, at twenty-six, Jackie is young, he is confident and tough—already a hard case. He is not at all intimidated by Eddie's story about his broken fingers. Shortly after hearing it, he says, "I got guns to sell. . . . I done a lot of business and I had very few complaints. I can get you four-inchers and two-inchers. You just tell me what you want. I can deliver it" (7). In addition, Jackie holds his own in the negotiation with Eddie about the price of the guns. But Jackie makes a young man's mistake when he brags to Eddie about selling machine guns.

As I noted above, Higgins uses Eddie's story about his broken fingers to initiate his audience into his handling of the relationship between conversational and authorial disclosure (as Eddie warns Jackie, Higgins also marks Eddie as a small-timer in a vulnerable position). Nevertheless, throughout his dialogue with Jackie, Eddie comes off as appropriately careful, as knowledgeable about why Jackie can be so confident ("You got somebody in the plant" [7])—and as curious about Jackie's other customers. When Jackie boasts that he has someone interested in machine guns, Eddie asks, "What color was he?" (8). Jackie's youth and his unproven status with Eddie in combination with Eddie's story about his broken fingers establish the initial instability: can Eddie trust Jackie? At the same time, because the conversational disclosure does not extend to why Eddie wants to buy guns—he doesn't tell, and Jackie doesn't ask, since the use of the guns is not relevant to their deal—Higgins constructs a tension of unequal knowledge: he and Eddie know, and we readers, unlike Jackie, want to know.

In the second chapter, the audience learns that Eddie is about a month away from his sentencing hearing and that he desperately wants to avoid a return to jail. As he says to Foley, "I got three kids and a wife at home, and I can't afford to do no more time. . . . Hell, I'm almost forty-five years old" (13). Higgins's skill is especially on display in the closing exchange, as he immediately complicates both the instability from chapter 1 and the global instability.

"Yeah," the stocky man said. "Suppose you had a reliable informer that put you onto a colored gentleman that was buying some machine guns. Army machine guns, M-sixteens. Would you want a fellow like that, that was helping you like that, would you want him to go to jail and embarrass his kids and all?"

"Let me put it this way," the agent said, "if I was to get my hands on the machine guns *and* the colored gentleman *and* the fellow that was selling the machine guns, and if that happened because somebody put me in the right place at the right time with maybe a warrant, I wouldn't mind saying to somebody else that the fellow who put me there was helping uncle. Does the colored gentleman have any friends?"

"I wouldn't be surprised," the stocky man said. "Thing is, I just found out about it yesterday."

"How'd you find out?" the driver said.

"Well, one thing and another," the stocky man said. "You know how it is, you're talking to somebody and he says something and the next fellow says something, and the first thing you know, you heard something."

"When's it supposed to come off?" the driver said.

"I'm not sure yet," the stocky man said. "See, I'm right on the button with this one, I come to you soon as I heard it. I got more things to find out, if you're—if you think you might be interested. I think a week or so. Why don't I call you?"

"Okay," the driver said. "Do you need anything else?"

"I need a good leaving alone," the stocky man said. "I'd as soon not have anybody start thinking about me too much on this detail. I don't want nobody following me around, all right?"

"Okay," the driver said, "we'll do it your way. You call me when you get something, if you do, and if I get something, I'll put it in front of the U.S. Attorney. If I don't, all bets're off. Understood?"

The stocky man nodded.

"Merry Christmas," the driver said. (15–16)

In the first part of this passage, the conversational disclosure is straight-forward: Eddie wants to know whether informing on Jackie (though of course he does not name him) and his customer will persuade Foley to put in a good word for him in New Hampshire, and Foley makes it clear how much information he would need. The authorial disclosure, however, communicates a discrepancy between what Eddie thinks Foley is promising him and what Foley actually promises. Eddie wants a stay-out-of-jail card and thinks Foley is telling him that supplying the information will get him one, but Foley promises only to say "something to somebody" about Eddie "helping uncle"—even as Foley emphasizes how much information he needs. Higgins conveys the discrepancy by showing that Eddie does not at all pick up on it. He does not object to Foley's requirements or ask for a greater guarantee but instead allows Foley to steer the direction of the conversation with the next two questions (about who else and when). Eddie is all too ready to mistake Foley's limited promise for something greater. Foley, of course, is aware of what he is and is not promising. In communicating the discrepancy to his rhetorical readers, Higgins is also complimenting them on being smarter than Eddie.

Additional significant authorial disclosure comes from reading across the conversations in chapter 1 and chapter 2. This disclosure leads to our first reconfiguration of the plot dynamics. We now see that Eddie's question to Jackie, "What color was he?," was motivated by more than idle curiosity or even knee-jerk racism. Indeed, Higgins invites rhetorical readers to recognize that Eddie has initiated this meeting with Foley precisely because of Jackie's mention of this potential customer, and thus, the whole conversation in chapter 2, including Eddie's posturing about buying skis, and then later Foley's opining that Eddie could be facing up to five years in jail, has been leading up to this moment.[3] The first reconfiguration involves our understanding of

---

3. The earlier conversation also provides an excellent lesson in how to use conversational disclosure for the authorial disclosure of necessary background: Higgins uses Eddie's protestations of innocence and Foley's skepticism as the mechanism for conveying the facts of Eddie's crime and its likely consequences to us. In this regard, Higgins is more skillful than O'Hara,

the instability in Eddie's relation to Jackie Brown: it's not just a question of whether Eddie can trust Jackie but also a question of whether Eddie can *use* Jackie. Even as Eddie schools Jackie in the importance of Eddie's being able to trust him, Eddie begins looking for a way to exploit Jackie for his own advantage. This reconfiguration introduces a pattern of ironic reversals that will become increasingly significant as the narrative continues.

Reading across the conversations also leads rhetorical readers to recognize a third authorial disclosure: Eddie has jumped to unwarranted conclusions—or at least to the conclusions that he thinks will be most attractive to Foley—with his reference to a "colored gentleman," since Jackie never answered his question about race. This jump highlights the casual racism underlying his assumption either that the purchaser must be connected with the Black Panthers (Higgins here taps into the paranoia about the Black Panthers that existed in the late 1960s and early 1970s) or that Foley would be more interested if that were the connection. More than that, it highlights how eager Eddie is to have something to offer Foley. This disclosure, along with Eddie's willingness to overlook the limits of Foley's promise, conveys how much the looming presence of the sentencing hearing affects Eddie's behavior.

In the second part of the passage—from Foley's question, "Does the colored gentleman have any friends?," to the end—the conversation unfolds as a kind of sparring match, with Foley on offense and Eddie on defense, until Foley decides to let up on Eddie and give him some breathing room. Again, it is helpful to look at the conversational disclosures in light of each speaker's purpose. Foley's questions (who else and when) indicate that he wants to know how solid and how detailed Eddie's information is, while Eddie's speculative and evasive answers indicate that he does not have specifics and that he is primarily interested in knowing what Foley would be willing to do for him, if he could provide those details. Foley's shift to asking, "Do you need anything else?" suggests that he understands the relation between what Eddie wants and what Eddie knows. The more natural follow-up to Eddie's "the first thing you know, you heard something," would be "Did you hear anything else?" By asking instead, "Do you need anything else?," Foley implies that he knows Eddie does not have any more information and that he has already given Eddie a lot of what he needs to get more, namely the appropriate incentive. Finally, by ending with his ironic "Merry Christmas," a wish that Eddie conspicuously does not return, Foley reminds Eddie of who has the upper hand.

---

whose initial exchanges between Lois and Howard Ambrie seem less fully motivated by the mimetic context than by the need to disclose necessary information to the audience.

For his part, Eddie plays good defense, and indeed, his skill suggests that he has at least some awareness of Foley's purposes. Eddie's remark, "I wouldn't be surprised [about others] . . . [but] I just found out" both makes the information potentially more valuable and allows him to back off from promising too much. His "I'm right on the button with this one" is as good a play as he can make, given how little he knows, and given that earlier in the conversation Foley had chided him for delivering information too late to be useful. Finally, his "I need a good leaving alone" is an even better play, since it gives him the room to maneuver that he wants.

Since Foley and Eddie exhibit this awareness of each other's purposes, the conversational and authorial disclosures overlap to a large degree. But again, reading across the conversations adds a layer to the authorial disclosure. While Eddie puts his request for a good leaving alone in terms of "this detail," we know from chapter 1 that he wants to keep doing his other business with Jackie. Foley, as Higgins's audience soon learns, is smart enough to know that Eddie has additional reasons for wanting to be left alone, but, unlike those readers, Foley does not know what they are. This authorial disclosure has the additional important consequence of adding another complication to the developing instabilities: can Eddie simultaneously succeed in his new criminal operation and escape the impending jail sentence by cozying up to law enforcement? In other words, the instabilities now include whether Eddie will be able to successfully juggle his relationships in these different networks.

By establishing significant parallels between chapter 1 and chapter 2—in each, Eddie negotiates a deal with one other person outside his own immediate network—Higgins's authorial disclosure across the chapters guides rhetorical readers to additional aspects of configuration and reconfiguration. First, those readers can recognize the rough equivalence between the commodities of exchange in each deal: guns and money, on the one hand, and information and influence, on the other. Second, with regard to affect and ethics, rhetorical readers recognize that in this world, interpersonal relationships are built primarily on self-interest. At best, the ethics governing interpersonal relationships are those referred to in the phrase "It ain't personal, it's just business." Eddie needs guns, Jackie needs buyers, they negotiate a price. Eddie needs a break, Foley needs information, they negotiate a deal. But at worst, the interpersonal relationships are ones in which self-interest is so strong that other people get reduced to objects that can be used for one's own benefit. The most obvious example is Eddie's eagerness to use Jackie to stay out of jail. Although Eddie and Foley are not exploiting each other in this way, each is less interested in what he can do for the other than in what the other can do for him. Eddie is not a good citizen out to help law enforcement, but rather a crook wanting to know just how much information he has to give Foley in order for Foley to make the call to New Hampshire. For his part, Foley wants as much information as possible in exchange for doing as little as possible for Eddie. If Eddie misses this dimension of the deal, Foley is not going to point that out. Later, after Eddie does turn in Jackie and the New Hampshire U.S. attorney tells Foley that's not good enough to affect the sentencing, Foley reminds the distraught Eddie that he only promised to make the call and that Eddie ought to grow up. As Jackie says, "This life's hard, but it's harder if you're stupid" (78).

Higgins uses these authorial disclosures through the conversations and the restricted role of the narrator to establish his own—and his audience's—affective distance from the characters and the action. Eddie's plight has the potential to make him a sympathetic character, but Higgins's own clear-eyed portrayal of Eddie's participation in the ethics of exploitation renders Eddie unsympathetic. Higgins's audience does not attach in any powerfully affective way to any of the characters, even as that audience is drawn in to the complexity of Eddie's situation and his effort to stay on the tightrope. The implied Higgins emerges as a dispassionate examiner of Eddie and the world in which he moves. Higgins projects neither affection nor disdain for his characters but instead a clear-eyed view of this world's values—self-interest, money, information—and the way they intersect and interfere with each other. The greatest effect of this clear-eyed view is that it fuels Higgins's penchant for irony, a point I'll return to below.

HIGGINS AND DILLON

Dillon appears as a speaker in chapters 6, 11, 23, 26, 28, and 29, and he appears as the subject of other people's conversations in chapters 3, 14, and 24. All of these conversations are worthy of analysis, but I believe I can capture the key features of Higgins's communications by summarizing several and then looking more closely at a few. In chapters 6, 11, and 23, Higgins shows Dillon speaking with Foley about Eddie. Dillon's reports of Eddie's activities in and around Dillon's bar further complicate the instabilities associated with Eddie, since these reports raise Foley's suspicions about Eddie's current criminal activity. In addition, Higgins uses the structural similarity between the Eddie-Foley conversations (chapters 2, 16, 21, and 25) and the Dillon-Foley conversations—a member of the mob turns informer—to add an additional irony to Eddie's situation: the rat gets ratted on. Thus, part of the authorial disclosure is that Eddie is as mistaken in trusting Dillon as Jackie is in trusting Eddie. As for Dillon himself, his conversation in chapter 6 makes him appear to be even more beleaguered than Eddie, as he explains to Foley the fear that keeps him from testifying before the grand jury. The most salient relationship between authorial and conversational disclosure involves the connection between this conversation and the first mention of Dillon in chapter 3—Scalisi and Eddie say they hear something about Dillon and the grand jury that they don't like. The implication is that Dillon is going to testify. But once chapter 6 reveals that he is not, Higgins uses the authorial disclosure across conversations to reveal that the information that travels across the criminal network is not always reliable.

At the end of the conversation in chapter 6, Dillon gives Foley a teaser about Eddie, saying that Eddie and Jimmy Scalisi are calling his bar leaving messages for each other—but that he does not know what is actually going on. In chapter 11, he extends the tease with a dramatically told story about how distressed one of his customers is to get a message that Scalisi needs to talk to him about something important, revealing only at the end that the customer is Eddie. By chapter 23, Dillon has become much more assertive with Foley. After telling another story of Eddie's behavior at the bar—he displays a roll of bills and gives a few to somebody whom Dillon won't identify—he urges Foley to go and "think about how come a little fish has got a lot of money all of a sudden" (149).

Higgins also uses the structural parallel to highlight two major differences between the Eddie-Foley and the Dillon-Foley conversations: (1) Higgins makes Eddie's motive for informing on Jackie clear from the outset (Eddie wants his stay-out-of-jail card), but he does not disclose Dillon's motive for informing on Eddie. (2) Higgins uses Eddie's informing on Jackie to significantly complicate the global instability—Foley arrests Jackie, and his phone call to the New Hampshire prosecutor does not yield any clemency for Eddie—but Dillon's informing on Eddie does not have any such consequences. Although Foley uses the information to get himself transferred back from drug enforcement to monitoring the mob, he never gets enough evidence to go after either Eddie or Scalisi. As a result, Higgins uses these scenes to introduce and complicate a tension about Dillon's motives for telling. Higgins very slowly resolves this tension, as he gradually discloses the complexities of Dillon's character and his place in the crime network.

Dillon's growing assertiveness with Foley and Foley's own comments to his colleague Waters that he feels as if Dillon is playing him are part of Higgins's gradual revelation that Dillon is a far more artful poser with Foley than Eddie is. But the pivotal authorial disclosure comes in chapter 24, in a conversation between Scalisi and his partner Fritzie Webber as they drive to the bank job during which they get arrested.

[WEBBER]: "I wonder what the fuck it was got Dillon so stirred up then?"
[SCALISI]: "He was worried about Coyle. I believe him. He was wondering
if maybe Coyle was swapping us for that thing he's got going up in New
Hampshire, there." (151)

Although the conversation does not resolve the tension about Dillon's initial
motives for informing on Coyle, this authorial disclosure of Dillon's place in
the criminal network has a ripple effect on our reconfigurations. Rather than
being a marginal figure like Eddie, Dillon is well connected. He knows about
Scalisi's bank jobs, and he knows that Eddie also knows about them. (Eddie,
by contrast, does not know that Dillon knows about either Scalisi's operation
or his own involvement in it.) Dillon is not so obviously powerful that Scalisi
and Webber take his advice, since Scalisi reasons that even if Eddie is smart
enough to know about their operation, he has no way of knowing when and
where this job is.

Understanding Dillon's central place in the network also leads Higgins's
rhetorical readers to recognize another contrast between his conversations
with Foley and Eddie's with Foley. Eddie pretends to know more than he actually does in order to get what he wants from Foley. Dillon pretends to know
less than he does in the interest of keeping Foley on his side while also pro-
tecting himself and those he favors—a strategy that, however, makes Eddie a
sacrificial lamb. Higgins's rhetorical readers can recognize that in the chapter
23 conversation, both Dillon and Foley are pretending to know less than they
do in order to find out how much the other knows.

[DILLON]: "I think Eddie thinks probably he isn't gonna go to jail there, and
I wonder why he thinks that."
"I wonder where he got the money," Foley said. "That's what bothers me.
I always understood he was just getting by. I wonder what he's been doing
to get all that money." (149)

Dillon doesn't share Foley's wonder about where Eddie got the money because,
as we learn in the next chapter, Dillon knows that Eddie has been selling guns
to Scalisi. Foley doesn't share Dillon's wonder about why Eddie might think
he's not going to jail because Foley knows that he is going. But neither will
enlighten the other. Foley won't tell Dillon that Eddie tried and failed to get
the stay-out-of-jail card because he doesn't want Dillon to know that Eddie
is a fellow informer. Dillon won't tell Foley where Eddie got his wad of cash
because then he'd reveal that he is far more connected and knows way more
than he pretends to know.

At the same time, Higgins manages the authorial disclosure across conversations for an additional communication here, one he triggers through Dillon's speculation that Eddie was using his wad of money to buy "a color tee-vee" (147). Earlier, in chapter 18, Eddie, while commiserating with Scalisi about how difficult women can be, tells him that he hit the number and won $650 and that he changed his plans to buy his wife a color television with the money because she complained about a smoky oil burner when he came in the door the other night. Chapter 23 transforms this earlier conversational disclosure, a side comment to the more dramatic interchange between Dillon and Wanda, into the authorial disclosure that Dillon is wrong about what Eddie was doing with his money. Higgins's more general disclosure is that Dillon—and by extension, the network along which news travels in the underworld—are at least partly unreliable in their reports about characters and events and especially in their interpretations of them.

A little later, once Dillon accepts the job of killing Eddie, Higgins guides us to further reconfigure the events of chapter 23. As each character pursues his self-interest, Eddie remains in jeopardy. If Foley were to tell Dillon about Eddie's unsuccessful play for clemency, Dillon would have to revise his hypothesis that Eddie knows he's not going to jail. If Dillon were to tell Foley that Eddie's money comes from supplying guns to Scalisi and that he believes Eddie has informed on them, Foley would have reason to correct Dillon—and to pursue the arrests of Eddie and Scalisi. But since self-interest dominates here, as it does everywhere else in this world, Eddie becomes collateral damage.

In chapter 26, much of the remaining tension about Dillon's character gets swiftly resolved through conversational disclosure, as he talks with the mob boss's representative about eliminating Coyle and demands that he get to do the job on his own terms. But again, the conversation includes additional authorial disclosure that guides rhetorical readers' configuration and reconfiguration. The following excerpt comes after Dillon tells the rep that he tried to warn Scalisi about a possible informer:

"This guy," the man said, "anybody we know?"

"Could be," Dillon said. "We hadda break him up a while back here. He set up Billy Wallace there with a gun that had a history. We hadda teach him. I thought he learned his lesson. I threw a little work his way myself now and then."

"Name of Coyle?" the man said.

"That's the one," Dillon said. "I had him driving a truck for me and a fellow up in New Hampshire there and he got hooked with it. Which was why he was coming up. He didn't talk then, but he had a fall coming and he knew it. I thought maybe he was thinking about dumping me, but of course he wouldn't do that without making a will first. So I guess he dumped Jimmy and Artie instead. Bastard."

"He's the one the Scal mentioned," the man said. "LeDuc give his name to the man. Coyle. Eddie Fingers. That's the one."

"You want him hit?" Dillon said.

"The man wants him hit," the man said. (163)

Because rhetorical readers know from chapter 22 that Scalisi's girlfriend Wanda has done the informing, the authorial disclosure framing the whole scene is that Dillon is unreliably interpreting Eddie's role. Part of the reason, Higgins suggests, is that these men cannot even conceive that a woman would be responsible for anything happening in their world. In this respect, Higgins combines his depiction of the sexist assumptions of the criminal underworld, especially evident in the Scalisi-Wanda relationship ("My kid brother talks about his goddamned Mustang the same way you talk about me," she objects [110]), with his predilection for dramatic irony. This dimension of the scene also helps set up the authorial disclosures that arise from Higgins's juxtaposition of chapter 29, which recounts Dillon's extremely professional and efficient execution of Eddie, who goes to his grave thinking that Dillon is his friend, and chapter 30, which emphasizes the flaws in the way the official legal system will deal with Jackie Brown. As I discuss in more detail in chapter 1, the authorial disclosure across the chapters is that the flaws in the official system are ultimately preferable to those in the more efficient mob system.

There are other key authorial disclosures in this conversation in chapter 26. Dillon's interlocutor apparently takes Dillon's report about Coyle as confirmation of the information that Scalisi gave the mob lawyer LeDuc. But of course Scalisi's source is Dillon. Consequently, the authorial disclosure is that Dillon acts as *witness, prosecutor, judge, and eventually executioner* of Eddie. The simultaneous conversational and authorial disclosure that Dillon hired Eddie to drive the stolen whiskey subtracts several more degrees from Dillon's increasingly cold blood. Rather than feeling any responsibility for Eddie's plight or any sense of gratitude or loyalty for Eddie's taking the rap without informing on him, Dillon remains suspicious of him. Indeed, Eddie's getting "hooked" there and his earlier mistake with the traceable gun lead Dillon to think of him as less than fully trustworthy—and therefore expendable. It is this logic that underlies his conversations with Foley: let me trade the weak, mistake-prone Coyle for whatever protection Foley can give me. Poor Eddie, rhetorical readers now realize, never had a chance.

But to say "poor Eddie" is to overlook the knowledge that Eddie's self-interest has put him on the verge of doing what Dillon accuses him of doing. In that respect, Higgins's rhetorical readers have another layer of irony to add to their reconfiguration: Eddie takes the fall for Wanda's betrayal of Scalisi—but only because she beat him to the punch.

THE AFFECTIVE, THE ETHICAL, AND THE IMPLIED HIGGINS

Indeed, by the end of the novel, Higgins's dispassionate dissection of the interaction between self-interest and the unreliable flow of information across the criminal network leaves his audience with a highly negative view of that network not only because the criminals prey on law-abiding citizens but because they also prey on each other. It's not just Eddie who has no real friends, because the ethic of self-interest means that in this world, finally, it's every man for himself. This ethic of self-interest exists alongside a faith in information that travels along the network, but this faith is often misplaced. Foley and his colleagues do not live by the same ethic as the mob, but they, too, are hard cases who will use others for their own ends—even as they have only a limited success in achieving those ends. Higgins does not invite rhetorical readers to grow progressively more sympathetic or otherwise attached to Eddie, though Higgins does guide those readers to remain fascinated by the intricacies of the networks and to develop a grudging respect for those who are able to manage their own survival. Ultimately, the ethical and the affective dimensions of the progression lead back to the implied Higgins, who exposes the way this world works by letting his characters act and especially speak in pursuit of their own ends and then guiding rhetorical readers to share his dispassionate judgments of them. Higgins is not an implied author who endears himself to his audience through the affection he displays for his characters and his storyworld but rather one who commands his audience's respect for his clear-eyed, uncompromising vision of a Hobbesian world in which life for most is nasty, brutish, and short. Indeed, that uncompromising vision leads him—and his rhetorical readers—to the cold consolations of dramatic irony.

AUTHORIAL DISCLOSURES ACROSS CONVERSATIONS IN "APPEARANCES"

Higgins was himself an admirer of John O'Hara's use of dialogue, and, indeed, it was reading Higgins's comments in *On Writing* about "Appearances" that led me to the story (I'll have more to say about those comments below). O'Hara does not have space for any Higgins-like arias, and his dialogue calls far less attention to itself than Higgins's. Nevertheless, he is equally interested in developing the interplay between conversational disclosures, authorial disclosures, and authorial disclosures across conversations. Examining O'Hara's character-character dialogue will expand our understanding of how skillful authors can use this resource.

"Appearances" consists of three conversations among the members of the Ambrie family—husband, Howard; wife, Lois; and their divorced daughter, Amy—with each conversation involving only two of the characters: first Howard-Lois, then Howard-Amy, and finally, Lois-Amy. These conversations all occur one Friday night in the fall of 1961 (John F. Kennedy is in the White House and the book is published in 1962), though they refer to backstory involving the early years of Howard and Lois's marriage. O'Hara's arrangement of the sequence demonstrates how he adapts the typical pattern of character-audience relationships: while Howard and Lois know much more than the audience at the beginning of the first conversation, the audience knows much more than all three characters by the end of the third. In other words, while each character is simply participating in two conversations that take place on that Friday night, O'Hara indirectly constructs and his audience actively reconstructs a narrative that extends over a much longer time frame and culminates in the events of these three conversations. Furthermore, O'Hara's disclosures give intriguing nuance to the pattern: Lois and Amy share knowledge about the past that Howard does not have (or that they believe he does not have, a qualification I will return to), and then Lois refuses to share other knowledge when Amy asks her a leading question about the past. Thus, it seems that Lois knows the most, Amy the next most, and Howard, the character whom O'Hara begins with, the least. But the story is not called "Appearances" for nothing, because, as we shall see, it also gives the audience reason to question this apparent hierarchy. Both the questions and the more secure knowledge greatly influence our understanding of each character and of the Ambrie family as a whole.

"Appearances" begins with a brief passage of exposition that efficiently accomplishes several purposes: (1) it establishes Howard as the character whose experiences we initially track; (2) it locates the action on a clear, warm night; and (3) it identifies the Ambries as a well-to-do couple (they live in a house with a "porte-cochere") with an apparently careless daughter (she leaves the door of her MG open and the light on in the garage). In the first conversation, we continue tracking Howard and begin to track Lois, as the two of them discuss his plan to play golf in the morning rather than go to the funeral of his lifelong acquaintance, Jack Hill. In the second conversation, we continue to follow Howard and substitute Amy for Lois as our secondary interest, as father and daughter discuss why her marriage broke up and what her future holds. In the third conversation, we cease tracking Howard and shift over to tracking both Lois and Amy as they discuss why Howard never liked Jack Hill. Although there is no compelling reason within the logic of the characters' actions for the conversation between mother and daughter to follow rather than precede the one before father and daughter, the logic of O'Hara's communication to his audience makes this sequence the most effective. In other words, O'Hara recognizes that the interaction of textual and readerly dynamics is more powerful with this arrangement of the sequence. With the shift away from Howard in the third conversation, O'Hara makes his major moves to give the audience knowledge about events that Howard seems to have no access to. Those disclosures—that Amy's marriage broke up because she had an affair with Hill and that Amy suspects Lois had her own affair with Hill shortly after she married Howard—add layers to the authorial disclosures across conversations because they shed retrospective light, and, indeed, all but require the audience to reinterpret the previous conversational disclosures.

To put this point another way, because the plot dynamics proceed more through tensions than instabilities, and because the third dialogue is the one that partially resolves the tensions as it completes the authorial disclosure across conversations, the readerly activities of configuration and reconfiguration are especially important to the progression. More generally, the sequence of conversations does not trace a story of change but rather gradually discloses the relation between the present and the past in the service of painting a group portrait of the Ambrie family with Jack Hill as a shadowy presence in the background. And the most significant strokes in that portrait result from the privileged authorial disclosure about events in the third conversation. For that reason, I shall give more attention to that conversation, but first I want to highlight some salient features of the authorial and conversational disclosures in the first two scenes of dialogue.

The only instability of any significance in the Narrative Now is located in the initial conversation between Lois and Howard—she wants Howard to attend Hill's funeral and he does not want to—and it is decisively resolved by the end of that conversation, when Howard submits to Lois's repeated entreaties. But O'Hara uses the conversational disclosures to create tensions about why Howard is so set against going to Hill's funeral and why Lois is so insistent that he go. Although the conversational disclosures suggest that they speak frankly as they offer their reasons—Howard says, "I never liked Jack and he never liked me," and Lois says, "I don't want Celia [Hill's wife] knowing that you stayed away" (5–6)—O'Hara uses the initial strength of their respective positions in combination with his title to invite his audience to wonder whether they each have motives that they do not reveal to the other.

O'Hara complicates the tension with the movement to the dialogue between Howard and Amy, even as it "appears" to be about different subjects. When Amy comments that she is comfortable living home again, in part because she enjoys reading their many detective stories, and Howard responds that they have "early Mary Roberts Rinehart" (8)—who is known as the American Agatha Christie and is credited with the phrase, "The butler did it"—O'Hara's authorial disclosure is that his audience should be on the lookout for some mystery-solution structure in his own tale, which, after all, introduces the dead body of Jack Hill early on.

Again, the conversational disclosures between father and daughter suggest that they are speaking candidly. When Howard advises the divorced Amy to have children right away if she remarries because children can help a couple stay together, Amy notes that he implies that the advice comes from his own experience. Howard agrees: "I know what I'm implying. And I know you're no fool. You know it's often been touch and go with your mother and I. You've seen that" (8). For her part, Amy explains that "nothing" would have kept her marriage intact because she had an affair with a married man, a man that she had been seeing even before her marriage. Amy also admits that she is no longer seeing that married man, that she now agrees with her father that he was a "son of a bitch" (10), and that she is currently sleeping with Joe, the doctor she has been dating and might soon marry. At the same time, for all its candor (and it's worth noting that in 1961 a daughter's telling her father about extramarital sex is racy stuff), the conversation calls attention to issues that Amy does not want to discuss. When Howard starts to ask for more details about Amy's history with that man, she says, "Don't ask me any more questions, please" (9). From that point on, Howard offers judgments about the man ("He sounds like a real son of a bitch" [10]), but he does not seek any more information about his identity. Consequently, O'Hara uses the conversation to create the tension about his identity.

In the crucial final conversation, O'Hara gives us four exchanges where the relation between conversational disclosure and authorial disclosure, especially authorial disclosure across conversations, is especially salient. The first comes right at the beginning of the conversation after Lois asks whether Howard said anything to Amy about Jack Hill:

> "I'll be glad when Jack is buried and out of the way."
> "I know," said Amy.

"Your father is getting closer to the truth, Amy."

"I guess he is."

"I had a very difficult time persuading him to go to the funeral tomorrow."

"Why did you bother?"

"Appearances. 'Why didn't Howard Ambrie go to Jack Hill's funeral?' They'd be talking about that for a month, and somebody'd be sure to say something to Celia. And then Celia'd start asking herself questions."

"I wonder. I think Mrs. Hill stopped asking questions a long time ago. She should have. I wasn't the only one he played around with." (11)

Here O'Hara uses this conversational disclosure to resolve tensions from the first two conversations—about Lois's motivation in persuading Howard and about the identity of Amy's lover. As noted above, O'Hara uses this exchange to firmly establish that he, his audience, Lois, and Amy now all share information that Howard (apparently) does not. In addition, the revelation begins the process of reconfiguration because it not only confirms the hypothesis that "Appearances" would follow the mystery-solution pattern of a detective story but does so in a way that ties the first two conversations together. Furthermore, the authorial disclosure across conversations reveals that both previous scenes involving Howard were significantly less candid than they appeared and significantly less candid than this one: Lois and Amy share significant confidences with each other that neither shares with him.

In addition, certain moments in both of the previous conversations take on greater significance. In the first, Howard couples his consent to attend the funeral with the question of why Lois cares so much about whether Celia would know about his presence, but Lois responds only to his agreement: "But you will go?" (6). O'Hara uses this conversational disclosure to reveal why she was so selective. In the second conversation, when Howard asks whether the man with whom Amy had her affair has "gone out of [her] life," "she looked at him sharply" before answering yes. And it is when he follows up by asking whether she met him at Cornell that she tells him to stop asking more questions. O'Hara now allows his rhetorical readers to recognize that Howard apparently does not suspect that Amy suspects that he knows about her affair with Hill.

These reconfigurations rooted in the authorial disclosure across conversations also have consequences for rhetorical readers' larger construction of the family portrait and their affective and ethical responses to each member. Amy is not just a careless woman who will neglect to close the door of her expensive sports car and turn out the light in her garage but also someone who takes her marriage vows lightly. Lois is more concerned about keeping up appearances than about Amy's actual behavior. And both women conspire to keep Howard in the dark. Consequently, Howard emerges as the most sympathetic character, especially since he also has consented to Lois's request to attend the funeral. But the readerly dynamics continue to evolve as this conversation does—and they evolve to a point at which it will be necessary to return to this first exchange.

The second especially salient exchange occurs right after Amy tells Lois that now that Jack is dead, she feels that she can go ahead and marry Joe and settle down.

> "He [Jack Hill] was no good," said Lois Ambrie. "Strange how your father knew that without knowing why."
>
> "I know why," said Amy. "Jack was the kind of man that husbands are naturally suspicious of. Father was afraid that Jack would make a play for you. Instead he made a play for me, but Father never gave that a thought."
>
> "I suppose so. And in your father's eyes it would have been just as bad for me to cover up for you as it would have been for me to have had an affair with Jack. I'll be glad when he's out of the way. Really glad when you can marry Joe." (12)

The conversational disclosures in this collaborative exchange not only add to the gap between Howard's knowledge and the audience's knowledge but also further reveal the two women's intimacy as they build on each other's thoughts and conclusions about the two men. It is especially striking that Lois is talking about her husband this way with her daughter, since O'Hara gives us no similar conversation between Lois and Howard about Amy's judgments. In addition, O'Hara uses the conversational disclosure to add another layer to Lois's motives for keeping up appearances: she is as concerned about Howard's judgment of her as about his judgment of Amy. I will comment below on Lois's curious equation of covering up Amy's affair with having her own affair with Jack Hill.

The third salient exchange switches from the focus on Jack, Howard, and the past to one on Amy, Joe, and the future, as Lois asks Amy whether she will have to convert to Catholicism to marry Joe. This shift has three main effects: (a) it signals at least a temporary end to the configurations and reconfigurations about the past, (b) it introduces some significant differences between the previously intimate Lois and Amy, and (c) it influences our ethical judgments of both Lois and Amy. Where Lois is fixated on what a "feather in their cap" (13) it will be for Joe's Catholic family to make an alliance with the Ambries,

Amy has no such concerns and, indeed, is able to imagine that Joe's family is likely not to regard his marrying a divorced woman so positively: "They may not see it that way. I understand they can be very tough about some things." Indeed, she is willing to accommodate Joe's family: "When the time comes, whatever they say I'll do" (13). In order to underline Lois's unquestioned assumptions about the superiority of her WASP identity and the way her judgments of others are tied to those assumptions, O'Hara gives her the final word about Catholics with a topical reference to John Fitzgerald Kennedy: "I still can't get used to the idea of having one in the White House" (13). By marking this difference between Lois and Amy, O'Hara uses the conversational disclosures to shift our ethical judgments: the careless Amy is capable of seeing at least some of her own flaws, whereas Lois remains within the tunnel vision accompanying her class privilege. In addition, Lois's casual assumption about the superiority of the Ambrie family to Joe's not only breaks the intimacy between Lois and Amy but is sufficiently annoying to Amy that she embarks on the final exchange in the story.

This exchange gives a further twist to rhetorical readers' reconfigurations, as it turns back to past events. In addition, it invites rhetorical readers to revisit the first exchange in this scene. This final exchange begins with Amy's apology and then itself takes a sudden turn:

> "I'm sorry I caused you and Father so much trouble. You especially. All those lies you had to tell."
>
> "Oh, that's all right. It's over now. And it was really harder on your father. He never knew why he didn't like that man."
>
> "And *you* couldn't tell him, *could* you, Mother?"
>
> "What?"
>
> "Oh, Mother."
>
> Lois Ambrie looked at her daughter. "Is that another detective story you're reading? You mustn't get carried away, Amy." She smiled. "Goodnight, dear," she said, and closed the door. (13–14)

The conversational disclosures are simultaneously rich in authorial disclosures that make this exchange a brilliant end to the progression. Amy's move from sincere apology to sly insinuation about Lois's affair with Jack adds another significant element to the gap between Howard's knowledge and everyone else's, including the audience's. At the same time, Lois's nondenial denial introduces an element of differential knowledge between Lois and the audience on the one side and Amy on the other. Amy can have her suspicions, but she does not have confirmation of them. I will take up the audience's relation to those suspicions shortly, but first I want to note how O'Hara uses Amy's insinuation as part of his larger disclosure about her character. Lois is right to note that Amy has been playing detective, but Amy's choice to reveal her suspicions shows that she is quite confident that they are well grounded and that she believes she has something to gain by expressing them. Either she and Lois will have something else to share—or she can learn something further by the manner of Lois's denial.

Furthermore, in a case of authorial disclosure *within* conversation, Amy's insinuation prompts O'Hara's audience to reconfigure the initial dialogue in this scene. Amy's comments there now all seem to have an additional, covert layer that Lois is not aware of. Amy's "I know" in response to Lois's "I'll be glad when Jack's gone" now looks like a serious understatement, and her "I wasn't the only one [Jack] played around with" now appears far more pointed. As a result, Amy emerges from O'Hara's managing of the relations between her conversational and his authorial disclosures as a character who is by turns careless, immoral, aware of her faults, grateful, shrewd, and bold. Joe, her future husband, is likely in for some surprises of his own.

In order to assess what Lois's response to Amy's insinuation reveals about her, we need to consider how O'Hara uses the authorial disclosures across conversations to guide his audience's detective activities and how that guidance affects the audience's reconfiguration of both character and events. O'Hara gives his audience considerable evidence that Amy gets it right: Lois does not confirm Amy's suspicions, but O'Hara confirms those of his audience. From the first and third conversations, the audience knows that Jack did not start disliking Hill only recently but rather that he "never" liked Hill. From the first conversation, the audience also knows that Hill was as an usher at Howard and Lois's wedding. Consequently, they would have been in each other's orbit during the early years of Howard and Lois's marriage, the time when, according to Howard, they stayed together for Amy's sake. Moreover, the audience knows that if Amy is right, Lois has even more reason to keep up appearances so that Celia—and others—don't start asking why Howard would not go to Hill's funeral. In fact, the audience can recognize that, in light of Hill's age, this motive of keeping her own affair a secret from Howard and Celia becomes at least as compelling, since people would be more likely to suspect that Hill had been involved with Lois than with Amy. In addition, Lois's own curious judgment earlier in this conversation, that covering up Amy's affair would have been as bad in Howard's eyes as her having an affair with Jack herself, now seems less curious: she wants to minimize her own transgression and maximize Amy's. Furthermore, in terms of the overall sequence of the story, Amy's inference provides a nice final twist to the mystery-solution pattern: although that pattern seemed to be completed with the revelation about Amy and Jack Hill, the audience now discovers, at the very end of the story, another, deeper layer to the pattern.

In light of these conclusions, O'Hara's audience has further reason to interpret Lois's response as a nondenial denial, one in which she stops short of telling Amy that she did not have the affair even as she tries to discourage Amy's conclusion. With this nondenial denial, Lois refuses Amy's implicit invitation toward a greater intimacy based on their similar experience, a choice that reinforces what O'Hara has already disclosed about her character. Lois is committed to keeping up appearances, and she has appeared to be the concerned mother helping her daughter keep her daughter's affair from Howard. She is far more comfortable being Amy's older, wiser confidant than she is being Amy's equal.

At this point, the audience does not have any privileged access to events with respect to Lois, except for the exact details of Howard's conversation with Amy. But O'Hara's concluding with another reference to detective stories and to the mystery-solution pattern invites some further reflection. Might Howard, who after all is the original reader of the detective stories and the one who mentions Mary Roberts Rinehart to Amy, know more than Lois and Amy give him credit for knowing? If Lois and Amy are committed to keeping up certain appearances, isn't it plausible to wonder about the extent to which Howard is similarly committed, especially in light of his sudden capitulation to Lois's request that he go to Hill's funeral? Does Lois's suspicion that he is getting nearer the truth stop too soon—has he perhaps figured it out? Is Howard's question to Amy about the man having "gone out of [her] life" what she initially suspects it is, a covert reference to the recently deceased Hill?

No less a practitioner of dialogue narrative than George V. Higgins believes that Howard knows about both affairs and "torment[s] his women-folk by making veiled references designed to keep them constantly on the edge of fear of public humiliation, while lacking the guts to confront either of them or Jack Hill directly" (*On Writing* 120–21). As much as I admire Higgins's own writerly skills, I find that he is seriously overreading the story here, as his leap from conversations in the privacy of their home to possible "public humiliation" indicates. (Higgins also overreads Lois's role in Amy's affair when he says that "she connived in her daughter's seduction" by Hill [121].) Neither Higgins nor O'Hara provides any evidence of Howard's knowledge equivalent to the pattern of hints O'Hara supplies to confirm Amy's insinuation about Lois's affair with Jack. And if O'Hara wanted his audience to have a degree of confidence about Howard's knowledge comparable to the one he gives that audience about Lois's affair, he could easily have planted such evidence—given Howard a reference to Hill whose veil was more transparent or introduced a revealing discussion between Howard and Amy about whether she was going to the funeral, or something else along those lines. Instead, O'Hara gives his audience enough evidence to suspect that Howard knows more than Lois and Amy give him credit for, but not enough evidence to confirm any suspicions with anything approaching the confidence the audience achieves about Lois's affair with Hill. In this way, O'Hara harnesses the power of a limited ambiguity in his overall portraiture of the family.

Indeed, the result of O'Hara's rich authorial disclosures through the various conversational disclosures is a very complex and very intriguing family portrait, one that his audience can see more clearly than any of its subjects. To be sure, the figures of Lois and Amy emerge more clearly and sharply than the figure of Howard, but the overall portrait emphasizes each character's interest in keeping up appearances and the way that interest increases the distance among them. Lois clearly hides the most from the other two, even as she works hardest to manage how they all look to the outside world and retains a sense of her own superiority. Amy is both dependent on her parents and capable of seeing through them. Howard might be either the most put-upon or the most devious of the three characters.

At the level of readerly dynamics, O'Hara's audience partially sympathizes with each family member even as it makes some strong negative ethical judgments about each, with the strongest of these directed at Lois (though any final judgment of Howard must be tentative and provisional given the ambiguity about what he knows). The Ambries are not a family to admire, but they are a family that demonstrates not only human frailty but humans' complicated ways of responding to their frailties.

Finally, the ethics of O'Hara's telling provides a striking contrast to the ethics of the told. Where the Ambries value appearances more than actualities, to the point that their apparent frankness with each other covers both withholding of information and active deception, O'Hara values communication about actualities even as he is content with leaving some questions unanswered. He especially values collaborative communication, the ways in which he and his audience can, by working together, see past appearances to the complexities of how family members often avoid such collaboration. All in all, "Appearances" is a rich indirect communication from somebody to somebody else by means of what still other somebodies communicate (or fail to communicate) to each other.

CHAPTER 10

The Implied Author, Deficient Narration, and Nonfiction Narrative

JOAN DIDION'S *THE YEAR OF MAGICAL THINKING*
AND JEAN-DOMINIQUE BAUBY'S *THE DIVING BELL
AND THE BUTTERFLY*

TO THIS POINT, when I have focused on the "somebody else" of rhetorical poetics, I have primarily focused on rhetorical exchanges in which actual audiences become members of the authorial audience—and thus play the role of what I have called rhetorical readers. Playing that role is what I regard the first step of successful rhetorical reading. In the discussion of *Lolita* in chapter 5, I also noted that there are rhetorical exchanges in which the relationship between actual and authorial audiences itself becomes an important object of analysis, something crucial to an account of the effects of the narrative communication. In this chapter, I turn to consider situations in which the actual audience finds good reason, after it recognizes the position of the authorial audience, not to occupy it. In this way, I foreground the second step of rhetorical reading: evaluating the experience of reading in the authorial audience. More specifically, I shall focus on what I call deficient narration, a phenomenon that can be usefully understood in relation to unreliable narration. In both unreliable and deficient narration, actual audiences who perceive the authorial audience position find something off-kilter in the narration. The difference is that unreliable narration is deliberately off-kilter and deficient narration is inadvertently so. In unreliable narration, author, authorial audience, and actual audience align as they recognize what is off-kilter about the narrator. In deficient narration, author, narrator, and authorial audience align, but the actual audience views all three of them as off-kilter.

This chapter also continues the discussion of chapter 3 about the differences for readerly response that follow from a narrative's status as fictional or nonfictional. I argue that the judgments of deficiency in my two case-study memoirs, Joan Didion's *The Year of Magical Thinking* and Jean-Dominique Bauby's *The Diving Bell and the Butterfly,* are dependent on the actual audience's assumptions that they are reading nonfiction. In addition, my treatment of Didion complements the discussion of her memoir in chapter 3.

Finally, since I am grounding the difference between unreliable and deficient narration in the actual audience's reading of the implied author's intended communication, and since the issue of intentionality has been implicitly present in every chapter of this book, I take it up explicitly here. More specifically, even as I develop a case for the practical value of the concept of the implied author, I subordinate that case to a more fundamental argument for the validity and viability of a rhetorical understanding of intentionality.

As I explained in the introduction and chapter 1, rhetorical poetics is more invested in the phenomenon of authorial agency than it is in the concept of the implied author, but it still finds that concept useful. Furthermore, rhetorical theory's investment in authorial agency runs counter to the dominant anti-intentionalism of contemporary critical theory, a stance that dates back at least to the mid-twentieth century, when W. K. Wimsatt and Monroe Beardsley declaimed against "The Intentional Fallacy." In narrative theory, Wayne C. Booth pushed back against that anti-intentionalism with the concept of the implied author, by which he meant a "second self" that the author constructed through all the choices (conscious or intuitive) she made in the writing of a work. Since then, for the most part, the participants in the debate about the concept of the implied author have focused on fiction (see Booth, Genette, Chatman, Rimmon-Kenan, Lanser, Hansen, Ansgar Nünning, Vera Nünning, Kindt and Müller, Richardson, and Shen, as well as the 2011 special issue of *Style*), while some participants in the closely related debate about unreliable narration have turned to nonfiction (see especially Shen and Xu and Phelan, *Living to Tell*). But to my knowledge, no one has yet done what I shall attempt to do here: use nonfiction narrative as the central focus of a discussion that brings together the debates about the implied author and about unreliable narration.

ELBOW ROOM FOR INTENTIONALITY

I start with a small debate I have been having with two leading theorists of lifewriting, Sidonie Smith and Julia Watson. In *Living to Tell about It,* I argue that the first edition of Smith and Watson's valuable book *Reading Autobiog-*

raphy (2001) offers a helpful analysis of four autobiographical "I's" (the historical-I of the real author, the narrating-I, the narrated-I, and the ideological-I) but that the analysis leaves an unfortunate gap between the real author and the narrating-I. Since Smith and Watson contend both that the real author is ultimately unknowable and that the narrating-I may have multiple voices, I suggest that their model should fill the gap with the implied authorial-I. This implied authorial-I would be the agent responsible for choosing which of the multiple voices of the narrating-I to employ at which points in the narration. This implied authorial-I would also be able to communicate whether the narrating-I was a reliable or unreliable spokesperson.

In the very impressive second edition of *Reading Autobiography,* Smith and Watson respond to my suggestion by politely rejecting it. They contend that the "narrating and narrated 'I's are temporally too interlinked to both be effects of an implied author, and the project of self-narration is too involved with its own process of reading and interpretation to sustain, or require, this third term" (76). As long as the model of autobiographical telling emphasizes that both the narrating-I and the narrated-I are potentially mobile, the concept of the implied author is unnecessary: "Phelan's model of positing a triangular situation (with narrating 'I,' narrated 'I,' and implied author) seems to depend on a narrating 'I' fixed in one temporal plane. We would argue that the dynamism of much autobiographical work, its ability to put the narrative situation into play, makes such a category redundant" (76).

From my perspective, what Smith and Watson's response demonstrates most powerfully is something that any advocate for the concept of the implied author ought to be aware of: among many narrative theorists, resistance to the concept runs deep. The most telling evidence of Smith and Watson's resistance is that their response only obliquely addresses the specific argument I make about the gap in their schema, that it leaves them with no clear way of accounting for changes in the narrating-I. Rather than directly showing how their model deals with that gap, Smith and Watson appeal to the complexity of the interrelations of the narrating- and narrated-I's and the potential dynamism of both, and go from there to the conclusion that the concept of the implied author is redundant.

But a little reflection on the example I use to extend my proposal for the utility of the implied author, Frank McCourt's *Angela's Ashes,* calls that conclusion into question. In McCourt's memoir, the narrating-I is very mobile, as McCourt employs the vision and voice of his younger self at multiple ages from three to nineteen.[1] Within Smith and Watson's model, we have two

---

1. In this connection, I find it puzzling that Smith and Watson claim that my model depends on the narrating-I being fixed in one temporal plane, since my discussion of *Angela's Ashes* emphasizes the shifts in the vision and voice of McCourt's narrating-I.

options for locating the agency of the shifts in the narrating-I's voices: one or more of the successive "Frankies" or the more mature narrating-I who appears at the beginning of the memoir. The first option is implausible since it would lead to such hard-to-process conclusions as "three-year old Frankie decides to yield the floor to five-year old Frankie," and the second option goes against Smith and Watson's interest in freeing the narrating-I from a fixed temporal position, a position that McCourt seems to share.

In addition, saying that the narrating-I is responsible for the shifts in his or her own voices also assumes that the narrating-I always performs the dual functions of telling and of orchestrating the telling. This assumption may be justified with some self-conscious narrating-I's, but it effectively rules out uses of a genuinely naïve narrating-I, since the orchestrator would have to be only pretending to be naïve. But McCourt and others have shown that memoirists can not only employ genuinely naïve narrating-I's but also use them in the construction of very moving narratives.

If, however, we add the implied author to Smith and Watson's schema, then we have a much more persuasive and elegant model of autobiographical narration, one that allows us to unpack the complex "project of self-narration" and the temporal connections between narrating- and narrated-I's. The historical-I of the real author can remain ultimately inaccessible (though I would suggest that in many cases we can draw probable conclusions about the historical-I); the narrating-I retains the potential for maximal dynamism; the narrated-I retains a similar potential as well as its multiple functions as protagonist; the ideological-I remains the concept of personhood available to the narrating-I in her cultural moment; and the implied author becomes the orchestrator of the shifts in the narrating-I's voices, in the various representations of the narrated-I, and of their temporal interrelations. This implied author can choose, within the limits of her own imagination as both constrained and stimulated by her cultural moment, to employ any kind of narrating-I—one in a fixed temporal location, one whose temporal location constantly shifts, one who is naïve, one who is sophisticated and self-conscious, and so on—and can show the stages of the narrated-I's temporal progression in any order. What's not to like?

From Smith and Watson's perspective, what's not to like can be found in what I detect as the two deeper reasons for their polite rejection of my proposal, reasons shared by many others who are skeptical of the concept of the implied author: (1) Adding the concept to a model that already includes four autobiographical I's seems to violate Ockham's Razor. It's this reason, I believe, that underlies Smith and Watson's objection to the alleged redundancy of the concept. (2) Adding the concept opens the model to a significant role for intentionality in our understanding of autobiographical telling, and such a role is incompatible with the dominant orthodoxy of contemporary theory. It's this reason, I believe, that underlies or at least influences Smith and Watson's move from the complexity of "the project of self-narration" to the rejection of the concept. In their view, that project is too complex to be contained within the intentionality of any one agent, regardless of its label. In order to make my broader case, then, I need to address these two widely shared objections. Consequently, I will turn, first, to make room for a valid and viable notion of intentionality in interpretation, an argument that is ultimately prior to a case for the implied author, even as it is central to the conception of narrative as rhetoric. Once I've argued for this elbow room, I will turn to explain why Ockham need not reach for his Razor whenever he hears the words *implied author*.

As I noted above, contemporary theory's general suspicion of intentionality goes at least as far back as the New Criticism. It was 1946 when W. K. Wimsatt and Monroe Beardsley began the process of turning suspicion into dogma in their famous essay on "The Intentional Fallacy," which effectively ruled out of court the author's take on the achievement and interpretation of her text. Despite counterarguments by the Chicago neo-Aristotelians and by E. D. Hirsch Jr., the suspicion only grew after the New Criticism lost its ascendancy. Some theorists contended that readers should be granted more interpretive power and authority (Holland, Iser, and Fish, "Literature"), while others, persuaded by post-structuralist arguments about language as a system of signs with no anchoring center, contended that language and, by extension, literary texts were ultimately indeterminate. Still others focused on the irreducible intertextuality of literature, pronounced the "death of the author" (Barthes), or distinguished between a historical author and an author function (Foucault). In my view, however, this anti-intentionalist orthodoxy is unpersuasive because (a) it is rooted in claims about language, readers, or interpretation that are at best only partially true, or (b) it often entails adopting an either/or position when a both/and one is preferable. To demonstrate these points, I turn to consider two of the main anti-intentionalist positions, Stanley Fish's theory of interpretive communities and Anglo-American deconstruction (for arguments along similar lines, see my "Data, Danda," part 1 of *Worlds from Words,* and the introduction to *Narrative as Rhetoric*).

Fish's theory of interpretive communities is the most extreme form of his attack on that other famous pillar of New Critical faith, Wimsatt and Beardsley's "The Affective Fallacy," but that attack simultaneously reinforces "The Intentional Fallacy." If, as Fish argues, the interpretive strategies of interpretive communities dictate the meaning of texts, then interpretive authority rests entirely with those communities—authors are essentially irrelevant. Fish's contention is persuasive only if the crucial assumption underlying it can be sustained, the assumption that texts do not provide resistance or recalcitrance to our interpretive efforts but instead are always amenable to the strategies of any interpretive community. I contend that the assumption cannot be sustained once we look more closely than Fish does at the nature of interpretation and the means by which we test interpretive hypotheses. Fish tests interpretive hypotheses only by seeking to confirm them, but such confirmation is a necessary but not a sufficient condition for establishing the soundness of an interpretation. It is not until we seek to disconfirm hypotheses by comparing them to alternatives that our testing becomes sufficient.

In "How to Recognize a Poem When You See One," Fish makes his larger case about the power of interpretive communities by telling a story that he regards as a particularly telling example of that power. When he asked the students in his seventeenth-century poetry class to interpret a list of authors he'd assigned to his previous class on stylistics, they were able to give a plausible account of the list as a religious poem. But the story only demonstrates a far less radical finding: those trained in allegorical interpretation can apply what they've learned to a list of names. If we shift from asking whether it is possible to interpret the list as a religious poem to asking whether the hypothesis that it is a poem is stronger than the hypothesis that it is a reading assignment, then everything changes. (Note that this shift is not a shift from one interpretive community to another but rather to a meta-interpretive inquiry: is it possible to choose between hypotheses generated by two different interpretive communities, that of the class in stylistics and that of the class in religious poetry?) The assignment hypothesis meets with no recalcitrance—it can account for all the textual details precisely and coherently—while the poem hypothesis, as Fish himself admits, has difficulty with one of the names (Hayes), and it offers a much looser fit between the textual details and the overall interpretation.

In this way, Fish's own example ends up providing strong support for the position that although our view of texts is mediated by our interpretive frameworks, texts have an existence independent of those frameworks. This position, in turn, provides the warrant for rhetorical theory's inquiry into why texts have one set of properties rather than another and to seek the answer in a hypothesis about the intentionality that governs their shape and supports their communicative purposes.

With Anglo-American deconstruction, the key issue is less the sustainability of the position's claims about the language of literary texts and more the consequences that follow from those claims. This version of deconstruction is a viable position to the extent that it is a response to one worthwhile question about a literary text—what can the language of this text possibly mean?—but its viability does not entail the conclusion that other kinds of questions, including questions about intentionality, should be ruled out of court. In other words, the deconstructionist position that language always undoes itself is compatible with its operative question about possible meanings, but that position and that compatibility do not undermine the equally valid question, "what did the person who wrote this text for this audience probably want to communicate?" Consider, for example, the famous first sentence of Jane Austen's *Pride and Prejudice*, "It is a truth universally acknowledged, that a single man in possession of a good fortune, must be in want of a wife." If we ask the Anglo-American deconstructionist question, our answers will include not only the incompatible ironic and nonironic meanings—the sentence is sending up those who believe its literal statement; no, the literal statement is right on target—but other incompatibilities as well. Consider the phrase "single man in possession of a good fortune." Even as the sentence clearly asserts the relation between the single man and the fortune (he possesses it), the sentence also implies that possessing the fortune inevitably creates the desire for the wife—and thus that the good fortune is simultaneously in possession of the man. This recognition, in turn, invites us to contemplate the incompatible meanings of the word *good*.

If, however, we ask rhetorical theory's question about intentionality, a question that can be translated as "what are the writer's reasons for using the language in this way rather than some other way in relation to some audience?," then we arrive at a very different view of the sentence. The question invites us to consider whether the sentence is designed to be ironic, nonironic, or somehow both—and a look at the design with all three possibilities in mind indicates that the teller probably meant it to be ironic. That hypothesis offers the most satisfactory explanation of the movement of the sentence from its initial signaling of some grand wisdom (not just "A universally acknowledged truth is" but "It is a truth universally acknowledged that") to its final delivery of a dubious proposition. That answer also recognizes that the teller's choice of irony establishes a much richer relation to her audience than the other options and that doing so at the beginning of a novel makes good sense. If the designer wanted the nonironic reading, she has not executed her intention particularly well, especially since she could have just written "It's widely assumed that any rich, single man in our society is on the lookout for a suitable woman to be his wife." If she wanted to insist on both meanings, she would have needed a way to make the nonironic hypothesis more plausible. (The same logic can be applied to Fish's example of the names on the blackboard: once we shift from asking if the names can possibly be interpreted as a religious poem to asking what the person who wrote the names on the board probably intended, then the assignment hypothesis becomes far more likely.)

In sum, the two different questions generate two different kinds of knowledge about the first sentence of *Pride and Prejudice*. Although I realize that some critics will prefer the Anglo-American deconstructionist question and others the rhetorical theorist's question, I contend that such a preference is not itself evidence that can be appealed to in order to decide what Austen's sentence means. To put this point another way, it would be a mistake for either the deconstructionist or the rhetorical critic to conclude that his ability to answer his question means that the other's is thereby rendered obsolete, naïve, or otherwise wrong-headed (though I can't help but point out that the deconstructionist position is limited in a way that the rhetorical is not: it operates with an a priori commitment to showing that language undoes itself, while the rhetorical model views such undoing as one of several ways that language can work).

Similar analyses could be done of other anti-intentionalist positions, but such analyses would not alter my larger point: neither the long tradition of an anti-intentionalist orthodoxy nor a close look at details of positions within that tradition undermines the viability and validity of the intentionalist position. Consequently, the intentionalist position ought to have sufficient elbow room in the territory of contemporary theory to do its work.

INTENTIONALITY FROM A RHETORICAL PERSPECTIVE

Paying attention to the anti-intentionalist positions underlines the need to be clear about what one means by intention and about the claims one wants to make for it. From the rhetorical perspective, intention is a mental state, a will to do something, including to mean something—and to deliver a multilayered communication to an audience. In this sense, intention is the force that takes potentially ambiguous matter and shapes it into one thing rather than another (even intentional ambiguity is ambiguous in some ways rather than others).

Identifying intention as a mental state allows us to recognize that it is not a synonym for "meaning," which still rests on the public norms governing language. If I intend to communicate the proposition that "'The Intentional Fallacy' is itself a fallacy" but instead carelessly write "'The Intentional Fallacy' is not itself a fallacy," then there is a contradiction between my intention and my meaning—or to be more precise, between my intention and the meaning of the sentence I chose to express that intention. In other words, successfully executing one's intention to mean something depends on the appropriate use of the available resources of language. At the same time, as the discussion of the first sentence of *Pride and Prejudice* shows, if we focus only on possible meanings, we miss entirely the ways in which intention can govern the use of those linguistic resources.

This distinction between intention and meaning is relevant to the principle that narrative communication involves a feedback loop among authorial agency, textual phenomena, and reader response. In the present context, the most important aspect of the metaphor is its stipulation that authorial agency—and more specifically, the intentionality of that agency—is accessible through textual phenomena and (partially) testable against reader response. Rhetorical theory is ultimately interested not in private intention but in public, textualized intentions.

The second crucial aspect of intentionality for rhetorical theory is that it operates at the level of the whole narrative communication. The intentionality of *Pride and Prejudice* is more than the sum of the intentions of the novel's individual sentences. Instead, that intentionality is a larger system of thought, the purposive design of the narrative that governs the entire set of the implied Austen's constructive choices. This set includes her choices about such things as how to handle the probability of events early and late (see the discussion in chapter 3) as well as how to arrange events when their arrangement is optional (for example, she orders the marriages of the Bennet sisters in climactic sequence—first Lydia's, then Jane's, then Elizabeth's); which narrative techniques to deploy at which points (for example, when representing Elizabeth's response to Darcy's letter, Austen gives us a lot of Elizabeth's direct thought in order to convey her appropriately harsh self-judgments); and more. All these choices contribute to the novel's purposive design of combining its critique of the marriage market with its tracing of the ethical maturation of both Elizabeth and Darcy so that the audience can take deep satisfaction in their engagement.

These two points—the distinction between intention and meaning, and the idea that intentionality operates at a global level—link up with the argument in chapter 2 about the temporal unfolding of the relation between textual and readerly dynamics and its effects on textual construction. Together these points and that argument highlight the importance of the temporal dimension of the narrative communication to the developing apprehension of a system of intentionality. As we read, we develop hypotheses about that system, and these hypotheses influence how we respond to new parts of a text, even as those new parts have the potential to alter our developing hypotheses. This understanding in turn allows us to recognize that not every sentence (or other part of the constructive design) will necessarily contribute to the positive realization of that design. Just as the meaning of an individual sentence may not be in accord with an utterer's particular intention, so too some elements of a narrative may work against rather than with its larger purposive design. I will return to this point when I discuss the passages from Didion and Bauby. For now I need to round off the discussion of the implied author.

FLESH-AND-BLOOD AUTHORS, IMPLIED AUTHORS, AND OCKHAM'S RAZOR

As noted above, the case for intentionality is independent of a case for the viability of the concept of the implied author (for this reason, I have been referring to the "writer" rather than the "implied writer"). In fact, some narrative theorists who would support the arguments I have made for elbow room for intentionality would still want to borrow that Razor from Ockham. Recently David Herman, while arguing for the necessity of what he calls the intentional stance, adds two other objections to the concept of the implied author: it concedes too much to the anti-intentionalists, and it encourages its user to lose sight of the fact that interpretive hypotheses should be defeasible. In light of these objections, why not locate authorial agency in the actual rather than the implied author?

The short answer is that I believe that Herman's objections don't have much purchase on the concept of the implied author as I define it and that the concept follows naturally from the case for intentions and purposes I have been making. Before I elaborate, though, I do want to reiterate the point that my case for elbow room for intentionality is ultimately more significant than my case for the efficacy of the concept of the implied author. Those who grant the first case are my theoretical allies, regardless of whether they grant the second. Thus, although Herman argues against the concept of the implied author, I very much welcome his case that "theories of narrative need to be calibrated with the assumption that stories are irreducibly grounded in intentional systems" ("Narrative Theory" 240). Since I'm more concerned with elbow room than with driving the anti-intentionalists out of the Hermeneutic Temple, I would just alter "need to be" to "can be productively."

As noted above, I want to locate the intentionality in the agency of the implied rather than the flesh-and-blood author because I believe that such a location is the appropriate extension of the case for intentionality I have just made. Rhetorical theory is interested not in the author's private intentions but rather in his or her public, textualized intentions, and that interest entails locating authorial agency in the implied rather than the actual author. From this perspective, Herman's objections are easily met: I have made my case by means of a direct engagement with prominent anti-intentionalist positions, and that case includes the principle that interpretive hypotheses need to be tested against alternatives. I submit, then, that Herman is addressing misuses of the concept more than the concept itself.[2]

Furthermore, by understanding the implied author as the agent responsible for the purposive design that governs the text, we can further clarify the nature of narrative communication—and in so doing, offer Ockham and his followers good reasons to keep their hands off his Razor. There are at least five significant clarifications that follow from locating intentionality in the implied rather than the flesh-and-blood author. This location helps explain or call attention to the following:

(1) The significant role of self-presentation in the construction of narrative, either fictional or nonfictional; a writer inevitably constructs one version of herself rather than another through her choices of technique, subject matter, ethical values, and so on.

(2) The sometimes surprising difference in ideological or ethical positions in texts by the same biographical author: despite their common flesh-and-blood author, such texts have different implied authors.

(3) The not uncommon situation when the flesh-and-blood author's discussion of his or her text runs counter to the purposive design governing the text. For example, Ernest Hemingway responded to a critic interested in his take on the debate about the apparent textual problems in the pre-1965 version of "A Clean, Well-Lighted Place" by saying that he reread the text and it seemed fine to him. The purposive design governing the story, however, indicates that the pre-1965 text is inconsistent in its attributions of dialogue to its two waiters, and we are thus justified in saying that the implied author of the story, unlike the flesh-and-blood author, would approve the post-1965 version of the story, which corrects the inconsistency.[3]

(4) The complicated authorial agency in collaborative and ghostwritten texts as well as that in hoaxes and fraudulent memoirs. In collaboratively written texts, the flesh-and-blood authors construct a hybrid version of themselves responsible for the purposive design of the text. In both ghostwritten texts and hoaxes, the flesh-and-blood author constructs a version of herself that purports to be a version of the author named on the title page. In ghostwritten texts, the author named on the title page authorizes the flesh-and-blood author to construct that implied version, while in hoaxes the author

---

2. For a fuller discussion, see the Phelan-Rabinowitz contribution to Herman et al.'s *Narrative Theory: Core Concepts and Critical Debates*.

3. See chapter 7 of my *Experiencing Fiction* for a fuller discussion.

named on the title page is left out of the loop. In a fraudulent memoir, the flesh-and-blood author constructs a version of himself that is itself at least partially fraudulent.

(5) Our sense that we both come to know an author through reading his or her text and to recognize that the author has a life independent of the identity projected in the text. This point is especially applicable to our reading of autobiographical narrative.

Conceiving of the implied author as a version of the flesh-and-blood author responsible for the purposive design governing the text also means that the implied author is an active agent rather than simply the product of the text or the reader's inferences. We ought not to confuse how we come to know an implied author with the implied author herself. In Dan Shen's helpful terms, the implied author encodes the text; the reader decodes it, and through that decoding comes to know the implied author.

THE IMPLIED AUTHOR, NONFICTION NARRATIVE, AND DEFICIENT NARRATION

As I noted in chapter 3, in *The Year of Magical Thinking* Joan Didion tells the story of her life during the year after the fatal heart attack suffered by her husband, John Gregory Dunne, in December 2003. During that year, Didion has to deal not only with her grief about John but also with the stress of her daughter Quintana's life-threatening illness. The implied Didion writes about her experiences with admirable frankness and insight, establishing her narrating-I as a reliable spokesperson and initially emphasizing the interpretive and occasionally ethical distance between that I and the narrated-I—or, as I prefer, experiencing-I—even as she insists on the continuity between them. The narrating-I exposes the experiencing-I's "magical thinking," the various mechanisms she used to keep from accepting the irreversibility of John's death: if she doesn't discard his shoes, for example, then he will be able to return for them. As the narrative progresses, the distance between the narrating-I and the experiencing-I diminishes until, finally, they converge in their joint affirmation of John's lesson that "you had to go with the change" (232). Crucial to this process of acceptance is the experiencing-I's response to the autopsy report, a response that both the narrating-I and the implied Didion endorse. This report, which did not arrive until "early December 2004" (199), is crucial because it allows the experiencing-I to accept that she was not responsible for John's heart attack, and with that acceptance she is able to extricate herself from much of her magical thinking. The problem, however, is that within the system of intentionality the implied Didion has established to this point, the narrating-I's and the implied author's endorsement of the experiencing-I's response to the report is, to put it kindly, inadequate.

By this point in the narrative, the narrating-I has reported that John had a history of heart trouble and of treatments for it, including an angioplasty in his left anterior descending artery in 1987. By this point, the narrating-I has also reported that the experiencing-I has been looking for evidence of something she or John could have done to prevent his heart attack. In fact, on the previous page she has emphasized how strongly this search affects the psychic life of the experiencing-I: watching a television commercial that claims Bayer aspirin can reduce the risk of heart attacks, she "was seized . . . by the possible folly of having overlooked low-dose aspirin" (206), even though she knows John is taking Coumadin. The implied Didion has the narrating-I conclude this section with these comments:

> As I recall this I realize how open we are to the persistent message that we can avert death.
>
> And to its punitive correlative, the message that if death catches us we have only ourselves to blame. (206)

The troubling passage then begins:

> Only after I read the autopsy report did I begin to believe what I had been repeatedly told: nothing he or I had done or not done had either caused or could have prevented his death. . . .
>
> Greater than 95 percent stenosis of both the left main and the left anterior descending arteries.
>
> Acute infarct in distribution of left anterior descending artery, the LAD.
>
> That was the scenario. The LAD got fixed in 1987 and it stayed fixed until everybody forgot about it and then it got unfixed. *We call it the widowmaker, pal,* the cardiologist had said in 1987. (206–7)

It is the clause "everybody forgot about it" that does not fit with the purposive design, the system of intentionality governing the narrative. The problem with the clause is not what it reports: the human mind has a remarkable ability to compartmentalize, and this forgetting can be read as another example of that ability. The problem is that, according to the purposive design of the narrative, with its frequent and recent signals about the experiencing-I's quest to find something that could have been done to prevent John's heart attack, the admission that "everybody forgot about it" should not lead the experiencing-I, the narrating-I, or the implied Didion to the conclusion that there was nothing she or John could have done: they—and his cardiologists—could have continued to monitor his LAD. Even if the implied Didion wants to make the case that such monitoring would ultimately not have mattered, the way she has set up the passage both globally and locally entails the necessity of her making that case. The implied Didion's missing the contradiction between the way she sets up the autopsy report and the way she treats the experiencing-I's response to it renders the narration off-kilter. Furthermore, the implied Didion's choice to have the narrating-I quote the cardiologist's ominous words after John's angioplasty (*We call it the widowmaker, pal*) only underlines the break in the purposive design.

Let me come at the same point from another direction: why would I or any reader notice that this clause is off-kilter? Because of our unfolding responses to the progression. In my own experience, the clause seemed to jump off the page because it ran so counter to the expectations and desires I had developed by attending to the narrating-I's quest for something that could have made a difference. Attuned to expect and desire some resolution to the quest, I was stunned that the narrating-I and the implied Didion both interpret this strong evidence that there was something that she and John might have done as grounds for the conclusion that there was nothing they could have done.

The actual reader's understanding of the memoir's status as nonfiction supports this analysis, as becomes clear in a thought experiment of taking the narrative as fictional. In that case, readers who have intuited the larger system of intentionality would regard as unreliable interpreting and evaluating the passage's conclusion that "nothing he or I had done or not done" would have made a difference. The setup, with its focus on the search for what could have been done, and the conclusion, with its quotation of the cardiologist, would be sure signs that the implied author is signaling the narrator's misinterpretation of the report. Readers would be likely to conclude that the implied Didion wants her audience to understand that the character narrator so deeply needs to end her search for something she could have done differently that she goes ahead and ends it even after she is presented with exactly what she has been looking for. Furthermore, this instance of misinterpreting would contribute to a larger design that depends on the development of distance between the implied Didion and her narrating-I for the rest of the fiction. As part of this design, the resolution in which the narrating-I and experiencing-I come together in the conclusion that they need to "go with the change" would signify not an important stage in the working through of the experiencing-I's grief but rather a short-circuit of that working through. This resolution would be an integral part of the implied Didion's purpose of exploring the connections between mourning and self-delusion.

However, because *The Year of Magical Thinking* is nonfiction, this hypothesis about distance between the implied Didion and the narrating-I is extremely difficult to sustain. In fiction, the implied author is ontologically distinct from the narrating-I and the experiencing-I, while in nonfiction, there is ontological continuity from one to the others. In Didion's case, this continuity gets expressed, first, in the alignment of the implied author and the narrating-I as able to recognize the magical thinking of the experiencing-I, and, second, in the gradual movement of the experiencing-I toward a union with the attitudes and understandings of the other two figures. It would be self-contradictory for the implied Didion to intentionally undermine this movement at this juncture of the narrative. To put these points another way, the larger design of the narrative underwrites the experiencing-I's movement toward some partial acceptance of John's death. Consequently, it makes sense to regard the implied Didion and the narrating-I as endorsing the conclusion that there was nothing that the experiencing-I could have done to have prevented John's heart attack. Thus, the off-kilter quality of the passage is unintended. I will return to the consequences of this judgment, but first I want to consider another example of unintended off-kilter narration.

Jean-Dominique Bauby's *The Diving Bell and the Butterfly* is an account of living with "locked-in syndrome," a condition in which one's body is almost completely paralyzed, while one's mind remains fully functioning. The passage I want to consider is from a chapter entitled "Twenty to One."

Neither of us was a racing fan, but the track correspondent valued us highly enough to treat us to lunch at the Vincennes restaurant and to give us the password to the Aladdin's cave of racing: a tip. Mithra-Grandchamp was a sure thing, he told us, a guaranteed winner, and since the odds on him were twenty to one, a fat little profit—much better than municipal bonds—seemed likely. [. . .]

We had eaten an enjoyable lunch that day in the restaurant overlooking the racetrack. The large dining room was frequented by gangsters in their Sunday suits, pimps, parolees, and other shady characters who gravitate naturally to horse racing. Sated, we puffed greedily on long cigars and awaited the fourth race. In that hothouse atmosphere, criminal records bloomed like orchids all around us. [. . .]

At Vincennes, we lingered so long in the dining room that the race came and went without us. The betting counter slammed shut under our noses before I had time to pull out the roll of banknotes the people back at the paper had entrusted to me. Despite our attempts at discretion, Mithra-Grandchamp's name had made the rounds of the newspaper. Rumor had turned him into a mythic beast, and everyone was determined to bet on him. All we could do was watch the race and hope. . . . At the last turn, Mithra-Grandchamp began to pull away. Entering the final stretch, he had a lead of five lengths, and we watched in a dream as he crossed the finish line a good forty yards ahead of his closest pursuer. Back at the paper, they must have been going wild around the TV screen. (91–92)

In this passage, the jarring sentence is "At Vincennes we lingered so long in the dining room that the race came and went without us." And again a big part of the problem is that the implied author chooses to have the narrating-I mention something of major consequence within the developing purposive design, something that calls for substantial additional commentary, but then has the narrating-I simply move on. Again, imagining that the narrative is fictional helps clarify the readerly response. In that case, I'd hypothesize that the sentence is an instance of underreporting, one deliberately creating ethical distance between implied author and character narrator and inviting the audience to wonder what exactly happened in the dining room populated by those shady characters. We might even expect that the implied author would eventually supply that explanation. But the frame of nonfiction and the larger context work against the conclusion that the implied Bauby is using the sentence to create distance from the narrating-I. Furthermore, the implied Bauby ends the chapter with a strong signal that his narrative will not return to what happened in the dining room:

> Frankly, I had forgotten Mithra-Grandchamp. The memory of that event has only just come back to me, now doubly painful: regret for a vanished past and, above all, remorse for lost opportunities. Mithra-Grandchamp is the women we were unable to love, the chances we failed to seize, the moments of happiness we allowed to drift away. Today it seems to me that my whole life was nothing but a string of those small near misses: races whose result we know beforehand but in which we fail to bet on the winner. By the way, we managed to pay back all our colleagues. (94)

This passage reveals that the implied Bauby's main purpose in the chapter is to thematize the dramatic narrative of the missed opportunity, to make it the emblem of a life filled with near misses. Given that purpose, we might try to justify the lack of explanation by noting that the *event* of failing to get to the window on time is more important than the reasons for the failure, and that the difficulty of producing the narrative—the flesh-and-blood Bauby worked out a system in which someone would read letters to him and he would blink when they reached the letter he wanted—means that he will stay focused on the most important aspects of any events he narrates. But that justification is finally not satisfactory because this story of Mithra-Grandchamp is not only about the experiencing-I's own near miss but also about his responsibility for the near miss of the others. Thus, not getting to the window on time is as much of an ethical failure to follow through on his agreement to place the bets of his coworkers as it is a near miss for himself. Consequently, the implied Bauby needs to have his narrating-I address his failure to get to the window. Thematizing the event without addressing this ethical failure partly undermines that thematizing. The implied Bauby's decision to conclude the chapter with the sentence about the experiencing-I repaying his coworkers indicates that he has some awareness of the ethics of the told in this situation, but that sentence does not remedy the problem in the ethics of the telling.

How, then, can we theorize these passages of unintended off-kilter narration from Didion and Bauby? Here are six proposals.

(1) This narration is not unreliable but *deficient,* precisely because its going awry is unintended. The different terms help us conceptualize the difference in the relationships of the actual audience to the implied author, the narrator, and the authorial audiences in both types of narration. In unreliable narration, the actual audience seeks to stand with the implied author and the authorial audience at some distance from the narrator whose report, interpretation, or evaluation goes awry. With deficient narration, the actual audience stands at some distance from the implied author, the authorial audience, and narrator, all of whom regard the narration as reliable.

(2) The emphasis on intentionality provides a basis for using the same criteria to make judgments of unreliability and deficiency whether we are reading fiction or nonfiction. An implied author of a nonfiction narrative who endorses a narrator's erroneous report about a historical event is constructing reliable narration just as much as an implied author of a fictional narrative who endorses a narrator's racist views.[4] As members of the flesh-and-blood audience, we should deem both kinds of narration deficient, but, again, such faultfinding is not an activity to which the implied author guides her audience.

---

4. In this respect, I depart from the model of unreliability proposed by Shen and Xu, since they would regard the erroneous report in the historical account as an instance of extra-textual unreliability. In my view, we capture the rhetorical dynamics of such a report more adequately if we view it as reliable but deficient.

(3) Even as unreliable and deficient narration can occur in both fiction and nonfiction, the factual status of the narrative, as my discussion of the passages from Didion and Bauby indicates, will influence (but not determine) the flesh-and-blood audience's judgments about whether the narration is unreliable or deficient.

(4) Because the judgment of deficiency is made by the actual audience and because the actual audience is free to judge any narration as deficient, I find it worth distinguishing between judgments rooted in intratextual and para-textual signals, such as the ones I make about *The Year of Magical Thinking* and *The Diving Bell and the Butterfly*, and judgments rooted in extratextual matters, especially in discrepancies between the actual audience's values and those of the implied author. Thus, for example, deeply religious readers are likely to choose to judge any narration that endorses an existentialist view of the world as deficient, but nonreligious readers are not nearly as likely to do so. The responses of those religious readers to the existentialist narrative have their own interest as examples of actual readers rejecting the position of the authorial audience. But my main point here is that their judgments of defi-ciency are based on criteria imported to rather than derived from the implied author's purposive design of the narrative—as I claim my judgments are. Or, to return to *The Year of Magical Thinking*, many readers object to passages in which Didion displays a lack of awareness about her class privilege. These readers find the narration in these passages deficient not because it breaks from Didion's purposive design but because it conveys an ethically problem-atic sense of entitlement.[5]

(5) The case of deficient narration in nonfiction can further support the case for distinguishing between the flesh-and-blood author and the implied author, as a thought experiment about *The Diving Bell and the Butterfly* can show. Imagine that the flesh-and-blood Bauby, when "Twenty to One" was read back to him, recognized the deficiency in the narration but decided that it did not rise to the level of a flaw that would be worth the extensive labor it would require—from him and his collaborator—to revise the chapter. In this scenario, the flesh-and-blood author would have a different view of the narra-tion from the implied author. Indeed, the flesh-and-blood author would agree

---

5. This point opens the door for another essay devoted to this critique of Didion's memoir, one that would closely examine both its grounds and its consequences. I will not go through that door here but instead just say that I find Didion's lack of awareness of her privilege to be a genuine flaw in the memoir but one that does not overpower its affective, thematic, and ethical force.

with the actual audience that the implied author has introduced a deficiency into the narration.

(6) Deficient referential narration involves misreporting, misinterpreting, and misevaluating about characters, places, and events referred to in nonfiction narrative. In other words, deficient referential narration involves discrepancies between the representation of extratextual reality in nonfiction and that reality itself. Again, given reporting's fundamental role in narrative, the greatest deficiency involves misreporting. Deficiencies may be *inadvertent* or *deceptive.* Inadvertent deficiencies occur in situations where the author intends to report, interpret, or evaluate the external reality accurately but fails to do so. For example, an on-the-scene reporter of a developing news story typically will seek to report everything as accurately as possible but because of limited information may misreport, misinterpret, or misevaluate it. In cases where that happens, the newscaster's authorial audience is invited to accept her account as reliable, but as the additional information comes in, the actual audience will decline that invitation. Inadvertent deficiencies may have bonding or estranging effects, depending on the reasons for the deficiency.

Deceptive deficiencies occur in cases such as James Frey's *A Million Little Pieces,* where the author deliberately misreports events and the authorial audience is not supposed to detect the misreporting. Once the actual audience becomes aware of the deception—usually through one or more readers comparing the author's account to other evidence about the extratextual reality—the actual audience will typically opt out of the authorial audience. Deceptive deficiencies typically have estranging effects on the implied author–actual audience relationship.

I conclude by returning to the deficient narration in *The Year of Magical Thinking* and its consequences. My earlier commentary on how we might read the last part of the narrative if it were fiction is relevant here. But rather than the implied Didion undermining the accuracy of the character narrator's perceptions, we have a situation in which the actual audience comes to doubt whether the experiencing-I's partial working through of her grief is as successful as the implied author represents it. The actual audience recognizes that the representation includes a remarkable shortcut: rather than face the big question that the autopsy raises—how could John and I have forgotten about the LAD?—the experiencing-I has evaded it, and the narrating-I and implied author endorse the evasion.

Nevertheless, many members of the actual audience—and I include myself among them—are likely to find that the deficient narration has bonding rather than estranging effects. It functions as very powerful evidence of the depth of

Didion's grief and of her need to move beyond it. The implied Didion's usual sure-footed self-presentation falters here. This faltering is eloquent testimony to the painful effects of the trauma of John's death and of the virtual necessity of denial. That testimony in turn makes the rest of the implied Didion's construction of the narrative, with its various ways of naming, facing, and working through the experiencing-I's magical thinking, all the more impressive.

CHAPTER 11

Reliability, Dialogue, and Crossover Effects in Jhumpa Lahiri's "The Third and Final Continent"

T HIS CHAPTER, which analyzes Jhumpa Lahiri's "The Third and Final Continent," the rich and intriguing final story in her 1999 Pulitzer Prize–winning collection *Interpreter of Maladies*, brings together several threads of this book. First, as with my discussion of the relation between rhetorical poetics and cognitive narratology in chapter 8, I demonstrate the complementarity between my approach and another one, here postcolonial and cosmopolitan theory. Second, I return to the rhetorical exchanges of character narration, extending my account to the phenomenon of reliable narration. Third, I continue with attention to character-character dialogue, but focus here on the synergies between Lahiri's uses of dialogue and character narration. Fourth, I come back to the discussion of probable impossibilities and related phenomena in order to account for the remarkable climax of Lahiri's story.

"THE THIRD AND FINAL CONTINENT"

Lahiri's story is a moving tale about immigration: the Bengali character narrator tells the story of his relocation from Calcutta to London in 1964 and then from London to Cambridge, Massachusetts, in 1969. Lahiri constructs the progression of the story by intertwining two sets of instabilities: those involving the character narrator's adjustment to Cambridge and those involving his—and his wife Mala's—adjustment to their arranged marriage, which took place in Calcutta shortly before the character narrator departed for the United States. The character narrator's adjustment to both situations is also complicated by his recently having watched his own mother's very painful decline and death. But before Mala joins him in Cambridge, he lives for six weeks in a room he rents from a 103-year-old woman, Mrs. Croft. She initiates him into U.S. culture with what I will call the Splendid Ritual: she exclaims, "There is an American flag on the moon!" (182) and requires him to respond by shouting, "Splendid." Mrs. Croft also becomes what Judith Caesar calls the catalyst in the resolution of the intertwined instabilities, as she and the character narrator gradually come to respect each other across their differences, and they both extend that respect to Mala in a scene that functions as the turning point in the story.

Critics have used postcolonial and cosmopolitan theory to illuminate the story's fresh take on the political dimensions of immigration and naturalization.[1] These critics contend that Lahiri complicates standard postcolonial ideas about how large-scale power relations—between native-immigrant, first world–third world, white-brown, center-margin—operate in the immigrant experience. As Elizabeth Jackson puts it, Lahiri "deconstruct[s] simplistic binaries of power based on geographical origin, geographical location, and cultural identity" (113). Jackson identifies the turning point scene, where Mrs. Croft's and Mala's warm connection across their cultural differences leads to a new warmth between the character narrator and Mala, as a telling case in point.

In an insightful analysis, Susan Koshy argues that the stories in *Interpreter of Maladies* "reveal not only the growing relevance of relationships to those who are less than kin and more than stranger but also . . . the dislocation and consequent unreliability of the very categories through which we demarcate the familiar and the unfamiliar" (598). In addition, the collection explores what Koshy calls "minority cosmopolitanism" through its concern with "diasporic citizenship" and the process of naturalization. In Lahiri's stories, Koshy argues,

> the diasporic citizen inhabits an indeterminate space of belonging that aggregates the discrepant identifications and trajectories associated with contiguous words like *resident alien, immigrant, exile,* and *minority subject.* But it is the process of naturalization as much as a specific identity like immigrant or

---

1. Other issues have also been explored: see Caesar on space, Garg and Khushu-Lahiri on food, and Brada-Williams on the story's placement in the final position in the collection.

refugee that is the subject of Lahiri's fiction. Lahiri's stories explore naturalization not just as a formal process by which citizenship is acquired but also as a social process that extends beyond the conferral of formal citizenship and follows multiple, unpredictable pathways. (598–99)

Applying this framework to "The Third and Final Continent," Koshy makes three related points: (1) Lahiri uses the arranged marriage (rather than the more common choice of romantic love) as a metaphor for immigration and naturalization, thereby highlighting the difficulties of each. (2) Lahiri uses the turning point scene as an allegory for naturalization. The character narrator and Mrs. Croft develop mutual respect within an awareness of difference, and when they both extend that respect to Mala, they make possible the acceptance necessary for the successful marriage; a similar respect within the recognition of difference is necessary for naturalization. (3) Lahiri uses small events and "ordinary affects" as ways to mediate between individual subjectivity and larger social structures. Classifying "The Third and Final Continent" as an epic short story, in which the unnamed character narrator stands in for a whole generation of male Indian immigrants, Koshy notes that Lahiri nevertheless focuses on "quirky encounters and thick quotidian details to create the eventfulness of this journey" (604). As a result, the story "brings into view the dislocations produced by migration and globalization, but from a perspective far removed from macrostructural causes" (605).

From the perspective of rhetorical poetics, I find that Jackson and Koshy impressively elucidate key aspects of Lahiri's exploration of immigration and naturalization. I also note that their analyses proceed in the now time-honored fashion of politically oriented criticism: they use relevant concepts from cultural and political theory to thematize the characters and events of the story. While this method has amply proven its utility, it also leaves room for two rhetorically oriented questions: How does Lahiri use additional resources of narrative to contribute to her exploration of the immigrant experience? And how might Lahiri's practice feed back into our theoretical understanding of those resources? The first question is especially pertinent in light of Koshy's point that Lahiri provides "a perspective [on the dislocations of immigration] far removed from macrostructural causes." What better way to get further inside Lahiri's perspective than by analyzing how it develops through her careful crafting of multiple narrative elements of "Final Continent"? And such an analysis leads naturally to a consideration of the second question. For these reasons, I shall home in on Lahiri's handling of reliable narration, character-character dialogue, and the interaction of textual and readerly dynamics to generate a crossover effect at the story's turning point. My goals are to show that rhetorical theory can productively complement the conclusions of the postcolonial and cosmopolitan critics and that Lahiri's practice can further illuminate the synergies of narrative communication. I start by offering a rhetorical account of reliable narration.

FROM UNRELIABLE TO RELIABLE CHARACTER NARRATION

In discussions of character narration, reliable narration has served primarily as unreliability's unexamined Other. Since Wayne C. Booth distinguished the two kinds of narration in *The Rhetoric of Fiction* by saying that a narrator is "*reliable* when he speaks for or acts in accordance with the norms of the work (which is to say, the implied author's norms), *unreliable* when he does not" (*Rhetoric*, 158–59), theorists have devoted their attention to the devilish delights of unreliability. But the rhetorical principle that authors deploy resources in different ways for different effects points to the value of taking a closer look at reliability. Just as the rhetorical perspective leads to the understanding of unreliable narration as having various subtypes capable of generating effects along the spectrum from bonding to estranging, so too does the approach lead to a recognition that reliable narration is a more varied and nuanced resource than previous narrative theory has acknowledged. These conclusions, in turn, suggest that we should move toward thinking of unreliability and reliability as existing along a continuum rather than as clear binary opposites.

The essence of reliable character narration is the implied author's communicating reports, interpretations, or evaluations that she endorses through the filter of an ontologically distinct character. Authors adopt such filters because anchoring the reporting, interpreting, and evaluating functions of narration in the perspective and experiences of an actor in the storyworld can increase the thematic, affective, and ethical force and significance of the whole narrative. Just how authors adopt those screens can vary from one occasion to the next precisely because authors may give more or less prominence to the character narrator as filter and may use the teller's functions of reporting, interpreting, and evaluating in different combinations—sometimes one may be prominent, sometimes two, and sometimes all three. *The effects of any instance of reliable narration will then depend to a large degree on the specific interaction of the thickness of the character narrator filter with the particular narrating function(s).* Keeping this principle in mind, I still find it useful to group individual instances into three main subtypes: restricted narration, convergent narration, and mask narration.[2] (I will devote the next chapter to a comprehensive overview of character narration that lays out my overall view of the relations among reliable, unreliable, and deficient narration.)

In *restricted narration,* the implied author limits the character narrator's function primarily to reliable reporting and uses both the reliability and the restriction to convey interpretations or evaluations that the character narrator remains unaware of. In these cases, the narrating filter sometimes becomes thin, as the implied author directs primary attention to other characters or foregrounds the activity of the experiencing-I. Consider, for example, this passage from *Huckleberry Finn*: "Just then Sherburn steps out on to the roof of his little front porch, with a double-barrel gun in his hand, and takes his stand, perfectly ca'm and deliberate, not saying a word. The racket stopped, and the wave sucked back" (146). Twain uses Huck's reliable reporting and minimal interpreting to convey implicit interpretations and evaluations of Sherburn's imperious authority and the ultimate weakness of the lynch mob that Huck remains oblivious to. The narrating-Huck's filter is very thin, by which I mean that the focus is on the reliable report rather than the reporter. Twain even dials back Huck's vernacular here, with only the word "ca'm" calling attention to it. Since Twain's primary purpose here is to set the stage for the encounter between Sherburn and the mob from Bricksville, he does not want to call attention to idiosyncrasies of Huck's perspective.

But authors may also deploy restricted narration with a thick filter. They often use this combination when they want to take advantage of a character narrator's naïveté to defamiliarize a situation, to guide the authorial audience to active inferencing about that situation, or to convey an aspect of it that naïve interpreting or evaluating would either miss or render clumsily. In the following passage from Frank McCourt's *Angela's Ashes* (which I previously cited in *Living to Tell about It*), the naïveté of the child narrator is foregrounded almost as much as the events Frankie is reporting:

> Mam is moaning in the bed, her face pure white. Dad has Malachy and the twins out of the bed and sitting on the floor by the dead fire. I run across the street and knock on Aunt Aggie's door till Uncle Pat Keating comes coughing and grumbling, What's up? What's up?
> My mother is moaning in the bed. I think she's sick. (62)

As the reliable reporting of events continues, the implied McCourt makes clear that (a) Angela, Frankie's mother, is having a miscarriage, and (b) Frankie

---

2. In *Living to Tell about It,* I identify both restricted narration and mask narration, but I do not place them along the spectrum I propose here.

the child is too young and innocent to understand the event. Here the effect of the restriction is to highlight Frankie's naïveté in a way that Twain often does not do with Huck. Since one of Twain's purposes is to expose deficiencies of the values and actions of Mississippi shore society in the mid-1800s, he sometimes finds it to his advantage to do what he does in the passage above: foreground the behavior of those who live along the shore and background Huck as perceiver. McCourt, by contrast, wants to give a thick description of his experiences of growing up poor in Limerick, and thus always wants to keep Frankie's perspective front and center in his audience's consciousness. In this passage, McCourt effectively guides rhetorical readers' active inferencing about the gap between Frankie's astute awareness that something dire is happening to his mother and his understanding of just what that dire thing is.

In the next subtype, *convergent narration,* the implied author uses the character narrator as a thick filter who reports, interprets, and evaluates. The implied author's, the character narrator's, and the authorial audience's views of the reporting, interpreting, and evaluation coincide, and the experiencing-I (or some other character observed by the experiencing-I) is likely to be in the foreground. Consider, for example, Jane Eyre's description of her marriage to Rochester: "I have now been married ten years. I know what it is to live entirely for and with what I love best on earth. I hold myself supremely blest—blest beyond what language can express; because I am my husband's life as fully as he is mine" (500). The passage presents the narrating-Jane's report, interpretation, and evaluation of the marriage of experiencing-Jane, and it constitutes an affectively and ethically powerful summary precisely because the sentiments and judgments of the implied Brontë, narrating-Jane, and the authorial audience converge here. It's as if Brontë wants her audience to respond, "Narrator, you married him, and you're both happy—and we're happy for both of you."

In *mask narration,* the character narrator's reporting function recedes and the interpreting and evaluating functions move to the foreground as the implied author uses the character narrator to thematize one or more aspects of the narrative. As with restricted narration, the thickness of the filter can vary, but the implied author's voice is at most only slightly refracted through the mask. Consider, for example, Nick Carraway's famous interpretive and evaluative meditations at the end of *The Great Gatsby,* meditations that end with, "So we beat on, boats against the current, borne back ceaselessly into the past" (189). Nick's thematizing of the narrative is also the implied Fitzgerald's thematizing of it, one that gains power because it is rooted in Nick's prior experiences, observations, and reflections, all of which Fitzgerald's audience has shared.

LAHIRI'S SYNERGIES

At the core of Lahiri's story is the sequence of three scenes involving the Splendid Ritual. These scenes are crucial to her exploration of the politics of immigration and illustrative of her handling of reliable narration and dialogue. In addition, these scenes culminate in the crossover between readerly and textual dynamics at the story's turning point. Lahiri introduces the Ritual during the character narrator's first meeting with Mrs. Croft, when she assesses his suitability as a lodger. In the following passage, she juxtaposes restricted narration and dialogue:

> "There is an American flag on the moon!"
>
> "Yes, madame." Until then I had not thought very much about the moon shot. It was in the newspaper, of course, article upon article. The astronauts had landed on the shores of the Sea of Tranquility, I had read, travelling farther than anyone in the history of civilization. For a few hours they explored the moon's surface. They gathered rocks in their pockets, described their surroundings (a magnificent desolation, according to one astronaut), spoke by phone to the president, and planted a flag in lunar soil. The voyage was hailed as man's most awesome achievement. [. . .]
>
> The woman bellowed, "A flag on the moon, boy! I heard it on the radio! Isn't that splendid?"
>
> "Yes, madame."
>
> But she was not satisfied with my reply. Instead she commanded, "Say 'splendid'!" (179)

Lahiri uses the synergy between the restricted narration and the dialogue to communicate much more than the character narrator is aware of, in large part because the character narrator does not pick up on salient aspects of the authorial disclosure. First, by putting the focus of Mrs. Croft's exclamation on the planting of the American flag rather than, say, the "giant leap for mankind" that Neil Armstrong described, Lahiri constructs Mrs. Croft's exclamation as celebrating the extension of the imperial power of the United States from the earth to the moon. Second, Mrs. Croft's commanding the non-American character narrator who wants her approval to join in her salute is its own small-scale exercise of American imperial power, what we'd today call a micro-aggression. By giving Mrs. Croft a British name, Lahiri subtly adds a reminder of India's colonial past: she suggests that there's repetition with a difference in this exchange. In these ways, Lahiri dramatizes the macrostructural relations that underlie the personal relations between host and immigrant.

But, as Jackson and Koshy point out, Lahiri also wants to explore how such power relations break down or otherwise get complicated. Here she uses Mrs. Croft's dialogue to indicate that Mrs. Croft has a genuine, almost child-like ability to marvel at the moon landing and that she wants to share her pleasure in it with her new boarder. The authorial disclosure, in other words, is that her marveling at the moon landing is also a way to connect with this stranger whose age, sex, race, and nationality are so different from hers. (This inference also invites reflection on how the implied Lahiri enacts her connection with the character narrator across differences of gender and age.) Third, Lahiri uses the character narrator's restricted reporting of what he had read about the landing to convey her own sense of the mixed quality of the event: on the one hand, the astronauts had traveled "farther than anyone in the history of civilization," but on the other, they had found only rocks and a "magnificent desolation." By using the passive voice in the last sentence of the restricted narration, Lahiri distances both the character narrator and herself from the assessment that the voyage was "man's most awesome achievement."

Together these communications have multiple effects that give a significant texture to the politics of the scene. Lahiri guides her audience to view Mrs. Croft as a kind of benevolent, even endearing, dictator to whom the character narrator must pay tribute. She invites her audience to smile at the incongruities of the scene, even as it remains very serious for the character narrator. As the scene continues, Lahiri shifts from restricted narration to narration that is simultaneously reliable and unreliable:

> I was both baffled and somewhat insulted by the request. It reminded me of the way I was taught multiplication tables as a child, repeating after the master, sitting cross-legged . . . on the floor of my one-room Tollygunge school. It also reminded me of my wedding, when I had repeated endless Sanskrit verses after the priest, verses I barely understood, which joined me to my wife. I said nothing.
>
> "Say 'splendid'!" the woman bellowed once again.
>
> "Splendid," I murmured. I had to repeat the word a second time at the top of my lungs, so she could hear. (179–80)

The narration is reliable because the character narrator at some level registers the first layer of Mrs. Croft's command and evaluates it appropriately: as in the other situations, she is imposing her view of things on him, regardless of his own (lack of) connection to them. But the narration is unreliable because the character narrator misses the second layer of Mrs. Croft's communication. This misinterpretation has bonding rather than estranging effects because the occasion of the dialogue and all the differences between Mrs. Croft and himself position Lahiri's rhetorical readers to be extremely sympathetic. Lahiri calls attention to how far apart Mrs. Croft and the character narrator are at this early point in their relationship, even as he registers the similarity between her command and those other situations in which he has submitted to another's authority. Finally, Lahiri uses the comparison with the character narrator's marriage vows to provide a link between his distance from Mrs. Croft and his distance from Mala.

Once the character narrator rents the room, the Splendid Ritual becomes a daily occurrence. At the end of his first week, however, something changes:

> When I approached the bench she peered up at me and demanded:
> "What is your business?"
> "The rent, madame."
> "On the ledge above the piano keys!"
> "I have it here." I extended the envelope toward her, but her fingers, folded together in her lap, did not budge. I bowed slightly and lowered the envelope, so that it hovered just above her hands. After a moment she accepted, and nodded her head.
> That night when I came home, she did not slap the bench, but out of habit I sat beside her as usual. She asked me if I had checked the lock, but she mentioned nothing about the flag on the moon. Instead she said:
> "It was very kind of you!"
> "I beg your pardon, madame?"
> "Very kind of you!"
> She was still holding the envelope in her hands. (184)

The restricted narration thins the filter of the narrating-I, putting the emphasis of the scene on the character-character interaction itself. Lahiri then uses the synergy between the restricted narration and the dialogue, including the authorial disclosure across this conversation and the first one, to guide her audience's interpretations and evaluations of that interaction. Early in the scene, Mrs. Croft is again demanding and commanding, but this time the character narrator does not acquiesce. Instead he does what he thinks is right, countering her command ("On the ledge . . . !") with his assertion ("I have it here") and following through by making it easy for her to take the money. When she does, Lahiri guides her audience to infer that his ethically admirable action leads to a shift in their power dynamic. Later in the passage, Lahiri highlights one consequence of that shift. First, she briefly departs from the restricted narration to have the character narrator call attention to the fact that Mrs. Croft "mentioned nothing about the flag on the moon."

Then Lahiri again relies on the authorial disclosure across conversations to signal the significance of the difference in this night's exchange. It is not just that "It was very kind of you!" replaces "There is an American flag on the moon!," but also that Mrs. Croft pays the compliment twice, presumably because it was so unexpected the first time, the character narrator did not quite understand what "it" refers to. The larger communication, never directly expressed by the character narrator,[3] is that he and Mrs. Croft have now established a personal connection across their many differences, a connection rooted in each's admirable ethical response to the other. Although the power hierarchy has not disappeared, it has softened. The benevolent dictator has become a grateful host, and the subaltern lodger has become a man worthy of a compliment. Furthermore, these changes loom larger precisely because they arise out of the deviation from the ritual repetition of "Splendid!" and its implicit politics of interpellation. In other words, the character narrator's acting on his sense of what is right rather than acquiescing to Mrs. Croft's instructions has led her to see him in a different light and that vision, in turn, gives a new dimension to their relationship.

After the character narrator and Mala have been living together in their own apartment in Cambridge for a week, they are "still strangers" (192) to one another. He suggests they take a walk, and "without thinking" (193) he leads her to Mrs. Croft's, where they find her lying on the floor.

> "I broke my hip!" Mrs. Croft announced, as if no time had passed.
> "Oh dear, madame."
> "I fell off the bench!"
> "I am so sorry, madame."
> "It was the middle of the night! Do you know what I did, boy?"
> I shook my head.
> "I called the police!"
> She stared up at the ceiling and grinned sedately, exposing a crowded row of long gray teeth. Not one was missing. "What do you say to that, boy?"
> As stunned as I was, I knew what I had to say. With no hesitation at all, I cried out, "Splendid!"

---

3. Some close readers might ask whether we should attribute the larger effects of this passage not just to Lahiri but also to the character narrator's deliberate design. While I would not argue strongly against such a reading, I don't see enough other signs of the character narrator's self-consciousness and aesthetic control to make me find it more persuasive than my hypothesis that Lahiri moves him from one kind of narration to another according to the effects she seeks at any given point.

> Mala laughed then. Her voice was full of kindness, her eyes bright with amusement. I had never heard her laugh before. (194–95)

Lahiri begins with dialogue, mixes restricted narration with reliable interpretive commentary, and then moves to convergent narration. Once again the synergy leads to multiple communications, many of which the character narrator is not aware of. Here are the salient features of Lahiri's communication up to the character narrator's utterance of "Splendid!": (1) Mrs. Croft and the character narrator, despite all their differences and his having moved out of her house, converse as old friends. Her use of "boy" in this dialogue has a different tone and force than it did when she first said, "There's an American flag on the moon, boy!" He has moved from stranger to something closer to a surrogate son. (2) Mrs. Croft gives the character narrator more credit than during the previous enactments of the Splendid Ritual: earlier she had prompted him by asking, "Isn't it splendid?"; here she asks, "What do you say to that, boy?" (3). His ability to answer shows how well he knows her (at least in one way), a demonstration that in turn highlights the gap between him and Mala.

At the end of the passage, Lahiri shifts to convergent narration, as the character narrator reports, interprets, and evaluates Mala's response to his performance in a way that both Lahiri and her rhetorical readers warmly endorse. Just as he has never heard her laugh before, he has also never expressed this affective and ethical appreciation for her before. That expression deepens the audience's affective and ethical bond with him.

As the scene continues, Lahiri continues to build on the bonding effects of the convergent narration, making it the most affectively and ethically powerful scene in the story. Finally noticing Mala, Mrs. Croft commands her to stand:

> Mala rose to her feet, adjusting the end of her sari over her head and holding it to her chest, and, for the first time since her arrival, I felt sympathy. I remembered my first days in London, learning how to take the Tube to Russell Square, riding an escalator for the first time, being unable to understand that when the man cried "piper" it meant "paper," being unable to decipher, for a whole year, that the conductor said "mind the gap" as the train pulled away from each station. Like me, Mala had traveled far from home, not knowing where she was going, or what she would find, for no reason other than to be my wife. As strange as it seemed, I knew in my heart that one day her death would affect me, and stranger still, that mine would affect her. I wanted somehow to explain this to Mrs. Croft, who was still scrutinizing Mala from top to toe with what seemed to be placid disdain. . . . At last Mrs. Croft declared, with the equal measures of disbelief and delight I knew well:
>
> "She is a perfect lady!"

Now it was I who laughed. I did so quietly, and Mrs. Croft did not hear me. But Mala had heard, and, for the first time, we looked at each other and smiled. (195–96)

Lahiri continues the convergent narration with special emphasis on the character narrator's interpretations and evaluations. More specifically, the character narrator's reliable interpreting and evaluating is rooted in his empathetic response to Mala, one based less on his having previously undergone the scrutiny of Mrs. Croft than on his experience of adjusting to his second continent. It is an ethically admirable imaginative leap—and one that converts the opening section of the story, in which the character narrator briefly summarizes his time in London, from interesting backstory to events with ongoing relevance.[4] In addition, Lahiri invites her audience to make the link between Mala's travel and that of the astronauts: "far from home, not knowing where she was going or what she would find." Finally, the character narrator's empathetic drawing on his past to interpret Mala's present situation leads him to project a future in which each cares for the other.

As noted above, Mrs. Croft serves as the catalyst for the connection between the married couple. Her imperiousness evokes the character narrator's sympathy for Mala, and her clear approbation evokes the shared smile. But Lahiri builds another, subtler progression into the narration. After the character narrator thinks about his future with Mala, he comments, "I wanted somehow to explain all this to Mrs. Croft," a sign of how much he wants to continue to connect with her across their differences.[5] Yet after Mrs. Croft passes judgment on Mala, he laughs just loudly enough for Mala but not Mrs. Croft to hear, a signal from Lahiri that his main desire to connect now appropriately gets transferred to his wife.

THE PROBABLE IMPLAUSIBILITY; OR THE CROSSOVER LOGIC OF MALA'S LAUGHTER

My analysis so far has passed over the most radical feature of this scene, which I highlight here:

4. A full-scale rhetorical analysis would have much more to say about the role of the second continent in the narrative progression.

5. Lahiri's communication about the character narrator's relation to his mother, who became mentally unbalanced after her husband died, is worthy of more commentary. Suffice it to say that Mrs. Croft becomes a quasi-mother figure to him (at one point he has to remind himself that "I was not her son" [189]), and that his mother's response to her husband's death adds another layer to the character narrator's thoughts about how Mala's death would affect him and how his would affect her. See Caesar's good discussion of this issue.

As stunned as I was, I knew what I had to say. With no hesitation at all, I cried out, "Splendid!"

Mala laughed then. Her voice was full of kindness, her eyes bright with amusement. I had never heard her laugh before. (194–95)

In depicting Mala's laughter, Lahiri relies on a crossover effect to create a probable implausibility. Indeed, Lahiri's crossover effect is, in one sense, even more radical than Small's in *Stitches* (analyzed in chapter 2) because it is not a compressed representation of multiple events but an invented singular event. But, like Small's crossover effect, this probable implausibility will probably not be registered as such by most readers, and it will most likely be approved of by those who do notice it.

The laughter is not impossible in the sense of "it could never happen," but the law of probability and necessity suggests that Mala would be far more perplexed—and, indeed, further worried about her situation in this strange place with this strange man—than amused by her husband's interaction with Mrs. Croft. It's not just that she does not know—as Lahiri's readers do—the Splendid Ritual. It's also that she does not know Mrs. Croft from Adam's off ox, and she barely knows her husband, let alone why he would answer Mrs. Croft's question with "Splendid!" But the implied Lahiri relies on the readerly dynamics to guide her construction of the scene. Because she knows that her audience has followed the evolution of the Splendid Ritual, she can deliver this new variation and rely on her audience to laugh. Indeed, the Meta-Rule of Dominant Focus helps explain that the audience will initially be more attentive to the Ritual than to anything else in the scene. Once that attention generates laughter, Lahiri can rely on the Rule of Self-Assurance and simply write, "Mala laughed." In other words, Lahiri counts on her audience (a) laughing at the character narrator's "Splendid!" and (b) having their laughter cross over into the textual dynamics so that Mala's otherwise implausible laughter seems not just plausible but almost inevitable. Why does Mala laugh? Because Lahiri's rhetorical readers laugh first.[6]

Furthermore, Lahiri's elaboration of Mala's response extends the crossover effect: "Her voice was full of kindness, her eyes bright with amusement." That is, the readerly dynamics of the scene generate both amusement and kindness toward the character narrator and Mrs. Croft as they engage in their playful

---

6. Some readers may object that Mala's laughter is mimetically plausible without the crossover from readerly dynamics, contending that there is something intrinsically funny in the exchange between Mrs. Croft and the character narrator, and the laughter itself characterizes Mala as the kind of woman who would find humor in that situation. I do not want to dispute such readings unless they go so far as to deny the crossover effect. I also see them as rooted in the impulse to "preserve the mimetic," which I discuss in the introduction to *Living to Tell about It*.

Ritual. But the difference between audience and character means that Lahiri also guides her audience's responses to Mala's responses. As a result, the audience's sympathies for all three characters deepen even as their ethical approbation of all three increases, and thus, the convergent narration is even more affectively and ethically powerful.

MASK NARRATION

After the turning point, Lahiri has the character narrator cover, first, the "honeymoon of sorts" he and Mala enjoyed, and second, the next thirty years of his life, years that included their becoming parents to a son. Lahiri ends the story with a passage that morphs from the character narrator's thoughts about his son to mask narration, with the pivot occurring with his reference to the astronauts:

> In my son's eyes I see the ambition that had first hurled me across the world. In a few years he will graduate and pave his way, alone and unprotected. But I remind myself that he has a father who is still living, a mother who is happy and strong. Whenever he is discouraged, I tell him that if I can survive on three continents, then there is no obstacle he cannot conquer. While the astronauts, heroes forever, spent mere hours on the moon, I have remained in this new world for nearly thirty years. I know that my achievement is quite ordinary. I am not the only man to seek his fortune far from home, and certainly I am not the first. Still, there are times I am bewildered by each mile I have traveled, each meal I have eaten, each person I have known, each room in which I have slept. As ordinary as it all appears, there are times when it is beyond my imagination. (197–98)

Lahiri's narration employs a thicker filter than Fitzgerald's at the end of *The Great Gatsby,* but it too is mask narration because Lahiri uses it to thematize the character narrator's experiences. That thematizing is in line with Koshy's description of "Final Continent" as an "epic short story" in which the character narrator stands in for a whole generation of Indian men ("I am not the only man"). But what is especially effective here is Lahiri's reference to the astronauts. First, the character narrator's comparison sets up his double-sided interpretation of his experience, his assessment of it as both "ordinary" (unlike theirs) and "beyond [his] imagination" (like theirs). The comparison also points to the extraordinary temporal dimension of his immigration and naturalization, one that makes so much difference to his son. Second, the comparison also implicitly brings Mrs. Croft into the passage because she is so closely associated with the astronauts. Mrs. Croft is also present through the references to "each meal I have eaten, each person I have known, each room in which I have slept." In addition, the character narrator's attitude of wonder at his experience on three continents is similar to Mrs. Croft's wonder at the flag on the moon. Indeed, I would argue that the passage's implicit references to Mrs. Croft play a significant role in its persuasiveness. Above all, the mask narration effectively completes Lahiri's exploration of the complexities, idiosyncrasies, and wonders of immigration and naturalization.

CONCLUSION

This chapter sketches a different kind of partnership between rhetorical poetics and another approach than the one between rhetorical poetics and cognitive narratology in chapter 8. There the partnership is a collaboration, while here it is a complementarity. Postcolonial and cosmopolitan theory provide both key concepts and an attention to politics that illuminate Lahiri's thematic purposes. Rhetorical poetics provides a thicker description of the means by which Lahiri accomplishes those purposes, even as it adds to our understanding of the affective and ethical layers of Lahiri's story. At the same time, Lahiri's practice feeds back into a rhetorical understanding not only of reliable narration, character-character dialogue, and the synergies between them but also of probable implausibilities. In these ways, "The Third and Final Continent" provides valuable lessons in the rhetoric of narrative communication itself.

CHAPTER 12

Reliable, Unreliable, and Deficient Narration

TOWARD A RHETORICAL POETICS

THIS CHAPTER brings together in one short space the rhetorical view of reliable, unreliable, and deficient character narration in both fiction and nonfiction that I began to develop in *Living to Tell about It* and have elaborated on in this book.[1] Readers of those previous discussions will recognize some repetition here, but I hope that most readers will find the repetition offset by the advantages of seeing the separate strands of my inquiry woven together in this one place. In any case, this account seeks to be simultaneously capacious and supple: that is, it seeks concepts that can cumulatively provide the explanatory power of a comprehensive theory even as they individually offer the flexibility for a deep dive into the workings of particular uses of the technique.

I start with general points: (1) Reliable and unreliable narration are neither binary opposites nor single phenomena but rather broad terms and concepts that each cover a wide range of author-narrator-audience relationships in narrative. Furthermore, it makes sense to combine their two ranges into a single larger spectrum that runs from unreliable reporting on one end to mask narration on the other (details about these subtypes to follow). (2) Unreliable narration and deficient narration, by contrast, are radically different rhe-

---

1. For an alternative comprehensive account, see Sternberg and Yacobi, who criticize the rhetorical view on several points. Although I am not persuaded by their critique, I invite readers to compare the two accounts and draw their own conclusions.

torical phenomena, and deficient narration needs its own separate spectrum. Although both unreliable and deficient narration are what I have called "off-kilter"—that is, they both disrupt the alignment of authors, narrators, and audiences that characterizes most reliable narration—they have one fundamental difference: unreliable narration is deliberately off-kilter, while deficient narration is inadvertently off-kilter. In unreliable narration, author, authorial audience, and actual audience align as they recognize what is off-kilter about the narrator. In deficient narration, author, narrator, and authorial audience align, but the actual audience views all of them as off-kilter.

For purposes of expositional clarity, I offer two taxonomies and illustrate them by placing subtypes of reliable and unreliable narration along one spectrum and subtypes of deficient narration along another. At the same time, I want to emphasize that these taxonomies are not procrustean categories but rather heuristic devices designed to help explain the effects of different kinds of character narration on author-narrator-audience relationships. The application of the concepts to any one passage of character narration should proceed in a posteriori rather than an a priori fashion—from effects back to causes in the author-narrator-audience relationships, not from taxonomical categories to an account of effects. The distinction between bonding and estranging unreliability is another reminder of the need for a posteriori application: the distinction arises from the recognition that the same type of unreliability can have markedly different effects.

RELIABLE NARRATION

In *Living to Tell about It,* I argue that character narration is an art of indirection, in which an implied author uses a single text to address at least two different audiences (her own and the character narrator's narratee) to accomplish at least two different purposes (her own and the character narrator's). In *Living to Tell,* I also note that the main functions of narrators are to report, to interpret, and to evaluate, and that skillful implied authors can communicate to their audiences whether their purposes and those of their narrators converge, diverge, or do some of each.

The essence of reliable narration is the implied author's communicating matters that she endorses through the filter of an ontologically distinct character. Authors adopt such filters because anchoring the reporting, interpreting, and evaluating in the perspective and experiences of an actor and teller in the storyworld can increase the thematic, affective, and ethical force and significance of the whole narrative. But not all reliable narration establishes the same relationship between the character narrator's telling functions and her character functions. Indeed, attending to the variable relationship between these functions is crucial to understanding why reliable and unreliable narration are not binary opposites but convenient shorthands, each encompassing a range of character narration. To put this point another way, just how authors adopt the filter of an ontologically distinct character can vary from one occasion to the next precisely because authors may give more or less prominence to the filter itself and because they may use the teller's functions of reporting, interpreting, and evaluating in different combinations—sometimes one may be prominent, sometimes two, and sometimes all three. In unreliable narration, the filter is always thick (the distance between implied author and narrator depends on the filter introducing some distortion of the implied author's take on things), but in reliable narration, the thickness of the filter can vary. *Consequently, the nature and effects of any instance of reliable narration will depend to a large degree on the specific interaction of the thickness of the filter with the particular narrating function(s).* Nevertheless, I find it useful to identify three main subtypes of reliable narration: restricted narration, convergent narration, and mask narration.[2]

On the spectrum that goes from unreliability on one end (the left) to reliability on the other (the right), I locate *restricted narration* in the middle, because it is fundamentally reliable, yet its effects point to its affinities with both unreliable narration and other subtypes of reliable narration. In restricted narration, the implied author limits the character narrator's function to reliable reporting and uses both the reliability and the restriction to convey interpretations or evaluations that the character narrator remains unaware of. In restricted narration, the narrating filter of the character's mimetic function sometimes becomes thin, as the implied author directs primary attention to other characters or foregrounds the activity of the experiencing-I. Indeed, in some passages, the narration could seem to be coming from an undramatized noncharacter narrator. As I note in chapter 11, Mark Twain sometimes restricts Huck Finn's narration in this way. At other times, however, an author will keep the narrating filter thick, as Frank McCourt does with Frankie throughout *Angela's Ashes* (see chapter 11 for a specific example). A good rule of thumb is that the more the author wants to keep the focus on the character narrator's experience and the more naïve that character narrator is, the more likely the filter will be thick.

Further to the right along the spectrum, I locate *convergent narration*. In convergent narration, the implied author's, the character narrator's, and

---

2. In *Living to Tell about It*, I identify both restricted narration and mask narration, but I do not place them along the spectrum I propose here.

the authorial audience's views of the reporting, interpreting, and evaluating coincide even as the narrating filter of the character function is thick and the focus is on the experience of one or more characters. Convergent narration will typically have strong bonding effects because of this alignment of author, narrator, character, and audience. Convergent narration is especially likely to occur at high points in narratives that trace a character narrator's growth in maturity, wisdom, or some other desirable quality or qualities. For example, at the turning point of Jhumpa Lahiri's "The Third and Final Continent," the character narrator reports an action of his wife, Mala, who up until this moment has been a stranger to him, and he then interprets and evaluates it. Mala is responding to his interaction with his former landlady, Mrs. Croft:

> Mala laughed then. Her voice was full of kindness, her eyes bright with amusement. I had never heard her laugh before. (194–95)

This passage is an instance of convergent narration because the character narrator's filter is thick, and because Lahiri and her audience share not only in his interpretation and evaluation of Mala's laughter but also in the very positive affective and ethical undertones of the narration. In short, implied author, narrator, and audience are all aligned in this moment that marks the beginning of the character narrator's love for his wife following their arranged marriage. (For a fuller discussion, see chapter 11.)

At the right end of the spectrum I locate *mask narration.* In mask narration, the character narrator's reporting function recedes and the interpreting and evaluating functions move to the foreground as the implied author relies on the character narrator to thematize one or more aspects of the narrative for the audience. While the filter remains in place, it is thinner than in convergent narration, and the implied author's voice is only slightly refracted as a result. At the same time, the author relies on the audience's experience of following the character narrator's struggles and triumphs to give the thematizing its particular force. Mask narration is often at work in those lines from character narrators that get extracted from their context and attributed just to the author. Commentators on *The Great Gatsby* have no compunction about attributing the famous sentence, "So we beat on, boats against the current, borne back ceaselessly into the past" to F. Scott Fitzgerald rather than to Nick Carraway. Similarly, commentators on *The Long Goodbye* frequently attribute "To say good-bye is to die a little" to Raymond Chandler as much as (or even more than) they attribute it to Philip Marlowe. You can, I'm sure, think of other examples.

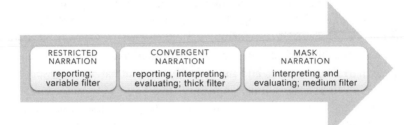

FIGURE 12.1. The spectrum of reliable narration.

To sum up, figure 12.1 is a diagram of the Spectrum of Reliable Narration. The direction of the arrow indicates the increasing degree of alignment between author and narrator (the authorial audience is always aligned with the author). Typically, reliable narration will have bonding effects.

UNRELIABLE NARRATION

Moving left from "restricted narration," we enter into the territory of unreliable narration. I reiterate that in this territory, the narrating filter of the character's mimetic function is always thick, because the unreliability is always linked to specific traits of the character. In *Living to Tell about It,* I identify six types of unreliability—*misinterpreting and underinterpreting, misevaluating and underevaluating, and misreporting and underreporting*—but I do not locate them along the spectrum of distance between author and narrator. I now locate misinterpreting and underinterpreting closer to the middle, misevaluating further along to the left, and misreporting at the far left end of the spectrum. I place misreporting at the far left for two reasons: (1) Since I view somebody-telling-somebody-else-that-something-happened as fundamental to narrative, I also view divergence between author and narrator about what happened to be more fundamental than divergences in interpretations or evaluations of what happened. (2) Misreporting is typically accompanied by misinterpreting or misevaluating, and so in practice the distance between author and narrator will be magnified. I locate misevaluating as further left than misinterpreting because I view ethical deficiencies as more significant than interpretive ones, and because I view misinterpreting as closer to what happens in restricted narration.

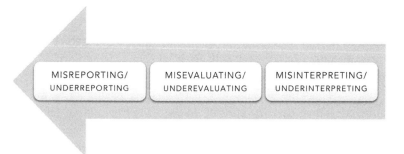

FIGURE 12.2. The spectrum of unreliable narration.

FIGURE 12.3. The spectrum of unreliable and reliable narration.

Figure 12.2 shows the spectrum of Unreliable Narration, with the arrow indicating the direction of increasing unreliability (though again, particular instances anywhere along this spectrum may have bonding or estranging effects).

Putting the two ranges together, we get the spectrum shown in figure 12.3, with the arrow indicating the direction of increasing reliability.

DEFICIENT NARRATION

In the spectrum of unreliability, author and authorial audience are always aligned, and the actual audience seeks to join that alignment. What varies is the degree of the author-audience alignment with the narrator. As noted above, deficient narration does not have a place on this spectrum because in it, author, narrator, and authorial audience are aligned, but the actual audience opts out of joining their alignment. Deficient narration can involve reporting, interpreting, and/or evaluating, and it can also have bonding or estranging effects, depending on our assessment of the reasons for the deficiency. However, those bonding and estranging effects operate primarily in the implied author–actual audience relationship rather than primarily in the narrator–authorial audience relationship, as they do in unreliable narration.

Any member of the actual audience is, of course, free to decide that any narration is deficient, especially along the axis of ethics, because any reader can resist or reject the ethical values that undergird an author's narrative. But as a rhetorical theorist, I am especially interested in two kinds of deficient narration, the first exclusive to nonfiction and the second appearing in both fiction and nonfiction. The first kind, which I call *deficient referential narration,* itself has two subtypes, the *inadvertent* and the *deceptive.* The second kind I call *deficient intratextual narration.* (For other treatments of character narration in which there is a discrepancy between the representation and external reality, see Hansen as well as Shen and Xu.)

Deficient referential narration involves misreporting, misinterpreting, and misevaluating about characters, places, and events referred to in nonfiction narrative. In other words, deficient referential narration involves discrepancies between the representation of extratextual reality in nonfiction and that reality itself. Again, given reporting's fundamental role in narrative, the greatest deficiency involves misreporting. Inadvertent deficiencies occur in situations where the author intends to report, interpret, or evaluate the external reality accurately but fails to do so. For example, an on-the-scene reporter of a developing news story typically will seek to report everything as accurately as possible but because of limited information may misreport, misinterpret, or misevaluate it. In cases where that happens, the newscaster's authorial audience is invited to accept her account as reliable, but as the additional information comes in, the actual audience will decline that invitation. Inadvertent deficiencies may have bonding or estranging effects, depending on the reasons for the deficiency.

Deceptive deficiencies occur in cases such as James Frey's *A Million Little Pieces,* where the author deliberately misreports events and the authorial audience is not supposed to detect the misreporting. Once the actual audience becomes aware of the deception—usually through one or more readers comparing the author's account to other evidence about the extratextual reality—the actual audience will opt out of the authorial audience. Deceptive deficiencies typically have estranging effects on the implied author–actual audience relationship.

Intratextual deficient narration, as I noted, can occur in fiction or in nonfiction, and it reveals its deficiency through some inconsistency or other flaw in the overall design of the narration. To put it another way, intratextual deficient narration is deficient in relation to the terms set by its own larger nar-

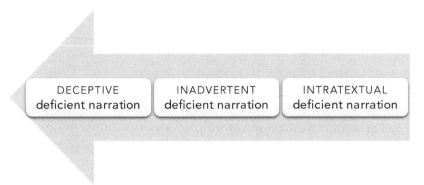

FIGURE 12.4. General kinds of deficient narration.

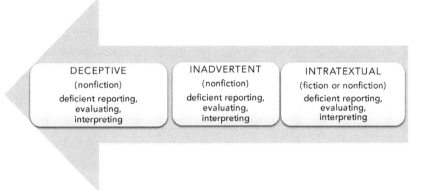

FIGURE 12.5. A detailed taxonomy of deficient narration.

rative. For example, Huck Finn's narration in the Evasion section of Twain's novel is deficient because its ethical endorsement of Tom Sawyer's plans for the Evasion, which entail a demeaning treatment of Jim, contradicts Huck's hard-won decision to go to hell rather than tell Miss Watson where she can find her slave. Here the deficient narration has estranging effects on many readers' relationship not only with Huck but also with Twain.

Typically, the deceptive subtype of deficient narration will have greater estranging effects than the inadvertent subtype. Hence the above spectra, with the second offering the more fine-grained description.

CONCLUSION; OR SO WHAT?

I offer two answers to the so-what question: (1) This account, like any synoptic view of diverse but related phenomena, allows us not only to see those phenomena as part of a coherent big picture but also to enhance our understanding of the individual phenomena. That is, we can understand each subtype of character narration more clearly and deeply when we see it in relation to all the other subtypes. (2) This account provides a springboard for a whole range of other projects. One could, for example, compare the uses of convergent narration in fiction and nonfiction as a way to compare the relations between implied authors and narrators in the two modes. Or one could consider how, if at all, the account would need to be modified for graphic narrative and film narrative. Or one could consider how the account can illuminate the workings of dialogue. And so on. In other words, to the extent that rhetorical poetics adequately describes character narration, it opens up additional lines of inquiry into the wonders of narrative communication.

CHAPTER 13

Occasions of Narration and the Functions of Narrative Segments in *Enduring Love*

I
N THIS CHAPTER, I move away from focusing primarily on explicit some-bodies who tell (narrators and characters) in order to take up two resources of narrative communication that deserve more attention from narra-tive theorists: occasions of narration and narrative segments. Ian McEwan's *Enduring Love* provides a rich site for this exploration for several reasons. McEwan constructs the novel in three segments, each with different tellers situated in different occasions, and he constructs synergies among tellers, segments, and occasions that are crucial to his overall communication to rhe-torical readers. The novel is also a rich site because McEwan overtly down-plays the significance of the final two segments by labeling them "Appendix I" and "Appendix II" while covertly signaling their importance in the overall progression.

More specifically, I shall consider the implied occasions of (a) the first, longest segment, Joe Rose's tale of how the erotomaniac Jed Parry disrupted Joe's relationship with his partner of seven years, Clarissa Mellon; (b) Appen-dix I, a fictional scholarly essay by Robert Wenn and Antonio Camia (the sur-names are an anagram for Ian McEwan) on erotomania in which the events of Joe's narrative are treated as a case study; and (c) Appendix II, an undelivered love letter from Jed to Joe, written from the hospital to which Jed has been committed after the events of Joe's story. In analyzing Joe's narrative, I shall discuss how its occasion relates to Joe's purpose in telling his story and to the shift in his tale from self-consciousness and reliability to unself-consciousness and unreliability; I shall also consider the relation between Joe's purpose in his telling and McEwan's purpose in his. In addressing the Appendices, I shall focus on how they function not as appendages to the novel but as integral parts of McEwan's telling. To put this point another way, although Joe Rose's narrative has two Appendices, McEwan's *Enduring Love* has none. More generally, McEwan's strategy enables him to combine the effects arising from his three distinctively different tellings with the effects arising from their interaction in order to give his rhetorical readers a powerful affective and ethical experience that ultimately serves one of his main thematic purposes: exploring the vexed nature of the relationship between love and logic.[1] Since the nature and consequences of McEwan's strategy become most evident in the Appendices, I will give substantial attention to them.

THE THREE TELLINGS IN *ENDURING LOVE*

I start with three initial observations about McEwan's three tellings. The third merely states the obvious, but I include it because I believe that the effects that follow from it are not so obvious.

(1) The authors of each telling remain ignorant of the existence of the others, and thus, McEwan's design for his novel foregrounds the importance of the overarching relationships between implied author and authorial and actual audiences, since only McEwan and his readers have access to all three texts. In other words, McEwan's structural design foregrounds the difference between Joe's story and McEwan's larger novel. In that way, *Enduring Love* is a close relative of the novel-within-a-novel design he will later employ in *Atonement*.

(2) McEwan does not present the three tellings in the temporal order of their composition. Jed's letter is written one thousand days after he's been hospitalized, and since McEwan tells his audience in a note preceding the letter that a photocopy of it was forwarded to Dr. Wenn, we can infer that Wenn obtained it while doing his research, and thus, that the scholarly essay itself was published at some point after that. Furthermore, since Joe's narration ends shortly after Jed's arrest, we know that it came first. Thus, the fabula order is

---

1. As the critical commentary on the novel amply demonstrates, McEwan has other important thematic purposes, including exploring conflicts among scientific, literary, and religious worldviews (Greenberg), the powers and limits of narrative itself (Greenberg, Randall, Edwards, and Malcolm), the problem of other minds (Green), and masculinity under pressure (Jago Morrison, Davies).

Joe's story, Jed's letter, and the scholarly article, while the sjuzhet order is Joe's story, scholarly article, Jed's letter.

(3) McEwan works with three different genres or modes of telling: a retrospective narrative, an article for a social science journal, and a letter that will never reach its addressee.

I now turn to look more closely at each telling.

JOE ROSE'S TELLING

Joe makes his living as a science writer, and McEwan makes it clear that (a) Joe is good at what he does in part because he understands a lot about the powers and limits of narrative, and (b) Joe is initially applying his craft to his own story of a balloon accident that killed a man, John Logan, and that brought Jed Parry into his life. Joe's first sentence is, "The beginning is simple to mark" (1), and the first three chapters are peppered with other comments that reflect his self-conscious construction: for example, "before I let [the gust of wind] reach us, let me freeze the frame" (12), and, at the beginning of chapter 2, "Best to slow down" (19). Perhaps most dramatically, McEwan has Joe narrate chapter 9 from Clarissa's "point of view. Or at least from that point as I later construed it" (85). But McEwan also uses the end of chapter 9 to mark a significant change in Joe's narration.

Chapter 9 recounts the scene between Clarissa and Joe two nights after the Sunday of the balloon accident when she returns from a frustrating day at the university where she teaches Romantic poetry. During this day, Jed has shown up outside their apartment building, called Joe on the phone, and otherwise established his harassing presence in Joe's life. With so much less exposure to Jed, Clarissa suspects that Joe is overreacting. For most of the chapter, Joe makes good on his effort to see things from Clarissa's perspective. Here is his account of Clarissa's arrival at their flat:

> When she steps into the hall, [Joe] is waiting for her by the door of his study. He has a wild look about him that she has not seen in some time. She associates this look with overambitious schemes, excited and usually stupid plans that very occasionally afflict the calm, organized man she loves. He's coming toward her, talking before she's even through the door. Without a kiss or any form of greeting, he's off on a tale of harassment and idiocy behind which there appears to be some kind of accusation [. . .] (86–87)

Joe's self-conscious crafting is impressive here because he consistently interprets and evaluates his actions through his reconstruction of Clarissa's perspective at the time of the action. Rhetorical readers can't, of course, know for sure that he has captured her consciousness, but they can know that he comes up with a plausible account and that the very effort is a sign of ethical generosity. At the same time, McEwan uses the passage—and the broader scene—to demonstrate how Joe's and Clarissa's different responses to Parry are creating a gap between them and that Joe is aware of the problem.

Now consider this passage from the end of the chapter:

> Clarissa, aware that her remarks might not bear up under discussion, is getting out while she's ahead, leaving the room while it's still delicious to feel wronged. "Well, fuck off, then," Joe shouts to her departing back. He feels he wouldn't mind picking up the dressing table stool and throwing it through the window. He is the one who should be walking out. After some seconds' hesitation, he hurries out of the room, passing Clarissa in the hallway, snatches his coat from its peg, and goes out, slamming the door hard behind him and glad that she was close by to hear its full force. (94)

In this passage, Joe fails to sustain his effort to narrate from Clarissa's perspective. Indeed, a closer look marks the trigger for the switch in Joe's report of his cursing, since it's in the very next sentence that Joe fully moves back to his own perspective. (Clarissa can't know that he feels like picking up that stool, since Joe doesn't actually do that. And if there is any lingering doubt about the switch, the next paragraph removes it, since it reports on Joe's movements after he leaves their flat.) Furthermore, Joe shows no awareness of his shift, but instead seems to revel in his representation of himself as the aggrieved party in their encounter. In other words, at this point, McEwan shows Joe not only inadvertently losing sight of his purpose in the chapter but also erasing the temporal difference between the experiencing-I and the narrating-I. The effort to narrate the highly charged and emotionally difficult scene makes the rational science writer lose rational control of his telling. Furthermore, despite his best efforts, the rational science writer can't help but betray his bias and his interest in making himself look right and Clarissa wrong. I will return to this point below. Finally, chapter 9 marks a significant turning point in Joe's narration: from this point forward, McEwan does not have Joe make any explicit comments on his construction of the narration. Instead, McEwan has Joe keep the primary focus on Joe's perspective at the time of the action, with occasional moves to Joe's present-tense scientifically based reflections on such issues as the way one's self-interest guides one's perceptions.

The most dramatic consequence of this shift occurs in Joe's narration in chapters 19 and 20 of Clarissa's birthday lunch and its aftermath. Jed, angry that Joe has not acknowledged his love, hires two men to shoot Joe in the restaurant where Joe, Clarissa, and Clarissa's godfather are celebrating her birthday. But Jed's plan goes awry when the killers mistakenly target a man at the next table. Here is an excerpt from Joe's account of the event:

> The two men who had stopped by the table next to ours seemed to have suffered burns to the face. Their skin was a lifeless prosthetic pink, the color of dolls or of Band-Aids, the color of no one's skin. They shared a robotic nullity of expression. Later we learned about the latex masks, but at the time these men were a shocking sight, even before they acted. The arrival of the waiter with our desserts in stainless steel bowls was temporarily soothing. Both men wore black coats that gave them a priestly look. There was ceremony in their stillness. The flavor of my sorbet was lime, just to the green side of white. . . .
>
> A variety of [possible explanations for the presence of the two men] unspooled before me at speed: a student stunt; vendors; the man, Colin Tapp, was a doctor or lawyer and these were his patients or clients; some new version of the kissogram; crazy members of the family come to embarrass. Around us the lunchtime uproar, which had dipped locally, was back to level. When the taller man drew from his coat a black stick, a wand, I inclined to the kissogram. (184–85)

Notice the power McEwan gives to Joe's perspective at the time of the action. Although Joe the narrator knows that the men were wearing latex masks, he describes them as having suffered from burns, as having skin the color of no skin. What's more, although Joe the narrator knows that the man withdrew a gun from his pocket, he calls it a wand, and he does not include a clarifying remark from his perspective at the time of the telling analogous to the one in the description of the men's faces. In fact, he goes on to say that the man "pointed his wand" at the man at the next table, Colin Tapp, and he only implicitly reports that the wand is a gun when he notes that "the silenced bullet struck through [Tapp's] white shirt at his shoulder" (185).

McEwan further emphasizes that Joe's perspective at the time of the narration governs his telling in chapter 20, when Joe records his dialogue with the police who are investigating the shooting. First, the authorial disclosure across the two scenes reveals discrepancies between Joe's account of the event and the account offered by the waiter:

Wallace (the police investigator): "Let's talk about the ice creams. Your waiter says he was bringing them to the table at the time of the shooting."

Joe: "That's not how I remember it. We started to eat them, then they were covered in blood."

"The waiter says the blood reached as far as him. The ice creams were bloodied when he set them down."

I said, "But I remember eating a couple of spoonfuls." (196)

Notice here how subtly McEwan's communication to his audience differs from Joe's communication to his uncharacterized narratee. Joe's focus on the details of *when* the shooting began means that he does not comment on the discrepancy between his earlier report that the dessert was sorbet and this conversation's presupposition that the dessert is ice cream. In case his audience has missed this discrepancy for the same reason as Joe, McEwan soon highlights it through Joe's reporting of additional dialogue:

Wallace was patiently repeating a question. "What flavor was the ice cream?"

"Apple. If the guy says it was anything else, then we're talking about two different waiters."

"Your professor friend says vanilla." (197)

Since Joe has previously reported that the dessert was lime sorbet, the authorial disclosure across conversations highlights both the discrepancy and Joe's complete unawareness of the discrepancy. Joe the self-conscious craftsman has become an unwittingly unreliable reporter of events. McEwan invites his audience to infer that there is some kind of contagion going on: the rational science writer is moving toward the kind of irrationality that governs Jed Parry's behavior. Furthermore, that irrationality exists both at the time of the action and at the time of the narration.

McEwan uses these developments—Joe's loss of control in chapter 9, his descent into unreliability, and his larger efforts at self-justification—to indicate that Clarissa's reservations about Joe's interpretations and evaluations of Parry are well justified.[2] That communication, in turn, raises the issue of whether McEwan wants his audience to regard Joe as reliable about the big picture. Of course, the events at the end of the narrative—and the case study in the scholarly article—settle that question very clearly in favor of reliability, but it's worth asking why McEwan wants his audience to entertain the possibility that the local unreliability is a sign of unreliability about the big picture.

---

2. For a debate on McEwan's handling of Clarissa's character, see Palmer, "Attributions" and Phelan, "Cognitive."

McEwan provides an answer in his implicit communications about the temporal occasion and the purpose of Joe's narrative, especially as that temporal occasion lines up with the occasions of the two appendices. Temporality first.

At the end of his narrative, Joe reports that he and Clarissa are living apart and that it is uncertain whether they will be able to forgive each other for what they each regard as the other's hurtful behavior during the period when Jed disrupted their lives. In the case study of Appendix I, Drs. Wenn and Camia report that "R and M were reconciled and later successfully adopted a child" (259). Notice that the "and later" suggests that Joe and Clarissa had a period, albeit one whose duration is not specified, in which they once again lived together before adopting a child and that the child has also been living with them for some duration, again not fully specified. In Appendix II, McEwan includes the information that Dr. Wenn had requested Jed's letter and that the letter was written on the one thousandth day of Jed's incarceration in the prison hospital. If we allow time for the completion of the article, its going through first the review process and then the production process, we can infer that the scholarly essay is published approximately four to five years after the end of Joe's story. In combination with Joe's ending his story by noting that both he and Clarissa "just did not know" (248) about their future, the Appendices indicate that Joe's own telling was shortly after the events it recounts. This inference has implications for our understanding of his purpose.

Because Joe is so close to the events, because their outcome remains uncertain, and because the events have been so traumatic, his decline from self-conscious reliable narrator to unwitting unreliable and even somewhat irrational narrator makes good psychological sense. The rational narration of the conscious craftsman gives way to the in-the-moment interpretations and evaluations of the middle-aged man under pressure from Jed, from Clarissa, and from himself, and he still suffers some of the effects of that pressure at the time of the telling.

But why does Joe tell this story to his uncharacterized narratee? Because the rational scientist whose stock-in-trade is narrative wants to understand what happened to him and Clarissa under the pressure of Jed's erotomania. He wants to get underneath the sequence of events and their surface causal links to deeper issues. Joe might have called his story "How Joe and Clarissa Came Apart" or "Why Our Allegedly Enduring Love May Not Endure." But because Joe is so close to the events, he also cannot help but give his audience his own sense of being more sinned against than sinning. So, a more accurate title would be "How Clarissa and I Came Apart and How It Was Mostly Not My Fault." Because he still suffers from the contagion of Jed's madness, he also cannot stay in full control of the narrative and he therefore falls short of achieving that purpose. Nevertheless, because Joe is sometimes able to step outside his own perspective—as in the beginning and middle of chapter 9— and sometimes able to see things more clearly from his perspective at the time of writing, McEwan also suggests that Joe's narrative is a step in the right therapeutic direction. In that regard, McEwan may even be suggesting that Joe's telling the tale helps him in his efforts to reconcile with Clarissa.

What, then, of McEwan's purposes? Why have Joe narrate on this temporal occasion rather than after he and Clarissa reconciled? A fuller answer depends on an analysis of the Appendices, but by the end of Joe's telling, McEwan has clearly established his thematic interest in the vexed relationship between love and logic.

Jed's erotomania is the extreme example of that vexed relationship, since it arises and continues without any encouragement on Joe's part. McEwan further underlines the gap by foregrounding Jed's belief that his love will lead Joe to God: love, like religious faith, always exceeds reason. In addition, the way in which McEwan uses the trajectory of Joe's telling to suggest that there's a contagion between Jed and Joe provides another dimension to the novel's thematics. Moreover, McEwan extends his thematic exploration well beyond Jed's obsession with Joe. Clarissa searches for a possible lost letter from a dying John Keats to Fanny Brawne on the assumption that he loved her so much that he would have wanted to express his feelings even if he couldn't see her; Joe thinks it is just as likely that Keats's love would have kept him from writing the letter. Joe extends these reflections to the "miraculous" quality of his relationship with Clarissa: "a beautiful woman loved and wanted to be loved by a large, clumsy, balding fellow who could hardly believe his luck" (7).

Finally, the most compelling example of how McEwan guides his audience's interest in the thematics of love and logic is his development of the subplot about John Logan and his widow, Jean. John died in the balloon accident that opens the novel and that provides the occasion for the first meeting between Joe and Jed. Jean develops a perfectly logical explanation of why John was the last man to hold on to the balloon when it was swept up into the air by a sudden gust of wind, thus letting himself be carried too high to survive his inevitable fall. Examining the woman's scarf and the picnic lunch found in John's car near the scene of the accident, Jean painfully concludes that John was showing off for a woman with whom he was having an affair. But Jean's logical conclusion turns out to be completely wrong, because the scarf belongs to the Oxford undergraduate Bonnie Deedes and the lunch to Bonnie and her much older professor James Reid. John had given them a ride to the Chilterns, but they had fled the scene because they were not yet ready to go public with their relationship. Reid happens to hold the Euler Chair in Logic (!) at Oxford University, and now that they have gone public, he will have to resign from his position—but he is perfectly willing to do so.

By the end of Joe's narrative, then, McEwan has used his audience's immersion in the concrete particularity of its multiple events as perceived through Joe's angle of vision and his thematizing of those events to complicate our understanding of both Joe and Clarissa's relationship and Jed and his condition. McEwan gives his audience a view that subsumes Joe's. For Joe, Jed is the erotomaniac who almost murdered him, who took Clarissa hostage, and whose entrance into his life led to what looks to be the end of his happy life with Clarissa. McEwan's communication guides his audience to say, "Yes, but" to Joe's view, with an emphasis on both words. Yes, Jed and his erotomania have wreaked havoc on Joe's life, but that erotomania exists along the same continuum of human relationships as the love between John and Jean Logan, that between James Reid and Bonnie Deedes, and that between Joe and Clarissa. Furthermore, despite where any couple is located on that continuum, their relationship will depend on some gap between love and logic. For that reason, Joe's interest in apportioning out blame for the disruption of his relationship with Clarissa is an understandable but far too limited response to the events. As for Jed's obsession with Joe, yes, it is markedly different from Joe's love for Clarissa, but it is also an extreme version of it—just as Jed is an extreme version of Joe. These "Yes, but" responses lead McEwan's rhetorical readers to contemplate the mystery of the relation between reason and feeling, love and logic, without denying that at some point love's unmooring from logic can lead to destructive consequences.

As this account suggests, McEwan might well have made his novel wholly coincident with Joe's telling and satisfied many of his readers. To be sure, there are loose ends: Joe's narrative does not report on what happens to Jed, and it leaves the future of Joe's relationship with Clarissa undecided. In addition, McEwan chooses to use Joe's narration of that undecided state as the penultimate rather than final passage of Joe's narrative. He devotes the final passage to a scene of Joe's bonding with John and Jean Logan's children. The scene does give the ending a more positive feeling, but, given the very minor role of the children in the narrative, their presence in this last scene is puzzling.

Still, such open-endedness and such a puzzle would be acceptable within the postmodernist aesthetics of literary fiction in 1997, an aesthetics that eschews strong resolutions. What value, then, does McEwan add by including the two Appendices? The short answer is that these additional structural units partially tie up loose ends, but even more, they complicate the interaction between the mimetic and thematic components of the authorial audience's engagement with the narrative, and in so doing enrich its affective, ethical, and aesthetic dimensions. The long answer follows.

APPENDIX I

The movement from Joe's narrative to the scholarly article is a radical shift in McEwan's mode of telling, so radical that it is affectively jarring. To help convey something of this effect, I will analyze the final section of Joe's narrative and the beginning of Wenn and Camia's article. Joe reports that after James Reid tells his story to Jean Logan, he asks for her forgiveness and then tries to comfort her in her distress at not being able to ask for her own forgiveness from John. Joe then continues:

> I caught Clarissa's eye and we exchanged a half-smile, and it was as if we
> were pitching our own requests for mutual forgiveness, or at least tolerance,
> in there with Jean's and Reid's frantic counterpoint. I shrugged as though to
> say that, like her in her letter, I just did not know. (248)

Although Joe describes small actions here—an exchange of glances, a half-smile, a shrug—the scene is affectively and ethically poignant. McEwan uses Joe's reporting and interpreting to convey both the strong connection and the deep rift between Clarissa and himself. They can understand each other with just a look and a half-smile, but that very capacity for mutual understanding only highlights their inability to forgive—or even tolerate—each other's behavior after Jed entered their lives. Joe's shrug, which he assumes that Clarissa will understand, nicely captures their plight, conveying doubt and uncertainty with a paradoxical confidence that the communication will be understood. On the ethical level, McEwan does not suggest that either character is more sinned against than sinning: each has been partially deficient and each has hurt the other, but neither of them has been fundamentally selfish or deliberately hurtful. Although Joe's shrug does not close off an eventual reunion, it does not move them toward one, either. After rhetorical readers' sympathetic immersion in their struggles, Joe's shrug pains those readers almost as much as it pains Clarissa.

As noted above, McEwan gives his audience some final affective counterbalance by continuing Joe's narrative until it ends with a small scene of his bonding with Jean Logan's children. But even here, their turning to him as a kind of surrogate father inevitably reminds the audience of the death of their real father and Jean's double grief over his loss and her misjudgment of his love. Indeed, the affective power of these last paragraphs contributes to the judgment that Joe's narrative would make a fine stand-alone novel.

But McEwan continues this way:

Appendix I

Reprinted from *The British Review of Psychiatry*

Robert Wenn, MB BCh. MRCPsych, & Antonio Camia, MA, MB, DRCOG, MRCPsych

A homoerotic obsession, with religious overtones: a clinical variant of de Clerambault's syndrome

The case of a pure (primary) form of de Clerambault's syndrome is described in a man whose religious convictions are central to his delusions. Dangerousness and suicidal tendencies are also present. The case adds to recent literature supporting the view that the syndrome is a nosological entity. (249)

The audience's sudden leap from the deep affective and ethical engagement with Joe's immersive narrative to Wenn and Camia's abstract academic discourse produces the jarring effect. The journal name and the listing of Wenn's and Camia's advanced degrees signal the radical change in voice and tone. The article's very formal title (which is also formulaic in its main title–colon–subtitle structure), followed by the passive voice and clumsy abstractions of the summary ("Dangerousness and suicidal tendencies are also present") then deliver that change, and the article itself sustains it.

In sustaining that change, the article has three major interrelated effects on the responses of rhetorical readers. First, it creates significant affective and ethical distance between McEwan's audience and Joe, Jed, and Clarissa. Instead of having access to the felt experience of the events, the audience gets an explanation of those events via the frame of a psychiatric "syndrome." On this first page of the article, Jed becomes a "case," and Joe and Clarissa all but disappear (we can perhaps dimly perceive them beneath the inelegant vagueness of "dangerousness"). When all three appear later in the article, they are only "P," "R," and "M." In this way, the move from Joe's narrative to Wenn and Camia's article is one from a reading experience in which the audience's mimetic interests in the characters and events are foregrounded to one in which those interests are set aside in favor of a thoroughly thematic view. Although Wenn and Camia indicate that "P," "R," and "M" refer to actual people, what is important about them is not their individuality but the way they perform representative roles in an illustrative narrative about erotomania.

Second, Wenn and Camia's article gives McEwan's audience a much clearer understanding of erotomania than Joe offers in his narrative. The article includes the history of de Clerambault's identification of the syndrome, summaries of what other (actual) researchers have found about its symptoms and possible treatment, and an analysis of the case of "P." As a result, the article persuasively accomplishes its purpose of establishing erotomania as a "nosological entity" (i.e., a distinct, classifiable disease), and that accomplishment in turn guides McEwan's audience to reconfigure Jed and his behavior within that psychiatric framework. Third, the article further validates Joe's interpretive judgments about Jed. Despite the deficiencies in some of Joe's own responses to Jed, McEwan assures his audience that in one important sense, Joe correctly read Jed. Indeed, if Joe were to come across the article at a time when he was in Clarissa's company, he would immediately hand it over to her. He wouldn't even have to say "I told you so" because the article implicitly says that as loudly as any implicit saying can. In all these ways, McEwan invites his audience to say "Yes" to the article's view of Jed and his condition.

Nevertheless, McEwan uses the interaction between Joe's narrative and Wenn and Camia's article, including the affectively jarring transition from one to the other, to guide his audience to add an emphatic "but" to that "Yes."[3] Because that audience moves from an account that values the concrete particularity of narrative to one that values the intellectual mastery of science and its penchant for classification, the audience has reason for some skepticism. To put this point another way, the interaction of the two tellings leads the audience to automatically translate Wenn and Camia's "P," "R," and "M" to "Jed," "Joe," and "Clarissa," and the gap signified by this different naming suggests that Wenn and Camia miss as much as they capture. They reduce the complex interplay between Jed's obsession and Joe's responses to them—and then Clarissa's responses to Joe's responses—to such descriptions as "within days this relationship [between R and M] was under strain from P's determined onslaught. Later they separated" (254). Yes, the psychiatric explanation does help McEwan's audience to understand P and his behavior, but it also radically oversimplifies Jed, Joe, and Clarissa. In a sense, the interaction McEwan sets up between Joe's narrative and Wenn and Camia's article demonstrates the problem of fully subordinating mimetic interests to thematic ones.[4] Further-

---

3. Here I depart from David Malcolm's assessment of the Appendix as primarily a validation of Joe's perspective. My position is closer to Greenberg's when he argues that the validation of Joe's interpretation of Jed does not resolve all the conflicts among worldviews.

4. At the same time, McEwan maintains his audience's interest in the mimetic component of the novel by shifting the focus of that interest from the characters to the essay itself, and he solidifies that interest by giving it the marks of a plausible contribution to the actual studies of erotomania listed in the "References" section. But he also gives his audience a not-

more, the interaction also points to a significant similar shortcoming in each narrative. Each teller's framework of experience (Joe's close encounters with Jed; Wenn and Camia's psychiatry) locks him/them into a particular perspective on Jed. Yes, each one's perspective yields some useful understanding about Jed and his condition, but each one's perspective also remains limited.

This "Yes, but" also applies to the article's final sentences:

> Patients with delusional disorders are unlikely to seek help, since they do not regard themselves as ill. Their friends and family may also be reluctant to see them in these terms, for as Mullen & Pathe observe, "the pathological extensions of love not only touch upon but overlap with normal experience, and it is not always easy to accept that one of our most valued experiences may merge into psychopathology." (259)

While the quotation from Mullen and Pathe, who are real scholars of erotomania, articulates McEwan's thematic point, the thrust of the article, with its emphasis on the syndrome as a "nosological entity," and its exclusively thematic treatment of Jed, Joe, and Clarissa, is that those who suffer from erotomania exist on the other side of a vast divide from their "victims." After signaling that Wenn and Camia reduce the human complexity of Jed and others who suffer from the disease throughout the essay, McEwan invites his rhetorical readers to find an unintentional irony in Wenn and Camia's conclusion.

McEwan's choice to use Wenn and Camia's article to deliver new information about Jed and about Joe and Clarissa highlights other effects that arise from the interaction between his structural units. The article informs McEwan's audience that Jed still suffers from erotomania, that he has been assigned to a secure mental hospital from which he writes daily to Joe, and that his letters are never delivered "in order to protect R from further distress" (255). From the perspective of Wenn and Camia, this information is important because it shows that the state has done what it needs to in P's case. From the perspective of rhetorical readers, the information is important because it resolves their lingering questions about Jed's fate, questions that Joe's narrative, with its preoccupation with Jed's effect on him and Clarissa, raises but does not answer. Furthermore, the specifics of the resolution lead McEwan's rhetorical readers to a more layered response than Wenn and Camia's, a response that includes an affective dimension missing from theirs. Yes, the

---

so-subtle synthetic wink by scrambling the letters of his own name to come up with names for the authors of the article. This wink further increases the audience's affective distance to Jed, Joe, and Clarissa and, thus, further sharpens the audience's focus on the characters' thematic functions.

state's actions are appropriate, but there's something profoundly sad about the intractability of Jed's delusion and the conditions of his day-to-day life.

The gap between rhetorical readers' view and Wenn and Camia's view of the new information about Joe and Clarissa is even wider. This new information comes as part of their concluding discussion about the range of outcomes among those afflicted by sufferers from de Clerambault's syndrome: "While in this case R and M were reconciled and later successfully adopted a child, some victims have had to divorce or emigrate, and others have needed psychiatric treatment because of the distress that patients have caused them" (258–59). Thus, for Wenn and Camia, the reconciliation is important only because it represents a relatively rare positive outcome. For McEwan's audience, however, the news brings some modicum of satisfaction and relief: Joe and Clarissa's love, whatever its flaws and defects, has been strong enough for them to reunite and to act on Clarissa's desire to become a mother. The information also leads McEwan's audience to reconfigure the significance of Joe's bonding with the Logan children: that experience gives him—and McEwan's rhetorical readers—the confidence that he can be a good parent. At the same time, the audience's affective response to this outcome is muted both by McEwan's tucking it into a subordinate clause in this academic article and by all that the audience does not know about the reconciliation, the adoption, and Joe and Clarissa's current life.

McEwan wants this muted response because of his thematic emphasis on the vexed relation of love and logic rather than on a mimetic marriage plot involving Joe and Clarissa. I can extend this point by reflecting on McEwan's choice for the occasion of Joe's narration. Why not have Joe narrate after the reconciliation, when the complications that followed Jed's "onslaught" had been resolved? For reasons having to do with the interrelation of the mimetic and thematic components of the novel. If Joe were to narrate after marriage and parenthood, he would have a wholly different perspective on his experiences with Jed, and that perspective would necessarily alter his purposes in a way that would not serve McEwan's purposes nearly as well. Joe's implicit title would change from "How Clarissa and I Came Apart and Why It Is Mostly Not My Fault" to something like "How Clarissa and I Weathered a Crisis in Our Relationship and Are Now Happier Than Ever." McEwan, I'm sure, could have Joe write an appealing narrative with that purpose, but he would have a much harder time shaping that narrative to explore the relation of love and logic and especially to generate the multiple "Yes, but" responses to the exploration that Joe's current narrative evokes.

APPENDIX II

The new information in Wenn and Camia's article about Jed and about Joe and Clarissa also sets up some significant interactions among Joe's narrative, Appendix I, and Appendix II. With Jed's final letter to Joe, McEwan returns to foregrounding the mimetic component of our interests, but the letter itself does not tell a story as much as it captures the spontaneous overflow of Jed's powerful feelings for Joe. Its one long paragraph is worth quoting in full:

Dear Joe,

I was awake at dawn. I slipped out of bed, put on my dressing gown, and without disturbing the night staff went and stood by the east window. See how willing I can be when you're kind to me! You're right, when the sun comes up behind the trees they turn black. The twigs at the very top are tangled against the sky, like the insides of some machine with wires. But I wasn't thinking about that, because it was a cloudless day and what rose up above the treetops ten minutes later was nothing less than the resplendence of God's glory and love. Our love! First bathing me, then warming me through the pane. I stood there, shoulders back, my arms hanging loosely at my sides, taking deep breaths. The old tears streaming. But the joy! The thousandth day, my thousandth letter, and you telling me that what I'm doing is right! At first you didn't see the sense of it, and you cursed our separation. Now you know that every day I spend here brings you one tiny step closer to that glorious light, His love, and the reason you know it now when you didn't before is because you are close enough to feel yourself turning helplessly and joyfully toward His warmth. No going back now, Joe! When you are His, you also become mine. This happiness is almost an embarrassment to me. I'm meant to be a prisoner. The bars are on the windows, the ward is locked at night, I spend my days and nights in the company of the shuffling, muttering, dribbling idiots, and the ones who aren't shuffling have to be restrained. The nurses, especially the men, are brutes who really ought to be inmates and have somehow scraped through to the other side. Cigarette smoke, windows that won't open, urine, TV ads. That's the world I've described to you a thousand times. I ought to be going under. Instead I feel more purpose than I've ever known in my life. I've never felt so free. I'm soaring, I'm so happy, Joe! If they'd known how happy I was going to be here, they would have let me out. I have to stop writing to hug myself. I'm earning our happiness day by day and I don't care if it takes me a lifetime. A thousand days—this is my birthday letter to you. You know it already, but I need to tell you again that I adore you. I live for you. I love you. Thank you for loving me, thank you for accepting me, thank you for recognizing what I am doing for our love. Send me a new message soon, and remember—faith is joy.

Jed (262)

We can begin to unpack the effects of this letter by comparing it with the first letter that Jed wrote to Joe and that Joe incorporated into his narrative as chapter 11. Here is its first paragraph:

Dear Joe,

I feel happiness running through me like an electrical current. I close my eyes and see you as you were last night in the rain, across the road from me, with the unspoken love between us as strong as steel cable. I close my eyes and thank God out loud for letting you exist, for letting me exist in the same time and place as you, and for letting this strange adventure between us begin. I thank Him for every little thing about us. This morning I woke and on the wall beside my bed was a perfect disk of sunlight and I thanked Him for that same sunlight falling on you! Just as last night the rain that drenched you drenched me too and bound us. I praise God that He has sent me to you. I know that there is difficulty and pain ahead of us, but the path that He sets us on is hard for a purpose. His purpose! It tests us and strengthens us, and in the long run it will bring us to even greater joy. (101)

This juxtaposition highlights the remarkable formal similarity between the two letters.[5] Although the Appendix II letter presupposes a greater knowledge of Joe, in just about every other way, it presents variations on the themes of the first. In each letter, Jed expresses his happiness, his conviction that he and Joe are deeply in love, and his joy that this love will bring Joe closer to God. In each, Jed exhorts Joe to stay the course. And in each, Jed refers to the morning of the day it was composed, and he connects his love of Joe to nature, especially to the light of the sun.

What my juxtaposition of the letters cannot capture is even more remarkable: how in the progression of McEwan's novel they evoke radically different responses. The audience's response to the first letter is governed in large part by McEwan's including it as part of Joe's narrative. This inclusion comes at a

---

5. Jed's second letter, reproduced in chapter 16, has a different tone. After disputing Joe's scientific worldview, as revealed in his writing, Jed implicitly threatens Joe: "Show me your fury or bitterness. I won't mind. I'll never desert you. But never, never try to pretend to yourself that I do not exist" (148). McEwan uses this letter to show that Jed is indeed dangerous. For a good discussion of the three letters, see Childs.

point where Jed's presence has already seriously disrupted Joe's relationship with Clarissa and at a point where rhetorical readers' relationship to Joe and his judgments about Jed need some shoring up. Prior to the letter, McEwan has used Joe's account of his own behavior (e.g., concealing from Clarissa Jed's first phone call to him the night after their chance meeting, erasing Jed's many messages from the answering machine) in conjunction with scenes of dialogue between Joe and Clarissa, including their serious row in chapter 9, to show how deeply and negatively Joe the character is affected by Jed and to open the possibility that Joe the narrator is at least partly unreliable in his interpretations of Jed as a dangerous stalker. While the letter does not resolve all the audience's questions about either Joe's behavior or his reliability, McEwan uses it both to confirm that Joe is right about Jed's obsession with him and to demonstrate that Joe's efforts to correct Jed's perceptions of him are futile. Since the audience's sympathies lie strongly with Joe, Jed's expression of his delusional attachment functions as an instance of estranging unreliability that deepens the audience's connection with Joe and further distances it from Jed.

Jed's letter in Appendix II, however, exists alongside—and after—the two other segments of the novel rather than inside one of them, and as a result, its formal similarities to the first letter have different, more layered effects. Coming to it at the end of the novel, McEwan's audience once again registers the colossal nature of Jed's delusion as reflected in his unreliable reporting, interpreting, and evaluating. Every claim Jed makes about Joe lacks connection to reality in the storyworld. Joe has no interest in being led to God. Joe does not love Jed. Joe does not accept Jed. Joe does not recognize what Jed is doing. Joe does not communicate with Jed. As a result, the unreliability again has estranging effects.

But McEwan's audience also recognizes that Jed's delusion enables him to rise above the unsavory conditions of his life in the institution, and this recognition leads to some bonding effects. Indeed, there is something deeply touching about Jed's effusions, something simultaneously uplifting and sad: he experiences a deep, even enviable joy, yet that joy depends on a delusion so powerful that he belongs in this secure hospital.

On the ethical level, Jed's unreliability also has both estranging and bonding effects. Since the audience has seen the consequences of Jed's obsession, we can't help but find something disturbing in Jed's emphasis on the duration of his love (one thousand days with no response). At the same time, because the audience knows from Appendix I that Jed's letter will never be delivered and that Joe and Clarissa have reconciled, we can find something admirable in Jed's expression of the continuing purity and intensity of his unselfish love. In this respect, Jed's letter conforms to the description of a possible letter from

Keats to Fanny Brawne that Clarissa has been unsuccessfully trying to track down: "a cry of undying love not touched by despair" (238).

These layered responses create a very effective ending for McEwan's novel because they reimmerse the audience in the mimetic component of the novel even as that reimmersion extends his thematic exploration of the vexed relation of love and logic. Yes, Jed's lyric effusions powerfully capture his seemingly unending delusion. But they simultaneously capture the purity and intensity of wholly other-directed love. Yes, they capture that purity and intensity, but are such purity and intensity sustainable over time only for the deeply delusional? McEwan does not answer that question directly, but his novel invites his audience to contemplate it.

CONCLUSION

This attention to the interpretive, affective, and ethical dimensions of rhetorical readers' responses to the two Appendices—and especially to their interactions with Joe's narrative and with each other—suggests that McEwan has used them to add considerable value to his novel. His strategy of double indirection works to considerably deepen his rhetorical readers' engagement with multiple dimensions of his communication, and especially the engagement with his thematic exploration of the vexed and varied relations between love and logic. That deeper engagement significantly enhances the ethical and aesthetic achievement of the novel, our sense that the quality of life we live while engaged in McEwan's communication rewards the time and thought that communication invites us to invest.

Reflections on the How and Why of Rhetorical Poetics

ROUND OFF this inquiry with a few reflections on the project of rhetorical poetics. First, I return to a point I made in the preface about the ever-evolving nature of the project by way of Henry James's famous remarks in the preface to *Roderick Hudson* about the difficulty of concluding. "Really, universally," James wrote, "relations stop nowhere, and the exquisite problem of the artist is eternally but to draw, by a geometry of his own, the circle within which they shall happily *appear* to do so" (*Art of the Novel* 5; emphasis in original). For the rhetorical interpreter, really, universally, relations between the somebodies who tell and the somebodies who listen, relations mediated by the multiple resources of any individual narrative, are, if not infinite, then certainly too numerous to address in any one analysis. The rhetorical interpreter's exquisite problem is to fashion, by a logic of his own, a reading within which those relations shall happily *appear* to be satisfactorily addressed. Similarly, the rhetorical theorist's exquisite problem is to shape an account that shall happily *appear* to approach comprehensiveness, even as he remains cognizant that the resources of narrative are themselves so plentiful and that the somebodies who tell continually find, in cooperation with the somebodies who listen, both new resources and new uses for already existing ones.

These problems of interpretation and theory construction are exquisite in part because they can never be completely solved. They are also exquisite because they are not so intractable that they render progress impossible. For the interpreter, progress often involves recognizing the teller's orchestration of the interactive effects of various resources, including the trajectory of rhetorical readers' responses. To return briefly to McEwan's *Enduring Love*, Joe Rose's unreliable character narration interacts with its occasion, with the character narrations and occasions of the two Appendices, and with McEwan's sequencing of all three segments, and these interactions have major consequences for rhetorical readers' evolving engagements with the mimetic, thematic, and synthetic components of the narrative—or to put it another way, with its cognitive, affective, ethical, and aesthetic dimensions. Furthermore, the analysis of these interactions prepares the way for a closer look at McEwan's handling of other resources, such as Clarissa's character narration in her letter to Joe after the row that leads to their separation, and even the strange events connected with Joe's procuring a gun. The findings emerging from those examinations would then feed back into the analysis of the other interactions, potentially leading to some revision of its conclusions. And so on and so on until the rhetorical interpreter is ready to cry, "Hold, enough."

A similar pattern applies to the rhetorical theorist's progress. Consider, for example, the analysis of character narration across the various chapters of this book. Progress in the understanding of some aspects of that resource has ripple effects on our understanding of other aspects. The more we get inside the rhetoric of unreliable narration, the more we can understand the rhetoric of both reliable narration and deficient narration. Just as important, progress with one resource often has ripple effects with another. My work on character narration, for example, sheds light on the rhetorical dynamics of character-character dialogue, and the more we understand about each of these resources, the more we can appreciate synergies between them. And so on. In addition, the accumulated theoretical insights can then inform rhetorical interpretation even as the workings of individual narrative can lead to revisions in the theory. To put this point another away, the activities of configuration and reconfiguration are important not only in reading narrative but also in constructing rhetorical narrative theory.

BEYOND THESE methodological issues that render the problems of rhetorical poetics exquisite is something even more important for the project: a belief in the value and power of narrative itself. The motivation for the somebody who tells is not far to seek: to come to terms with some aspects of human experience; to communicate ideas, attitudes, values, and convictions to anyone who will listen; to create something of lasting beauty. And more. But why be the somebody else? Rhetorical poetics answers by pointing to the positive effects that can flow from engaging with a powerful telling. The project believes in the potential efficacy of the cognitive, affective, ethical, and aesthetic dimensions of experiencing narrative, and especially of the two-step process of giving oneself over to mimetic, thematic, and synthetic components of the teller's communication and then assessing the teller's mind, emotions, values, and sense of quality. The goal of rhetorical poetics is to help individual readers perform that two-step process as skillfully as possible so that they can turn from the act of rhetorical reading to enriched acts of living. Indeed, rhetorical poetics wants to break down the border between reading and living. It believes that reading narrative, whether fictional or nonfictional, does not, in Michael Bamberg's phrase, put "life on holiday" (63), but rather functions as a rich and rewarding way of living life. To be sure, reading narrative does not by itself constitute a full life, but it is a valuable way to spend time that can greatly enhance other ways of spending it. Thus, the better rhetorical readers we can become, the better lives we can lead. Consequently, the ultimate purpose of rhetorical poetics is to contribute to human flourishing.

WORKS CITED

Abbott, H. Porter. *Real Mysteries: Narrative and the Unknowable.* Columbus: Ohio State Univ. Press, 2013.

Abel, Elizabeth. "Black Writing, White Reading: Race and the Politics of Feminist Interpretation." *Critical Inquiry* 19.3 (1993): 470–98.

Alber, Jan, Henrik Skov Nielsen, and Brian Richardson, eds. *A Poetics of Unnatural Narrative.* Columbus: Ohio State Univ. Press, 2013.

Alber, Jan, Stefan Iversen, Henrik Skov Nielsen, and Brian Richardson. "Unnatural Narratives, Unnatural Narratology: Beyond Mimetic Models." *Narrative* 18.2 (2010): 113–36.

Amis, Martin. *Time's Arrow, or, The Nature of the Offense.* New York: Harmony Books, 1991.

Aristotle. *Poetics.* Translated by S. H. Butcher. New York: Macmillan, 1895.

Armstrong, Lance (with Sally Jenkins). *It's Not about the Bike: My Journey Back to Life.* New York: Berkley Trade Publishers, 2001.

Austen, Jane. *Persuasion.* 1817. Oxford: Oxford Univ. Press, 1963. Vol. 5 of *The Novels of Jane Austen.* Ed. R. W. Chapman.

———. *Pride and Prejudice.* 1813. Oxford: Oxford Univ. Press, 1963. Vol. 2 of *The Novels of Jane Austen.* Ed. R. W. Chapman.

Baetens, Jan, and Katherine Hume. "Speed, Rhythm, Movement: A Dialogue on K. Hume's Article 'Narrative Speed.'" *Narrative* 14.3 (2006): 349–55.

Bakhtin, Mikhail. "Discourse in the Novel." *The Dialogic Imagination.* Ed. Michael Holquist. Trans. Caryl Emerson and Michael Holquist. Austin: Univ. of Texas Press, 1981. 259–422.

———. *Problems of Dostoevsky's Poetics.* Ed. and trans. Caryl Emerson. 1929/1963. Minneapolis: Univ. of Minnesota Press, 1984.

Bamberg, Michael. "Biographic-narrative Research, Quo Vadis? A Critical Review of 'Big Stories' from the Perspective of 'Small Stories.'" *Narrative, Memory, and Knowledge: Representations, Aesthetics, and Contexts.* Ed. K. Milnes, C. Horrocks, B. Roberts, and D. Robinson. Huddersfield: Univ. of Huddersfield Press, 2006. 63–79.

Barthes, Roland. "The Death of the Author." *Image-Music-Text.* Trans. Stephen Heath. New York: Hill and Wang, 1977. 142–48.

Bauby, Jean-Dominique. *The Diving Bell and the Butterfly.* Trans. Jeremy Leggatt. New York: Vintage Books, 1998.

Berman, Russell A. "Tradition and Betrayal in 'Das Urteil.'" *A Companion to the Works of Franz Kafka.* Ed. James Rolleston. Rochester: Camden House, 2002. 85–100.

Booth, Wayne C. *The Company We Keep: An Ethics of Fiction.* Berkeley: Univ. of California Press, 1988.

———. *The Rhetoric of Fiction.* 1961. 2nd ed. Chicago: Univ. of Chicago Press, 1983.

Brada-Williams, Noelle. "Reading Jhumpa Lahiri's *Interpreter of Maladies* as a Short Story Cycle." *MELUS* 29.3–4 (2004): 451–64.

Brontë, Charlotte. *Jane Eyre.* 1847. New York: Penguin, 1996.

Browning, Robert. "My Last Duchess." *The Major Works.* 1842. Ed. Adam Roberts. New York: Oxford Univ. Press, 2009. 101–2.

Caesar, Judith. "American Spaces in the Fiction of Jhumpa Lahiri." *English Studies in Canada* 31 (2005): 50–68.

Chandler, James. *An Archeology of Sympathy: The Sentimental Mode in Literature and Film.* Chicago: Univ. of Chicago Press, 2013.

Chatman, Seymour. "Backwards." *Narrative* 17.1 (2008): 31–55.

———. *Coming to Terms: The Rhetoric of Narrative in Fiction and Film.* Ithaca: Cornell Univ. Press, 1990.

———. *Story and Discourse: Narrative Structure in Fiction and Film.* Ithaca: Cornell Univ. Press, 1978.

Childs, Peter. "'Believing is seeing': The Eye of the Beholder." *Ian McEwan's Enduring Love.* Ed. Peter Childs. New York: Routledge, 2006. 107–22.

Cohn, Dorrit. "Discordant Narration." *Style* 34.2 (2000): 307–16.

———. *The Distinction of Fiction.* Baltimore: Johns Hopkins Univ. Press, 1999.

Conrad, Joseph. *Lord Jim: A Tale.* Oxford: Oxford Univ. Press, 2002 [1990].

Crane, R. S. "Criticism as Inquiry; or, The Perils of the 'High Priori Road.'" *The Idea of the Humanities.* Chicago: Univ. of Chicago Press, 1967. 25–44.

Crane, R. S., ed. *Critics and Criticism: Ancient and Modern.* Chicago: Univ. of Chicago Press, 1952.

Davies, Rhiannon. "Enduring McEwan." *Ian McEwan's Enduring Love.* Ed. Peter Childs. New York: Routledge, 2006. 66–76.

Didion, Joan. *The Year of Magical Thinking.* New York: Knopf, 2005.

Diedrick, James. *Understanding Martin Amis.* 2nd ed. Columbia: Univ. of South Carolina Press, 2004.

Donoghue, Emma. *Room.* New York: Little, Brown, 2010.

Easterbrook, Neil. "'I know that it is to do with trash and shit, and that it is wrong in time': Narrative Reversal in Martin Amis' *Time's Arrow.*" *Conference of College Teachers of English (CCTE) Studies* 55 (1995): 52–61.

Edwards, Paul. "Solipsism, Narrative and Love in *Enduring Love.*" *Ian McEwan's Enduring Love.* Ed. Peter Childs. New York: Routledge, 2006. 77–90.

Ellis, John M. "The Bizarre Texture of 'The Judgment.'" *The Problem of The Judgment: Eleven Approaches to Kafka's Story.* Ed. Ángel Flores. New York: Gordian Press, 1977. 73–96.

Faulkner, William. *As I Lay Dying.* 1930. New York: Knopf, 1990.

———. *The Sound and the Fury.* 1929. New York: Vintage, 1990.

Finney, Brian. "Martin Amis's *Time's Arrow* and the Postmodern Sublime." *Martin Amis: Postmodernism and Beyond.* Ed. Gavin Keulks. New York: Palgrave, 2006. 101–16.

Fish, Stanley. "How to Recognize a Poem When You See One." *Is There A Text in This Class? The Authority of Interpretive Communities.* Cambridge: Harvard Univ. Press, 1980. 322–37.

———. "Literature in the Reader: Affective Stylistics." *New Literary History* 2.1 (1970): 123–62.

Fitzgerald, F. Scott. *The Great Gatsby.* 1925. New York: Scribner's, 1992.

Ford, Andrew. "Literary Criticism and the Poet's Autonomy." *A Companion to Ancient Aesthetics.* Ed. Pierre Destreé and Penelope Murray. Malden, MA: Blackwell, 2015. 143–57.

Foucault, Michel. "What Is an Author?" *The Essential Foucault: Selections from the Essential Works of Foucault, 1954–1984.* Ed. Paul Rabinow and Nikolas Rose. New York: New Press, 2003. 377–91.

Frey, James. *A Million Little Pieces.* New York: Random House, 2003.

Garg, Shweta, and Rajyashree Khushu-Lahiri. "Interpreting a Culinary Montage: Food in Jhumpa Lahiri's *Interpreter of Maladies*." *Asiatic* 6.1 (2012): 73–83.

Genette, Gérard. *Narrative Discourse: An Essay in Method.* Trans. Jane E. Lewin. Ithaca: Cornell Univ. Press, 1980.

———. *Narrative Discourse Revisited.* Trans. Jane E. Lewin. Ithaca: Cornell Univ. Press, 1988.

Goldstein-Shirley, David. "Race/[Gender]: Toni Morrison's 'Recitatif.'" *Journal of the Short Story in English* 27 (1996): 83–95.

Green, Susan. "'Up There with Black Holes and Darwin, Almost Bigger than Dinosaurs': The Mind and McEwan's *Enduring Love*." *Style* 45.3 (2011): 441–63.

Greenberg, Jonathan. "Why Can't Biologists Read Poetry? Ian McEwan's *Enduring Love*." *Twentieth-Century Literature* 53.2 (2007): 93–124.

Guérard, Albert J. *Conrad the Novelist.* Cambridge: Harvard Univ. Press, 1958.

Hansen, Per Krogh. "Reconsidering the Unreliable Narrator." *Semiotica* 165.1/4 (2007): 227–46.

———. "When Facts Become Fiction: Facts, Fiction and Unreliable Narration." *Fact and Fiction in Narrative: An Interdisciplinary Approach.* Ed. Lars-Åke Skalin. Örebro: Örebro Universitet, 2005. 283–307.

Harris, Greg. "Men Giving Birth to New World Orders: Martin Amis's *Time's Arrow*." *Studies in the Novel* 31.4 (1999): 489–505.

Hemingway, Ernest. "A Clean, Well-Lighted Place." *The Complete Short Stories of Ernest Hemingway: The Finca Vigía Edition.* New York: Scribner's, 1987. 288–91.

———. *A Farewell to Arms.* New York: Charles Scribner's Sons, 1929.

Herman, David. "Introduction: Narratologies." *Narratologies: New Perspectives on Narrative Analysis.* Ed. David Herman. Columbus: Ohio State Univ. Press, 1999. 1–30.

———. "Narrative Theory and the Intentional Stance." *Partial Answers* 6.2 (2008): 233–60.

Herman, David, James Phelan, Peter J. Rabinowitz, Brian Richardson, and Robyn Warhol. *Narrative Theory: Core Concepts and Critical Debates.* Columbus: Ohio State Univ. Press, 2012.

Higgins, George V. *The Friends of Eddie Coyle.* 1970. New York: Picador, 2010.

──. *On Writing: Advice for Those Who Write to Publish (or Would Like To)*. New York: Henry Holt, 1990.

Hirsch, E. D., Jr. *Validity in Interpretation*. New Haven: Yale Univ. Press, 1967.

Hogan, Patrick. *Narrative Discourse: Authors and Narrators in Literature, Film, and Art*. Columbus: Ohio State Univ. Press, 2013.

Holland, Norman N. *The Dynamics of Literary Response*. New York: Oxford Univ. Press, 1968.

Hughes, Kenneth. "A Psychoanalytic Approach to 'The Judgment.'" *Approaches to Teaching Kafka's Short Fiction*. Ed. Richard T. Gray. New York: MLA Publications, 1995. 84–93.

Hume, Katherine. "Narrative Speed in Contemporary Fiction." *Narrative* 13.2 (2005): 105–24.

Hurston, Zora Neale. *Their Eyes Were Watching God*. 1937. New York: Harper Perennial, 2006.

Iser, Wolfgang. *The Implied Reader: Patterns of Communication in Prose Fiction from Bunyan to Beckett*. Baltimore: Johns Hopkins Univ. Press, 1974.

Ishiguro, Kazuo. *The Remains of the Day*. New York: Vintage International, 1993.

Jackson, Elizabeth. "Transcending the Politics of 'Where You're From': Postcolonial Nationality and Cosmopolitanism in Jhumpa Lahiri's *Interpreter of Maladies*." *ARIEL* 43.1 (2012): 109–25.

James, Henry. *The Art of the Novel: Critical Prefaces*. 1934. Chicago: Univ. of Chicago Press, 2011.

Jones, Margaret B. *Love and Consequences*. New York: Riverhead, 2008.

Kacandes, Irene. *Talk Fiction: Literature and the Talk Explosion*. Lincoln: Univ. of Nebraska Press, 2001.

Kafka, Franz. "Das Urteil." *Ein Landarzt und andere Drucke zu Lebzeiten*. Frankfurt: Fischer Taschenbuch Verlag, 1994. 39–52. Vol. 1 of *Franz Kafka, Gesammelte Werke: Nach der Kritischen Ausgabe*. Ed. Hans-Gerd Koch.

──. "The Judgment." *Kafka's Selected Stories*. Trans. and ed. Stanley Corngold. New York: Norton, 2007. 3–12.

Karl, Frederick. *Franz Kafka: Representative Man*. New York: Ticknor and Fields, 1991.

Kesey, Ken. *One Flew over the Cuckoo's Nest*. New York: Signet, 1963.

Kincaid, James. "*Fiction and the Shape of Belief*: Fifteen Years Later." *Critical Inquiry* 6.2 (1979): 209–19.

Kindt, Tom, and Hans-Harald Müller. *The Implied Author: Concept and Controversy*. Berlin: De Gruyter, 2006.

Knoflíčková, Marie. "Racial Identities Revisited: Toni Morrison's 'Recitatif.'" *Litteraria Pragensia* 21 (2011): 22–33.

Koshy, Susan. "Minority Cosmopolitanism." *PMLA* 126.3 (2011): 592–609.

Kuhn, Thomas. *The Structure of Scientific Revolutions*. Chicago: Univ. of Chicago Press, 1962.

Lahiri, Jhumpa. "The Third and Final Continent." *Interpreter of Maladies*. New York: Houghton Mifflin, 1999. 173–98.

Lanser, Susan S. "(Im)plying the Author." *Narrative* 9.2 (2001): 153–60.

Lardner, Ring. "Haircut." *The Best Short Stories of Ring Lardner*. New York: Charles Scribner's Sons, 1957. 23–33.

Lehane, Dennis. Introduction. *The Friends of Eddie Coyle*. New York: Picador, 2010.

Leonard, Elmore. Introduction. *The Friends of Eddie Coyle*. New York: Henry Holt, 2000.

Levi, Primo. *If This Is a Man; and, The Truce.* Trans. Stuart Woolf. London: Abacus, 2003.

Lifton, Robert Jay. *The Nazi Doctors: Medical Killing and the Psychology of Genocide.* New York: Basic Books, 1986.

Lipking, Lawrence. "Arguing with Shelly." *Critical Inquiry* 6.2 (1979): 193–208.

Lockridge, Ernest. "F. Scott Fitzgerald's *Trompe L'Oeil* and *The Great Gatsby's* Buried Plot." *Journal of Narrative Technique* 17.2 (1987): 163–83.

Lothe, Jakob. *Conrad's Narrative Method.* New York: Oxford Univ. Press, 1989.

Lubbock, Percy. *The Craft of Fiction.* New York: Scribner's, 1921.

Malcolm, David. *Understanding Ian McEwan.* Columbia: Univ. of South Carolina Press, 2002.

McCarthy, Dermot. "The Limits of Irony: The Chronillogical World of Martin Amis' *Time's Arrow.*" *War, Literature, and the Arts* 11.1 (1999): 294–320.

McCarthy, Matt. *Odd Man Out.* New York: Viking, 2009.

McCourt, Frank. *Angela's Ashes.* New York: Scribner's, 1996.

McEwan, Ian. *Enduring Love.* New York: Anchor, 1997.

McGlothlin, Erin. "Theorizing the Perpetrator in Bernhard Schlink's *The Reader* and Martin Amis's *Time's Arrow.*" *After Representation? The Holocaust, Literature, and Culture.* Ed. R. Clifton Spargo and Robert M. Ehrenreich. New Brunswick: Rutgers Univ. Press, 2010. 210–30.

Miller, J. Hillis. *Fiction and Repetition: Seven English Novels.* Cambridge: Harvard Univ. Press, 1985.

Mitchell, David, and Sharon Snyder. *Narrative Prosthesis: Disability and the Dependencies of Discourse.* Ann Arbor: Univ. of Michigan Press, 2000.

Morrison, Jago. "Narration and Unease in Ian McEwan's Later Fiction." *Critique* 42.3 (2001): 253–68.

Morrison, Toni. *Beloved.* New York: Knopf, 1987.

———. "Recitatif." *Confirmation: An Anthology of African American Women.* Ed. Amiri Braka and Amina Baraka. New York: William Morrow, 1983. 243–61.

Nabokov, Vladimir. *The Annotated Lolita by Vladimir Nabokov.* Ed. with preface, introduction, and notes by Alfred Appel Jr. New York: Vintage Books, 1991.

Nielsen, Henrik Skov. "Fictional Voices? Strange Voices? Unnatural Voices?" *Strange Voices in Narrative Fiction.* Ed. Per Krogh Hansen, Stefan Iversen, Henrik Skov Nielsen, and Rolf Reitan. Berlin: De Gruyter, 2011. 55–82.

———. "The Impersonal Voice in First-Person Narrative Fiction." *Narrative* 12.2 (2004): 133–50.

Nielsen, Henrik Skov, James Phelan, and Richard Walsh. "Ten Theses about Fictionality." *Narrative* 23.1 (2015): 61–73.

Nünning, Ansgar F. "Deconstructing and Reconceptualizing the 'Implied Author': The Resurrection of an Anthropomorphized Passepartout or the Obituary of a Critical Phantom?" *Anglistik* 8.2 (1997): 95–116.

———. "Reconceptualizing Unreliable Narration: Synthesizing Cognitive and Rhetorical Approaches." *A Companion to Narrative Theory.* Ed. James Phelan and Peter J. Rabinowitz. Oxford: Blackwell Publishing, 2005. 89–107.

———. "Unreliable, Compared to What: Towards a Cognitive Theory of Unreliable Narration: Prolegomina and Hypotheses." *Grenzüberschreitungen: Narratologie im Kontext* [*Transcending Boundaries: Narratology in Context*]. Ed. Walter Grünzweig and Andreas Solbach. Tübingen: Gunter Narr Verlag, 1999. 53–73.

Nünning, Vera. "Unreliable Narration and the Historical Variability of Values and Norms: *The Vicar of Wakefield* as a Test Case of a Cultural-Historical Narratology." *Style* 38.2 (2004): 236–52.

O'Hara, John. "Appearances." *The Cape Cod Lighter*. New York: Random House, 1962. 3–14.

Olson, Greta. "Reconsidering Unreliability: Fallible and Untrustworthy Narrators." *Narrative* 11.1 (2003): 93–109.

Palmer, Alan. "Attributions of Madness in Ian McEwan's *Enduring Love*." *Style* 43.3 (2009): 291–308.

———. *Social Minds in the Novel*. Columbus: Ohio State Univ. Press, 2010.

Pascal, Roy. *Kafka's Narrators: A Study of His Stories and Sketches*. Cambridge: Cambridge Univ. Press, 1982.

Pearlin, Leonard, and Carmi Schooler. "The Structure of Coping." *Journal of Health and Social Behavior* 19.1 (1978): 2–21.

Petterson, Bo. "The Many Faces of Unreliable Narration: A Cognitive Narratological Reorientation." *Cognition and Literary Interpretation in Practice*. Ed. Harri Veivo, Bo Pettersson, and Merja Polvinen. Helsinki: Helsinki Univ. Press, 2005. 59–88.

Phelan, James. "Cognitive Narratology, Rhetorical Narratology, and Interpretive Disagreement: A Response to Alan Palmer's Analysis of *Enduring Love*." *Style* 43.3 (2009): 309–21.

———. "Data, Danda, and Disagreement." *Diacritics* 13.2 (1983): 39–50.

———. *Experiencing Fiction: Judgments, Progressions, and the Rhetorical Theory of Narrative*. Columbus: Ohio State Univ. Press, 2007.

———. *Living to Tell about It: A Rhetoric and Ethics of Character Narration*. Ithaca: Cornell Univ. Press, 2005.

———. *Narrative as Rhetoric: Technique, Audiences, Ethics, Ideology*. Columbus: Ohio State Univ. Press, 1996.

———. "Voice, Tone, and the Rhetoric of Narrative Communication." *Language and Literature* 23.1 (2014): 49–60.

———. *Worlds from Words: A Theory of Language in Fiction*. Chicago: Univ. of Chicago Press, 1981.

Rabinowitz, Peter J. "'Betraying the Sender': The Rhetoric and Ethics of Fragile Texts." *Narrative* 2.3 (1994): 201–13.

———. "Reading Beginnings and Endings." *Narrative Dynamics: Essays on Time, Plot, Closure, and Frames*. Ed. Brian Richardson. Columbus: Ohio State Univ. Press, 2002. 300–13.

———. "Toward a Theory of Cognitive Flavor." *The Oxford Handbook of Literary Studies*. Ed. Lisa Zunshine. New York: Oxford Univ. Press, 2015. 85–103.

Rabinowitz, Peter J., and Corinne Bancroft. "Euclid at the Core: Recentering Literary Education." *Style* 48.1 (2014): 1–35.

Rader, Ralph W. "The Dramatic Monologue and Related Lyric Forms." *Fact, Fiction, and Form: Selected Essays of Ralph W. Rader*. Ed. James Phelan and David H. Richter. Columbus: Ohio State Univ. Press, 2011. 134–54.

———. "The Emergence of the Novel in England: Genre in History vs. History of Genre." *Fact, Fiction, and Form: Selected Essays of Ralph W. Rader*. Ed. James Phelan and David Richter. Columbus: Ohio State Univ. Press, 2011. 203–17.

———. "Fact, Theory, and Literary Explanation." *Fact, Fiction, and Form: Selected Essays of Ralph W. Rader*. Ed. James Phelan and David Richter. Columbus: Ohio State Univ. Press, 2011. 31–57.

——. "The Literary Theoretical Contribution of Sheldon Sacks." *Critical Inquiry* 6.2 (1979): 183–92.

——. "*Lord Jim* and the Formal Development of the English Novel." *Fact, Fiction, and Form: Selected Essays of Ralph W. Rader.* Ed. James Phelan and David H. Richter. Columbus: Ohio State Univ. Press, 2011. 303–17.

Randall, Martin. "'I don't want your story': Open and Fixed Narratives in *Enduring Love*." *Ian McEwan's Enduring Love.* Ed. Peter Childs. New York: Routledge, 2006. 55–65.

Richardson, Brian. "Time, Plot, Progression." *Narrative Theory: Core Concepts and Critical Debates.* Columbus: Ohio State Univ. Press, 2012. 76–83.

——. *Unnatural Narrative: Theory, History, Practice.* Columbus: Ohio State Univ. Press, 2015.

——. *Unnatural Voices: Extreme Narration in Modern and Contemporary Fiction.* Columbus: Ohio State Univ. Press, 2006.

——. "The Implied Author: Back from the Grave or Simply Dead Again?." *Style* 45.1 (2011): 1–10.

Richardson, Brian, ed. *Implied Author: Back from the Grave or Simply Dead Again.* Spec. issue of *Style* 45.1 (2011).

Rimmon-Kenan, Shlomith. *Narrative Fiction: Contemporary Poetics.* 2nd ed. New York: Methuen, 1983.

Roth, Philip. "The Conversion of the Jews." *Goodbye, Columbus and Five Short Stories.* New York: Meridian, 1960. 139–58.

Ryan, Marie-Laure. "Cheap Plot Tricks, Plot Holes, and Narrative Design." *Narrative* 17.1 (2009): 56–75.

——. "Postmodernism and the Doctrine of Panfictionality." *Narrative* 5.2 (1997): 165–87.

Sacks, Sheldon. *Fiction and the Shape of Belief.* Berkeley: Univ. of California Press, 1964.

——. "The Psychological Implications of Generic Distinctions." *Genre* 1.2 (1968): 106–15.

Shen, Dan. "Booth's *The Rhetoric of Fiction* and China's Critical Context." *Narrative* 15.2 (2007): 167–86.

Shen, Dan, and Dejin Xu. "Intratextuality, Extratextuality, Intertextuality: Unreliability in Autobiography versus Fiction." *Poetics Today* 28.1 (2007): 43–87.

Shklovsky, Viktor. "Art as Technique." *Russian Formalist Criticism: Four Essays.* Trans. Lee T. Lemon and Marion J. Reis. Lincoln: Univ. of Nebraska Press, 1965. 3–24.

Sklar, Howard. "'What the Hell Happened to Maggie?': Stereotype, Sympathy, and Disability in Toni Morrison's 'Recitatif.'" *Journal of Literary and Cultural Disability Studies* 5.2 (2011): 137–54.

Small, David. *Stitches.* New York: Norton, 2009.

Smith, Sidonie, and Julia Watson. *Reading Autobiography: A Guide for Interpreting Life Narratives.* 2001. 2nd ed. Minneapolis: Univ. of Minnesota Press, 2010.

Speirs, Ronald. "Movement, Time, Language: Forms of Instability in Kafka's 'Das Urteil.'" *Forum for Modern Language Studies* 23.3 (1987): 253–64.

Springer, Mary Doyle. "Upon Rereading *Fiction and the Shape of Belief*." *Critical Inquiry* 6.2 (1979): 221–29.

Sternberg, Meir. "Point of View and the Indirectness of Direct Speech." *Language and Style* 15.2 (1982): 67–117.

——. "Proteus in Quotation-Land: Mimesis and the Forms of Reported Discourse." *Poetics Today* 3.2 (1982): 107–56.

Stenberg, Meir, and Tamar Yacobi. "Unreliability in Narrative Discourse." *Poetics Today* 36 (2015): 327–498.

Suleiman, Susan. "Performing a Perpetrator as Witness: Jonathan Littell's *Les Bienveillantes.*" *After Testimony: The Ethics and Aesthetics of Holocaust Narrative for the Future.* Ed. Jakob Lothe, Susan Rubin Suleiman, and James Phelan. Columbus: Ohio State Univ. Press, 2012. 99–119.

Sussman, Henry. "Kafka's Aesthetics: A Primer: From the Fragments to the Novels." *A Companion to the Works of Franz Kafka.* Ed. James Rolleston. Rochester: Camden House, 2002. 123–48.

Thomas, Bronwyn. *Fictional Dialogue: Speech and Conversation in the Modern and Postmodern Novel.* Lincoln: Univ. of Nebraska Press, 2012.

Twain, Mark. *The Adventures of Huckleberry Finn: A Case Study in Critical Controversy.* 2nd ed. Ed. Gerald Graff and James Phelan. Boston: Bedford/St. Martin's Press, 2004.

Vesterman, William. "Higgins's Trade." *Language and Style* 20 (1987): 223–29.

Vice, Sue. *Holocaust Fiction.* London: Routledge, 2000.

Walsh, Richard. *The Rhetoric of Fictionality.* Columbus: Ohio State Univ. Press, 2007.

Watt, Ian. *Conrad in the Nineteenth Century.* Berkeley: Univ. of California Press, 1979.

Weinstein, Philip. *Unknowing: The Work of Modernist Fiction.* Ithaca: Cornell Univ. Press, 2005.

Wharton, Edith. "Roman Fever." *Roman Fever and Other Stories.* 1934. New York: Scribner's, 1997. 3–20.

White, Hayden. *The Content of the Form.* Baltimore: Johns Hopkins Univ. Press, 1987.

Wimsatt, W. K., and Monroe C. Beardsley. "The Affective Fallacy." *The Verbal Icon: Studies in the Meaning of Poetry.* Lexington: Univ. of Kentucky Press, 1954. 21–39.

———. "The Intentional Fallacy." *The Verbal Icon: Studies in the Meaning of Poetry.* Lexington: Univ. of Kentucky Press, 1954. 3–18.

Wittgenstein, Ludwig. *Philosophical Investigations.* Trans. G. E. M. Anscombe. 3rd ed. Malden, MA: Blackwell, 2001.

Wolfe, Peter. *Havoc in the Hub: A Reading of George V. Higgins.* Lanham: Lexington Books, 2007.

Wright, Austin. *Recalcitrance, Faulkner, and the Professors.* Iowa City: Univ. of Iowa Press, 1990.

Zerweck, Bruno. "Historicizing Unreliable Narration: Unreliability and Cultural Discourse in Narrative Fiction." *Style* 35.1 (2001): 151–78.

Zetterberg Gjerlevsen, Simona. "A Novel History of Fictionality." *Narrative* 24.2 (2016): 174–89.

Zunshine, Lisa. *Getting inside Your Head: What Cognitive Science Can Tell Us about Popular Culture.* Baltimore: Johns Hopkins Univ. Press, 2012.

———. *Why We Read Fiction: Theory of Mind and the Novel.* Columbus: Ohio State Univ. Press, 2006.

INDEX

Abel, Elizabeth, 151n3

actual audience, xi, 7, 20, 27–28, 64, 81, 92, 115–16, 157–58, 195–96, 211–13

actual author, 26 table 1.1, 26–27. *See also* author; implied author

Adventures of Huckleberry Finn (Twain), 7, 44–48, 105–8, 219–20, 232, 237

Adventures of Tom Sawyer (Twain), 45n9

aesthetics, 10–11, 64, 78–79, 81, 83–84, 95, 118–19, 126, 130–31, 247–48

Affective Fallacy, 97, 199

agency: authorial, 6, 33, 39, 196, 203–6; of characters, 18; in "Das Urteil," 88, 90; intentionality and, 203; in *Lolita,* 110; of narrator, 18; in *Persuasion,* 71; readerly, 34; in *Time's Arrow,* 129

Alber, Jan, 51

ambiguity, 4, 25, 64, 84, 136, 154, 156, 169, 194, 202

Amis, Martin, 117–34

Angela's Ashes (McCourt), 10, 197–98, 219–20, 232

anti-intentionalism, 196

"Appearances" (O'Hara), 168, 173, 185–94

Aristotle, 32–36, 34n3

Armstrong, Lance, ix

"Art as Technique" (Shklovsky), 106

As I Lay Dying (Faulkner), 110

Atonement (McEwan), 94

audience(s), ix–x; actual, xi, 7, 20, 27–28, 64, 81, 92, 115–16, 157–58, 195–96, 211–13; authorial, 7–8, 26 table 1.1, 27; deficient

narration and, 213–14, 236; in fiction, 69–70; genre inferences made by, 36–43; narratee as, 7; narrative, 7–8, 26 table 1.1, 27–28, 69–70, 75; narrative judgments and, 83–84. *See also* readers, rhetorical

Austen, Jane, 9, 43, 70–71, 73–77, 73n2, 202–3

author: actual, 26 table 1.1, 26–27; constraints on, 77–81; in fiction, 69–70; freedom of, 77–81; implied, 13, 26 table 1.1, 26–27, 197–98, 204–14, 231; reliable narration and, 218

authorial agency, 6, 33, 40, 196, 203–6

authorial audience, 7–8, 26 table 1.1, 27

authorial disclosure, 16, 20; across conversations, 168–70, 175–80, 183–94. *See also* conversational disclosure; dialogue

backward narration, 117–24, 118n1, 129, 134. See also *Time's Arrow* (Amis)

Baetens, Jan, 92

Bauby, Jean-Dominique, 196, 209–13

Beardsley, Monroe, 196, 199

Beloved (Morrison), 94

Bierce, Ambrose, 94

bonding unreliability, 99–116; literally unreliable but metaphorically reliable, 101–5; in naïve defamiliarization, 106; in playful comparison, 105–6; within rhetorical approach to narration, 99–101; in sincere but misguided self-deprecation, 107; subtypes of, 101–10; through optimistic comparison, 109–10, 112. *See also* estranging unreliability

THEORY AND INTERPRETATION OF NARRATIVE

JAMES PHELAN, PETER J. RABINOWITZ, AND ROBYN WARHOL, SERIES EDITORS

Because the series editors believe that the most significant work in narrative studies today contributes both to our knowledge of specific narratives and to our understanding of narrative in general, studies in the series typically offer interpretations of individual narratives and address significant theoretical issues underlying those interpretations. The series does not privilege one critical perspective but is open to work from any strong theoretical position.